D0397140

FIT
for
GROWTH

FIT
for
GROWTH

A GUIDE TO STRATEGIC

COST CUTTING,
RESTRUCTURING,
AND RENEWAL

VINAY **COUTO** | JOHN **PLANSKY** | DENIZ **CAGLAR**

WILEY

Cover image: Paul McCarthy
Cover design: Wiley

Copyright © 2017 by PricewaterhouseCoopers Advisory Services, LLC. All rights reserved.

© PricewaterhouseCoopers Advisory Services, LLC. PwC refers to the U.S. member firm or one of its subsidiaries or affiliates, and may sometimes refer to the PwC network. Each member firm is a separate legal entity. Please see www.pwc.com/structure for further details.

Published by John Wiley & Sons, Inc., Hoboken, New Jersey.
Published simultaneously in Canada.

No part of this publication may be reproduced, stored in a retrieval system, or transmitted in any form or by any means, electronic, mechanical, photocopying, recording, scanning, or otherwise, except as permitted under Section 107 or 108 of the 1976 United States Copyright Act, without either the prior written permission of the Publisher, or authorization through payment of the appropriate per-copy fee to the Copyright Clearance Center, 222 Rosewood Drive, Danvers, MA 01923, (978) 750-8400, fax (978) 646-8600, or on the web at www.copyright.com. Requests to the Publisher for permission should be addressed to the Permissions Department, John Wiley & Sons, Inc., 111 River Street, Hoboken, NJ 07030, (201) 748-6011, fax (201) 748-6008, or online at www.wiley.com/go/permissions.

Limit of Liability/Disclaimer of Warranty: While the publisher and author have used their best efforts in preparing this book, they make no representations or warranties with respect to the accuracy or completeness of the contents of this book and specifically disclaim any implied warranties of merchantability or fitness for a particular purpose. No warranty may be created or extended by sales representatives or written sales materials. The advice and strategies contained herein may not be suitable for your situation. You should consult with a professional where appropriate. Neither the publisher nor the author shall be liable for damages arising herefrom.

For general information about our other products and services, please contact our Customer Care Department within the United States at (800) 762-2974, outside the United States at (317) 572-3993 or fax (317) 572-4002.

Wiley publishes in a variety of print and electronic formats and by print-on-demand. Some material included with standard print versions of this book may not be included in e-books or in print-on-demand. If this book refers to media such as a CD or DVD that is not included in the version you purchased, you may download this material at http://booksupport.wiley.com. For more information about Wiley products, visit www.wiley.com.

ISBN 978-1-119-26853-6 (cloth); ISBN 978-1-119-26854-3 (ePDF);
ISBN 978-1-119-26855-0 (ePub)

Printed in the United States of America
10 9 8 7 6 5 4 3 2 1

Contents

Preface

Many companies today are trying to jump-start flattening revenues and deliver higher returns to investors. Some are fighting off efforts by activist investors to gain control of their company. Others are simply trying to survive and regroup. A few are racing to fend off bankruptcy. More and more, enterprises of all kinds are realizing that the only way to unleash profitable growth is to *cut costs*—often dramatically. In the globally interconnected, digitally disintermediated, hypercompetitive markets of the early twenty-first century, there is no safe harbor when it comes to the bottom line. Companies need to focus on managing costs as rigorously as they concentrate on growing revenues. As with any living organism, there is no profitable growth without equally robust pruning.

We have 70 years of collective experience in helping companies succeed in challenging markets. The surest path to success, we have found, is for companies to become Fit for Growth. Companies that are Fit for Growth do three things consistently and continuously:

1. They focus on a few differentiating capabilities—the things they do better than any other company.
2. They align their cost structure to these capabilities.
3. They organize for growth.

Our research and client experiences—based on lessons learned at hundreds of companies across all business sectors worldwide—show that companies that follow this Fit for Growth formula generate the highest growth and financial returns.

This book is a definitive guide for senior executives and middle managers on how to align their company's costs and organization with their strategy, so that they can grow, create value, and continuously outperform their competitors. It provides a complete blueprint for running a large-scale Fit for Growth cost transformation, including concepts, ideas, analyses, real-life case studies, and specific hands-on advice. It can also serve as a definitive handbook of the most important methods for managing costs.

The book is organized into three parts, each focusing on different aspects of the Fit for Growth approach. Each can also be read on its own. Part I, "Introduction and Fit for Growth Overview," introduces the Fit for Growth approach, which explicitly connects a company's growth agenda with its organization and cost agenda. Through specific company examples, we give economic and business reasons why companies need to cut costs strategically to grow. We explore what it means to become Fit for Growth and the key elements of the restructuring and renewal journey: identifying differentiating capabilities, aligning the cost structure, and reorganizing for growth. Last, we share 10 best practices for CEOs and CxOs to guide their organizations through a Fit for Growth transformation.

Part II, "How to Cut Costs and Grow Stronger: A Manager's Guide," dives into tried and proven approaches to strategic cost reduction. Through case studies and best practices, we discuss the nine most important techniques, or "levers," for cost management: business portfolio rationalization, zero-basing, aligning the operating model, outsourcing, footprint optimization, process excellence, restructuring management spans and layers, strategic supply management, and digitization. We explain each lever with practical examples, suggest when it should be applied, and walk through a step-by-step approach on how to execute.

In Part III, "Coping with Cost Restructuring: How to Manage and Sustain the Change," we discuss restructuring and ongoing renewal, focusing on the Fit for Growth restructuring journey and sustainability. We start by discussing how to mobilize, scale, and run a successful Fit for Growth transformation. Then we turn to the people aspects: how to manage the organizational morale throughout a cost transformation journey, and what senior leaders must do to keep their organizations engaged. We also discuss how to get the people in the organization ready, willing, and able to change. We review basic change management techniques and discuss why these techniques alone are not enough, and detail how executives must enlist the organization's culture to motivate, enable, and sustain the change. Last, and perhaps most important, we focus on how a company can stay Fit for Growth by introducing tools and techniques to sustain the benefits of the transformation and avoid returning to old, inefficient behaviors.

Whether you are an executive looking to catalyze growth in your organization, or have recently found out that your own organization is preparing to go through a restructuring journey, in *Fit for Growth: A Guide to Strategic Cost Cutting, Restructuring, and Renewal* you will find strategies, specific examples, and hands-on advice about how to cut costs carefully and effectively—and emerge from the process stronger and ready for growth.

PART

I

Introduction and Fit for Growth Overview

1

Do You Need to Cut to Grow?

What is currently inhibiting your company's ability to grow? Is it simply the global economic headwinds all companies are trying to navigate? Or is it rising consumer expectations? Digital technology disruption? Increased regulatory scrutiny? Competitive pressure on margins? Commodity volatility? Or has an activist investor just taken a substantial stake in your company and demanded immediate and drastic cost savings?

It doesn't matter. The effect is the same. Whether they're trying to jump-start flattening revenues or facing imminent bankruptcy, companies across industries and geographies are realizing that the only way to unleash growth—profitable growth—is to cut costs, often dramatically. In the globally interconnected, digitally disintermediated market in which all enterprises operate today, there is no safe harbor when it comes to the bottom line. To protect and bolster it, companies need to focus on managing costs as rigorously as they concentrate on growing revenues. In fact, as with any living organism, there is no profitable growth without equally robust pruning.

Welcome to the New Normal.

So, are you fit to weather this tough competitive environment and come out ahead? We've devoted 70 years of collective experience to helping dozens of companies answer this question affirmatively: Are *you* Fit for Growth?

To be *fit* in this way means to be prepared as a growth enterprise. This is not just a matter of innovation prowess, entry into new markets, or acquisition savvy. It means to have your resources, and thus your cost structure, aligned to your company's overall strategy—deployed toward the right businesses, initiatives, and capabilities to execute your growth agenda effectively. Fit for Growth companies have the right amount of resources they need to compete effectively—no more, no less—at the right places. As we noted in the Preface, companies become Fit for Growth by doing three things consistently and continuously:

1. They focus on a few differentiating *capabilities*.
2. They align their *cost structure* to these capabilities.
3. They *organize* for growth.

To focus on a few differentiating capabilities, you must build a clear identity for your company, based on the things you do better than any other company. These differentiating capabilities—the three to six combinations of processes, tools, knowledge, skill, and organization that enable your company to outperform—are at the heart of the Fit for Growth approach. When you know what your company does well and base your strategy on it, it gives you a "lighthouse": a clearly defined, focused goal that everyone in the company can see that directs them all to fulfill the same objectives. In such companies, employees know what drives the company's strategy; indeed, outsiders know, too.

But too many companies have *not* achieved this focus, and you can generally tell by the distractions endemic to working there. Too many initiatives clog people's calendars. Managers go to multiple meetings on unrelated topics every day. The best talent is tasked on so many high-priority programs that they are burning out. The distractions drain financial resources as well, so it's no wonder that these companies routinely underinvest in the activities unique to their enterprise, where they have begun to build a distinctive edge.

If a company's cost structure is *not* aligned to the company's strategy, its leaders will base their spending on other factors—generally to the company's detriment. We often see companies struggle this way. You can spot them because of symptoms like these:

- They use benchmarking as a way to make allocation decisions. Every function from marketing to HR to risk management is pursuing an excellence agenda, spending significant money to be "best in class"— better than other companies, whether or not those functions are strategically critical to the company.
- Legacy programs with little impact continue to get funded—becoming self-sustaining organizations in their own right—while priority growth initiatives cannot get off the ground.
- The budget process is basically "last year plus 3 percent," and staffing levels are out of sync—they might have twice as many finance people counting the money as sales people bringing it in, for example. Every couple of years, they go through a "fire drill" cost-cutting program to reduce overhead, and then watch the costs steadily creep back.

Last, if a company is *not* organized for growth, inefficiencies proliferate and decision making becomes uncertain. The internal bureaucracy is so cumbersome that it takes a week to get a sales quote approved; meanwhile your competition wins the business. Decisions made weeks ago still have not been executed and, worse, frequently come back for reconsideration. Information moves haltingly through the organization and is not readily available to the people who need it. People are afraid to take calculated risks for fear of failure and career derailment, which stifles innovation. Managers actually "manage" fewer than four staff on average and are overinvolved in their subordinates' work. Incentives don't motivate behaviors that drive the company's strategic priorities.

You get the picture. Too many organizations are not Fit for Growth, and their employees, leaders, and shareholders are living with the consequences. In fact, the majority of institutions—both private and public—display some or all of these symptoms.

In the current business and economic context, company leaders cannot afford to let their organizations get or stay out of shape—not if their goals involve profitable growth. They need to focus on what they do best, align the cost structure, and organize to support the strategy. They need to accept the facts: they need to cut to grow.

And that is hard. It requires difficult choices and wrenching trade-offs. Not everything you do is a differentiating capability, which means that you are probably overinvesting in the rest of your processes, systems, and organization if you haven't made conscious choices on how to allocate costs. This is particularly true of large, mature companies that have settled into a complacent, comfortable rhythm. The lean structure and laser focus of their early years has dissipated, and it becomes increasingly difficult to get back in shape.

Consider the cautionary tale of consumer electronics retailer Circuit City.

Circuit City: The Ostrich Approach

Circuit City's precipitous fall from grace vividly illustrates what not to do in the quest to be Fit for Growth. Forced out of business in early 2009, the once thriving big-box chain careened from solvency to bankruptcy to liquidation in less than six months.

Why? Because management did not adhere to the Fit for Growth formula. They lost sight of their differentiating capabilities system, which was centered on the hand-holding, advisory relationship they had developed with middle-class consumers looking to buy big-ticket electronics devices. Therefore, when it came time to cut costs, they cut into this productive muscle—undermining the customer experience—instead of shedding other nonessential costs. Last, they did not make the changes to their organization necessary to protect and promote what they did best.

Serial entrepreneur Sam Wurtzel was onto something big in 1949 when he opened a television shop in the front half of a tire store in Richmond, Virginia. He foresaw the American public's fascination with the fledgling medium and helped put a TV set within lower-income families' reach by offering installment payment plans and free overnight in-home demonstrations.[1]

In the flush postwar 1950s, Wurtzel sensed the growing demand for refrigerators, washing machines, and electric stoves and capitalized on that wave by offering appliances in his stores. He spotted the trend toward big-box discounting and was one of the first retailers to build superstores. Over the decades, under continued astute management, Circuit City expanded its offerings from TVs to appliances and personal computers. By 2000, it was the dominant electronics retailer in the country with 60,000 employees at nearly 700 locations and annual sales of more than $12 billion. Circuit City was ranked in the top 200 of the Fortune 500 and was featured in management expert Jim Collins's bestseller *Good to Great.*[2]

Circuit City flourished for decades with a commissioned sales force trained to hand-sell expensive and complicated home entertainment systems and appliances, along with extended service plans. These salesmen in sports jackets were the cornerstone of the company's business model, and they felt a sense of pride and loyalty in the company. They were experts in their field, educating buyers and participating in the rewards. Circuit City built its value proposition around the customer experience this veteran sales force delivered.

But as the company advanced toward the end of the century, it lost sight of this differentiating capabilities system and did not evolve it to meet changing customer needs. Circuit City did not adjust its product assortment or store formatting to keep up with retail trends or the times, and failed to play to its strength in customer experience enabled by expert advice. It also strayed from its premium-customer-experience value proposition when it signed cheap real estate leases for "B"- and "C"-grade sites inconvenient to customers.[3]

You have only to look as far as Best Buy—which experienced steady growth as Circuit City's sales declined—to understand what Circuit City could have done differently.

It could have sought opportunities to keep its trust-based premium advisory capabilities front and center. It could have invested in locations more convenient to customers and attracted traffic by offering the full line of home theater systems, accessories, peripherals, and gaming software. It could have streamlined the shopping experience for busy customers and been earlier and bolder in capitalizing on the promise of the Internet, especially in the services arena, where it had a natural advantage. In fact, high-end advisory services—such as home entertainment system consulting and installation—were a natural market opportunity for Circuit City's expert sales staff.

Having already lost significant ground to Best Buy and Amazon, Circuit City was on its heels when it came to terms with the magnitude of its financial distress in the early 2000s—and then it made mistake after mistake. Instead of engaging in a proactive and strategic process to redirect resources to its differentiating capabilities, it reacted haphazardly with a series of ill-considered tactical moves.

In 2001, it exited the appliance business overnight—the company didn't even inform its suppliers before it announced the move. It scrapped a store remodeling initiative targeted to roll out a more consumer-friendly format. And most alarmingly, in 2003, it summarily fired thousands of its most tenured and knowledgeable commissioned sales staff and replaced them with inexperienced hourly employees. Circuit City projected at the time that the disruptive impact on morale and customer satisfaction would be over in one month. They could not have been more wrong.[4]

By late 2008, when the recession and credit crisis struck, Circuit City's stock price had plummeted 90 percent to 10 cents a share (versus Best Buy's $25),[5] prompting the NYSE to threaten delisting.[6] Vendors were refusing to supply the stores, given the backlog of inventory the retailer had failed to unload and vendors' doubts that Circuit City would be around to pay off its debts. And store employees were so disheartened by rounds of mishandled layoffs—while headquarters executives remained secure and well compensated—that there was no reservoir of goodwill to draw on to shore up sales. And no cash—the company had engaged in a lavish $1 billion stock buyback program between 2003 and 2007, leaving it without necessary reserves.[7]

This domino effect of bad decisions left Circuit City tragically unfit to survive the perfect storm of the Great Recession. It declared bankruptcy on November 10, 2008, and was forced into liquidation by its creditors within months. The last Circuit City store closed its doors on March 8, 2009.[8]

It's easy to play Monday morning quarterback, but when you are a senior manager in the midst of stalled growth and declining results, it is anything but easy to clear a way up and out. It's not hard to be Fit for Growth, in theory. But in practice, for many companies it's next to impossible.

For those companies that align their costs and organization with their distinctive and differentiating capabilities, however, the results are impressive and enduring.

IKEA: Elevating Cost Optimization to an Art Form

Here's the story of another big-box retailer, founded in the post–World War II era by an enterprising leader with a clear vision of how middle-class consumers wanted to live in their homes. Same context, different outcome.

Swedish home furnishings superstore IKEA has set a great example when it comes to focusing on what it does best and aligning its costs and organization, not only for itself, but also—quite explicitly—for the consumers that the IKEA Group and its franchisees serve in 386 stores in 48 countries worldwide (as of 2016). IKEA is globally known for its simple and elegant product design, its huge but inviting retail stores, and its almost impossibly low prices (which drop another 1.5 percent to 2 percent at the start of each fiscal year per company mandate).

Few brands have achieved such an iconic status, and fewer still command the devout customer loyalty that IKEA has earned, which is all the more remarkable when you consider the relative burden IKEA places on its customers to pick, carry, and assemble its flat-packed furniture themselves. But customers do it willingly, because they understand that IKEA passes the savings on to them, prizing consumer value and affordability above all else.[9]

IKEA embodies the Fit for Growth formula: It is laser-focused on its strategy and differentiating capabilities; it has firmly aligned its cost structure to reinforce those capabilities; and it is organized to enable profitable growth.

Founder Ingvar Kamprad's original vision—"to create a better everyday life for the many people"—is a lighthouse visible to every IKEA employee worldwide and guides every decision, however big or small. As Ian Worling, IKEA's former director of business navigation, explains it, "That means we offer home furnishings at such low prices that as many people as possible can afford to buy them. That colors everything we do."[10]

IKEA employees are relentless in searching for cost savings opportunities in everything but the quality of their merchandise, the customer experience in their stores, and the efficiency of their operations. These comprise IKEA's key capabilities and they safeguard them—in fact, its leaders plow savings they generate elsewhere back into them.

To enhance the customer experience in their stores, for example, IKEA's management has invested heavily in understanding how their customers live at home in various markets. They do home visits and even install cameras in the homes of volunteers to gain insight on what sort of issues their customers encounter, so they can design home furnishings to solve them. Ingvar Kamprad has been known to walk through stores asking customers, "What could we have done better today?"[11]

IKEA integrates customer engagement, supply chain efficiency, and pricing considerations into the design process itself, enabling it to offer price-conscious and stylish product design while increasing its margins. Designers not only create new products, they work on packaging to economize materials and space to fit more pieces into a container. This congruence between strategy and execution is rare in product design. Designers are generally not responsible for managing expenses. The designs are costed out by a separate group in the finance or supply-chain function, and the retail price is set by a third group in marketing, resulting in a series of trade-offs between competing interests . . . with no one truly representing the customer or the bottom line.

At IKEA, design, cost, and price are all considered together in the product innovation phase; there are relatively few trade-offs because everyone is seeking the same goals.

IKEA clearly focuses on its differentiating capabilities, aligns its cost structure to advance these capabilities, and enables all of this and its profitable growth through its organization. Its organization and culture are in lockstep when it comes to supporting and reinforcing what it does best. "We work hard to ensure that as new people come in, they understand who we are and what we're trying to do," says Worling. "The people who work here genuinely want to be here and share IKEA's core values of cost consciousness and humility." As Kamprad himself put it more bluntly: "Wasting resources is a mortal sin at IKEA. . . . Expensive solutions to any kind of problem are usually the work of mediocrity."[12]

People at every level recognize when someone is behaving counter to the company's values. If an employee visibly wastes resources or reprimands a subordinate for suggesting an idea, he or she will hear about it immediately, not just from higher-ups, but from everyone around that person. People know that their continued attention to each other's behavior makes the entire system work.

This rigorous and continuous focus on what they do best when it comes to allocating costs is what distinguishes IKEA from Circuit City. Nowhere is the contrast more striking than in how they both confronted the need to sharply reduce costs in the global recession of 2008, which hit both retailers' core markets (new homeowners and middle-class consumers) hard.

While Circuit City summarily exited core businesses and executed waves of demoralizing layoffs, IKEA returned to its guiding vision and simply amplified the cost fitness measures it already had in place. "We didn't focus on cutting costs, because that's the easiest thing to do in retail. You just lay people off, and cut back some of your capital expenditure, and it reduces your variable costs," says Worling. "But it also weakens you."[13]

Instead, the chain's leaders continued investing in the capabilities that differentiated IKEA—for example, its custom-designed stores with distinctive room settings, supervised children's playrooms, and convenient self-serve caterics—all designed to make customers feel at home. IKEA not only built new stores, it extended and expanded existing ones.

"To make up the difference, we had to become very good at four things: Lowering operational costs . . . increasing volume . . . developing an even better-functioning supply chain . . . and empowering our coworkers. We asked ourselves what we could do during this period to lower our costs and, instead of increasing the bottom line, turn every Euro back to lower prices for our customers," recalls Worling. (At other companies, even 25 percent reinvestment is considered remarkable).

With that goal in mind, IKEA sought further cost-savings opportunities in places customers didn't see. Its product designers collaborated with its factory engineers and suppliers even more intensively to uncover additional efficiencies. They worked even more diligently on reducing packaging. "Even a few millimeters can make a big difference in fitting more pieces into a container. We hate transporting air," says Worling. "In general, we always ask ourselves, 'Would our customers want to pay for that particular item themselves?' If the answer is no, then we try to find a way to do without it or to do it in a cheaper way."

And this is why IKEA is emblematic of the Fit for Growth philosophy and approach. It makes deliberate choices around a crystal clear value proposition that prioritizes its key capabilities. It's also why the IKEA Group has achieved the seemingly impossible: about 10 percent annual top-line growth since 2001, surpassing €30 billion in revenues in 2015, and stable margins despite the ongoing price reductions and economic pressure of the past several years.

Fit for Growth companies are lean and deliberate in spending money—every day. They manage their costs for both efficiency and effectiveness. In all their investments, they seek long-term value. This means continually pursuing the lowest-cost way to run their operations and organization, taking full advantage of economies of scale and scope. In our experience, companies that become Fit for Growth do not see cost optimization as a single, "big bang"–style event. Instead, they make it a continuous process, embedded in the daily fabric of business.

By choosing to cut costs proactively and continuously, IKEA has been able to operate from a position of strength, even in times of market stress. As a result, it has avoided the panic and aggression that overtook Circuit City's senior executives in its final days—and the fate of all too many other companies in recent years.

To adhere to the Fit for Growth formula, companies have to make tough decisions. Senior executives may decide to exit an entire business or product line that doesn't leverage the company's differentiating capabilities. They may decide to outsource a number of support functions that do not have to be world class to enable the strategy. They may realign compensation and incentives to drive performance in one area to the detriment of another. These decisions have real consequences for real people—it is the rare senior manager who finds making and executing these trade-offs comfortable or easy.

But the sense of purpose and energy that this sort of strategic clarity and coherence delivers to an organization cannot be overstated. It is those companies that stick to this guiding philosophy that demonstrate market-leading returns year after year.

The Fit for Growth Index

To demonstrate the truth of that statement, we developed the Fit for Growth[14] Index, a quantitative metric that measures companies' adherence to the three elements of the Fit for Growth framework: focus on a few differentiating capabilities, align cost structure, reorganize for growth.[15] Having seen these three elements create value in the market, we wanted to determine how important they are—collectively and separately—in driving results. So we correlated the index scores of about 200 companies

FIT FOR GROWTH COMPANIES
GENERATE HIGHER RETURNS

This diagram shows the comparative placement of 197 sample companies on scales showing performance (two-year normalized total shareholder return on the y-axis) and readiness for growth (the Fit for Growth Index score on the x-axis).

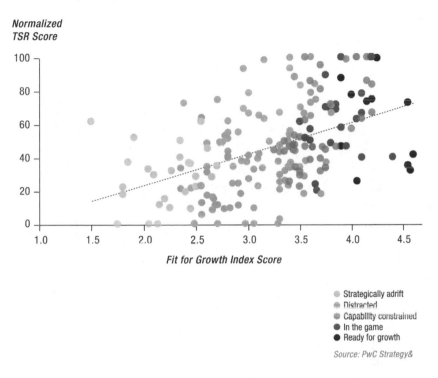

Figure 1.1

across various sectors with their financial performance, namely total shareholder return (TSR) adjusted for industry-specific factors.[16]

As Figure 1.1 illustrates, there is a clear correlation between how fit a company is for growth according to our index and its total shareholder returns. Almost three-quarters (73 percent) of companies with high index scores had high or medium-high TSR scores, and the reverse also proved true—those with low index scores generated lower returns. (See Figure 1.2.)

Having established the link between Fit for Growth Index scores and market returns, the next logical step was to isolate those specific attributes in

DISTRIBUTION OF NORMALIZED TSR SCORES BY FIT FOR GROWTH INDEX SCORE

Companies with higher index scores (at right) have better TSR profiles. The width of each column reflects the number of companies falling into that index score category.

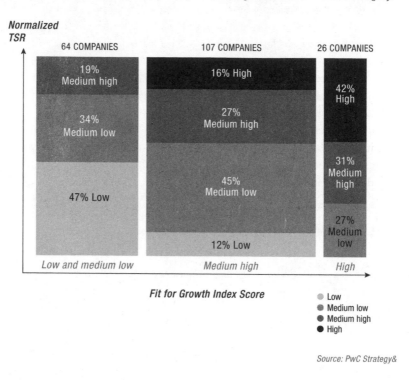

Figure 1.2

the index framework that best explained strong performance. (See "Calculating the Fit for Growth Index.") Our analysis highlighted the following six attributes across all three index dimensions: coherent strategy, strong capabilities, systematic investments, aligned initiatives, speed and decisiveness, and strong leadership.

Our research highlighted a number of other noteworthy findings:

High-performing companies tightly link their growth and cost agendas. They clearly understand what capabilities are truly critical to winning with their strategy, and they funnel the bulk of their resources to those differentiating capabilities.

Companies need to combine all three elements to unlock outstanding results. Those that integrate and align differentiating capabilities, cost structure, and organization generate the highest Fit for Growth Index scores and the highest financial returns. You cannot excel in only one of these elements and hope for the same result. For example, a company that does the hard work of identifying its few differentiating capabilities and aligning its cost structure will see costs creep back after a few years if it fails to adjust its organization to support the new regime. In our experience and research, companies stumble on the second imperative—they identify the right differentiating capabilities, but they don't have the heart or discipline to actually redirect resources to them from everyday activities.

Few companies are Fit for Growth. Although the formula for success is clear and its positive impact obvious, less than one-fifth of the companies we assessed seemed well-prepared for growth. Very few—only 6 percent—demonstrated strength in all three elements.

Calculating the Fit for Growth Index

The index assesses companies in three key areas: strategic clarity reinforced by an aligned system of capabilities, an aligned resource base and cost structure, and a supportive organization. Each company received a composite score from 1 to 5 based on its "fitness" in each of these areas (5 = the most fit). In calculating the scores, we weighted the three factors as follows: strategic clarity and coherence at 50 percent, resource alignment at 30 percent, and supportive organization at 20 percent. The second and third factors together constitute a company's execution capability. Thus, a company's index score is derived in equal parts from its strategy and its executional fitness. These weightings reflect our belief that strategy and execution are equally important in determining performance.

The three factors were in turn made up of several components, each with its own weighting:

- Focus on a few differentiating capabilities: coherent strategy (15 percent), strong capabilities (10 percent), strong/coherent product portfolio (10 percent), and presence in critical markets (15 percent)
- Align the cost structure: systematic investments in differentiating capabilities (10 percent), thoughtful cost reduction (15 percent), and improvement initiatives aligned with strategy (5 percent)

(continued)

> *(continued)*
>
> ■ Organize for growth: speed and decisiveness (10 percent), strong
>   leadership (5 percent), and supportive culture (5 percent)
>
> Our survey sample comprised 197 companies in 17 industries. Companies were chosen to yield a balanced sample including high, medium, and low financial performers in each industry, based on their total shareholder return over a two-year period. To supplement our knowledge of the companies, we examined information from research databases, analysts' reports, earnings call transcripts, and business periodicals.

So we know that companies that are Fit for Growth outperform. Their strategies are clear, differentiated, and well articulated. They have demonstrated resilience to market and environmental changes. Their most important capabilities are highly advanced and lead their industries; their resources are systematically directed to initiatives and opportunities with the highest strategic and financial returns; their organizational structures support key capabilities, with efficient decision making and talent in the right places; and their culture of cost management extends to the front line.

But we also know that most companies are *not* Fit for Growth. In the next two chapters, we will break down the journey to becoming Fit for Growth into its three basic steps—focus on a few differentiating capabilities, align the cost structure, and reorganize for growth—and provide an overview on how to achieve excellence in each. Part II provides a manager's guide on how to cut costs and grow stronger that presents in detail nine specific levers you can pull to reduce costs in a smart, strategic way—everything from automation to zero-basing. In Part III, we offer insight on how to actually manage a cost transformation from the top to the trenches—and then how to sustain the gains by aligning your organization and culture behind its new growth priorities.

We will show how companies like IKEA have not only restructured without wreckage but have actually enlisted their employees in the cost transformation process. Cost reduction does not have to conjure up images of mayhem and destruction—it can be a constructive, even uplifting exercise if managed adeptly and sensitively. Most important, it can make your company more competitive, more profitable, and better prepared to grow.

2

Becoming Fit for Growth

The Restructuring and Renewal Journey

As competitive and economic pressures mount, we are seeing companies anxiously searching for ways to bolster returns and grow their business. They are looking for breakthroughs to innovate new products and services, enter new markets, or offer more compelling customer value propositions—either organically or through mergers and acquisition.

To capture that increasingly elusive growth, companies need to be Fit for Growth. They need to have gone through the rigorous discipline of identifying the three to six distinguishing strengths (or, as we call them, differentiating capabilities) that give them a "right to win"—the ability to compete more effectively than competitors in the arenas where they choose to do business. Then they need to build their strategy—and hence their cost structure and organization—around that right to win.

As we've noted, this strategic exercise requires hard choices—about what markets to participate in, what products and services to keep or cut, what customers to serve, and what capabilities to invest in or prune. Until companies make those hard choices about the few things they can and should do exceptionally well to thrive in the competitive space they've chosen—and consciously divert resources from everything else—they will not be Fit for Growth.

How do you know if *your* company is fit or unfit for growth? Our diagnostic is deceptively simple.

1. Have you identified the differentiating capabilities that drive your growth strategy?
2. Are your resources—which determine your costs—deployed toward those capabilities?
3. Is your organization set up to enable and reinforce those capabilities?

A clear capabilities-driven strategy, cost alignment, and an enabling organization are the three pillars of the Fit for Growth model, and we will keep returning to them throughout this book. United they stand, divided you fall.

The World We Live In

Corporate leaders in every industry and region are contending with a generally deflationary economic environment in which it has proven difficult to find attractive markets and opportunities for capital investment. Emerging markets are still alluring but remain challenging and require patience to achieve scale. Many companies in this environment have implemented share buybacks to increase their stock price and offer a higher near-term return to shareholders.

Meanwhile, many companies are managing seismic disruption within their own industries. Media's transition from analog to digital, the impact of Obamacare on the delivery of medical care in the United States, and the rebuilding of balance sheets by global financial service companies under intense regulatory scrutiny are just three obvious examples.

In this environment of economic constraint and discontinuous change, traditional cost reduction programs are not enough. They invariably either spread the pain like peanut butter evenly across the company, or home in on obvious high-cost areas to the exclusion of worthier targets. Moreover, they are overly—sometimes exclusively—focused on short-term reductions, such as re-sourcing, working capital management, and headcount reduction. No careful thought is given to what costs are, in fact, "good" costs vital to the future growth of the business, and which are "bad" costs that divert resources from the company's critical capabilities.

So, what do you do if your company is missing one or more of these pillars?

What you don't do is what many have done for decades: wait for a crisis before paying attention to a bloated and inefficient cost structure, then enact drastic measures that not only eliminate fat but cut into productive muscle. Familiar options include across-the-board budget cuts, voluntary severance and retirement packages, and the perennial fallback, layoffs. Diet alone (and crash dieting particularly) will not help a company achieve fitness. Exercise— in this case the exercise of deciding where a capability needs to be best in class and where it can be good enough or stripped to the essentials—is integral to getting and staying in shape over the long haul.

A successful Fit for Growth agenda will be embedded in a company's overall strategy and culture and addresses each of the three pillars (see Figure 2.1):

1. Focus on differentiating capabilities
2. Align the cost structure
3. Reorganize for growth

Focus on Differentiating Capabilities

Achieving true cost fitness requires a more strategic perspective on what "cost" is. Costs are an outcome of the choices you make about where to invest your resources. The right way to think about costs is to align them with the strategic growth priorities of your business—those few capabilities that distinguish your company and contribute disproportionately to its success. Those capabilities should be fully funded, whereas other costs— those that are purely discretionary or may be necessary but are not differentiating—should be subject to stricter scrutiny and more intensive

FIT FOR GROWTH FRAMEWORK

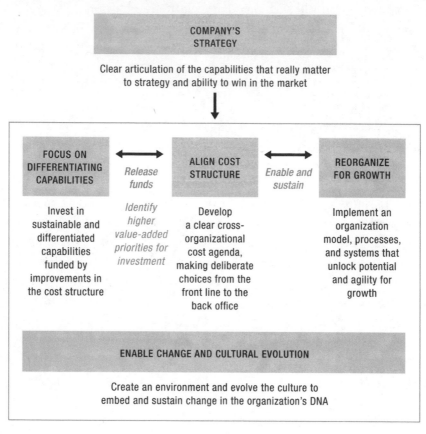

Figure 2.1

pruning. In capabilities-driven cost reduction, companies play clear favorites with finite resources.

The resulting approach is unique for each company, and delivers greater and faster cost takeout with less risk to the business, less chance of costs returning, and a greater likelihood that the company will emerge stronger and better positioned for growth. This approach involves a new way of thinking about capabilities—not as skill sets, core competencies, or individual corporate functions, but as combinations of processes, tools, knowledge, skills, and organization that enable a company to outperform.

A company's key capabilities drive most or all of its worthwhile discretionary costs. They can be counted on one hand, and almost always cross functional boundaries. Consider these examples: Walmart's "sharp-penciled" supply chain management, Southwest Airlines's energetic customer service and asset utilization, and P&G's open-architecture innovation model. These are examples of key capabilities in which these leading companies have consciously invested by directing resources away from less distinctive and differentiating activities.

It's not enough to have a single capability. Success derives from having mastered and institutionalized three to six capabilities, which come together in a distinctive, powerful, and mutually reinforcing way that is almost impossible to replicate. This is what we call a *capabilities system*.

Apple, for example, excels at more than exquisite product design. Its "secret sauce" is its combined ability to spot a burgeoning consumer need, bring technology to it (even if it's not theirs), make the interface intuitive and elegant, package and promote the result with a sleek simplicity, and, last, deliver it at a competitive price point—making it the default consumer standard. That's its winning capabilities system.

The first step in securing an enduring right to win in any industry is identifying the differentiating capabilities in your system. This will require clarity and consensus on the part of your senior management team. We discuss this strategic exercise in Chapter 4.

Align the Cost Structure

Developing a lean and deliberate cost structure naturally follows from the work the senior executive team has done to identify the company's key capabilities. In a perfect world, the cost structure builds on the growth priorities that emerge.

Fit for Growth companies manage their costs not only tightly but also thoughtfully; they recognize not all costs are bad. Indeed, costs that strengthen a company's differentiating capabilities are good costs. These companies sometimes may even increase good costs, while rigorously managing the rest of the cost structure. Through tight cost management, Fit for Growth companies increase profits and free up funds to further invest in differentiating capabilities.

There are many ways to ensure your cost structure is appropriately lean and thoughtful. When we support our clients, we often evaluate their costs in light of three questions:

1. *What do we do?* Start by analyzing everything you do. If an activity, process, or person furthers a differentiating capability, make sure it is adequately resourced and set up for success. Determine what non-priority capabilities and business segments can be eliminated or scaled back dramatically. Once these are determined, remove as much of the cost associated with them as possible.
2. *Where do we do it?* Review where your operations and people are located and explore opportunities to consolidate and gain scale efficiencies or scope economies. Relocate work and people to lower-cost locations. Take advantage of shared services models and consider outsourcing or offshoring.
3. *How* (and *how well*) *do we do it?* Streamline inefficiencies in company execution. Review and reengineer business processes to eliminate waste. Exploit and improve automation. Implement strategic sourcing to reduce direct and indirect material expense. Delayer the organization, optimize management spans of control, and ensure pay scales match the complexity of the job performed.

This exercise will quickly illuminate those costs associated with your company's truly differentiating capabilities and those that are not. We categorize these latter costs as "table-stakes" and "lights-on" costs. These are activities that you spend just enough on to stay in the competitive game or to literally keep the lights on in your operations, no more. You may find that some costs are candidates for complete elimination. Figure 2.2 reveals the reallocation of costs and the savings realized by a consumer products company that went through this resource alignment exercise.

You need to be thoughtful and deliberate in taking out costs, to avoid cutting into productive muscle. You want to change the way the company operates, redesign the business processes, and redefine how the work gets done so that unnecessary, non-differentiating costs go out and stay out.

You will find that systematically and objectively evaluating your cost structure releases dramatic savings, not only directly improving the bottom line, but also releasing cash for potential investment back into your critical capabilities and ultimately fueling growth.

IDENTIFYING "GOOD" COSTS AND "BAD" COSTS AT A CONSUMER PRODUCTS COMPANY

CAPABILITY MIX SHIFT

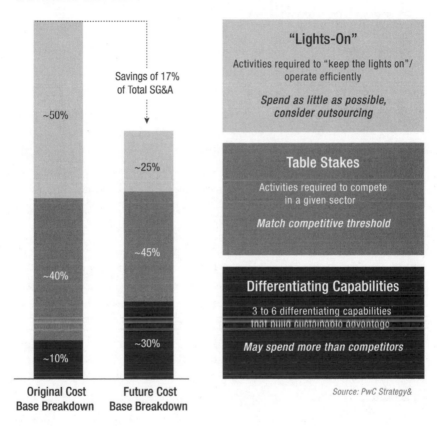

Figure 2.2

Of course, companies do not always have the mechanisms in place to systematically and incrementally adjust their cost structure. They find their backs pressed to the wall—under short-term pressure to cut costs dramatically and rapidly, perhaps as a response to recessionary pressures or declining overall profitability, or to accommodate a new strategy. In such situations, a company has to design and enact a large-scale cost transformation program in short order. It must put everything on the table and review all costs dispassionately: given our strategy and capabilities agenda, what must we absolutely do, and what is the best way of doing all that we do?

In Part II of this book, we will cover in greater detail the assessment of a company's cost structure and the various levers you can pull to optimize it.

Reorganize for Growth

A company's organization can either make or break a Fit for Growth transformation—or any transformation or major initiative, for that matter. In the context of a Fit for Growth transformation, a well-designed organization model enables fitness and growth in two ways: by enabling and sustaining cost reductions (which can then be redeployed as investments in differentiating capabilities) and by creating the right conditions for managers to drive growth.

In the first way, the well-designed organization model unleashes a number of cost reduction levers. In most large organizations, long-standing relationships have developed in an ad hoc fashion among the central core, the local business units, and the shared pools of resources that provide, for example, human resources and IT services. Local leaders may have too much power over functional activities (thus duplicating one another's efforts and promoting inconsistencies), or the central hub may be too controlling (which generates unnecessary work).

The solution typically involves redesigning the company to create more appropriate structures and spans of control. This may mean having more people report to each manager and reducing the number of hierarchical layers. Pay scales may be rationalized so that compensation matches the complexity of the job performed, or the company may take more deliberate approaches to sharing resources and outsourcing less-critical processes. When these measures are consistent and broadly understood, they are typically supported by people throughout the company.

In the second way, a well-designed organization model can fuel dramatic growth by empowering managers to act like owners of the business. The managers are given explicit financial and operational targets, along with clear decision rights that spell out what they can and cannot do by themselves to reach those targets. They are also given greater control over the resources assigned to them, and they can deploy these resources more flexibly. With incentives (like bonuses and promotions) aligned accordingly, business unit leaders align with the company's broader objectives in both the long term and the short term, and become accountable for results.

This tightly linked chain of empowerment, accountability, decision rights, and incentives allows the company to make decisions as close to the front lines as possible. Managers can capture opportunities in the market, while the corporate core focuses on building and maintaining the capabilities that all the business units share, and on driving the company's overall strategy and performance. Managers respond to opportunities quickly, collaborate across organizational boundaries seamlessly, make decisions resolutely, and execute effectively. Executives spend less time fighting political turf wars and more time thinking about their customers and competitors. Last, costs naturally decline, and the potential for growth improves, because the organization reinforces the practices developed through cost optimization.

Key to effectively executing any strategy is redesigning and aligning the organization with the articulated strategy. In our experience, there are four elements to consider when redesigning an organization.

1. The Operating Model

Before you embark on redesigning your organization, you need to sketch out its outlines. What are its natural elements, and how do these elements fit together? In other words, you need an operating model.

In summary, a company's operating model defines what work is performed by what organization units in the company and how these units work together. As you redesign your organization, you need to define these organization units, their roles, and how they interact. To do this, you may need to start from square one: what are your natural business units and how do they face off with customers and compete in the market? Once you define the natural business units, you'll need to carefully consider the role of and interplay among your business units, your corporate headquarters, and your administrative and support functions. For example, do product-based business units own the P&L, or do regions? Should headquarters act as a hands-off holding company, giving business units a lot of room to operate, or be more actively involved in operations? Do functional resources report to corporate or to individual business units? How deep into the organization should our matrix structure permeate? As we will discuss in Chapter 7, aligning the operating model with the capabilities system and cost structure is an essential step in a Fit for Growth transformation.

2. The Four Building Blocks of Organizational DNA

With the operating model defined, you can then design the organization. We have discovered four standard building blocks that define an organization and ultimately its effectiveness: decision rights, information flows, motivators, and structure. We call these the four building blocks of an organization's DNA.

1. *Decision rights:* A critical determinant of organizational performance, decision rights describe decision-making authority and accountability and where they reside in an organization. If decision rights reside at too high a level, the organization bogs down waiting for senior management to sign off on every decision. Conversely, overly decentralized decision rights also lead to inefficiencies and redundancies, as each division invents its own wheel. Unclear decision rights are possibly the worst of all, as decisions are either made everywhere—or nowhere.

2. *Information flows:* Properly allocated decision rights are great, but meaningless in the absence of appropriate and accurate information. Failure to furnish such information in a timely manner is a leading contributor to organizational inefficiency and hence higher costs, according to our research.

3. *Motivators:* Properly designed and implemented, motivators can be a valuable key to unlocking organizational efficiency. Many companies have failed to capitalize on this opportunity by perpetuating salary and benefit structures that are out of touch with current market practices. Instead of, say, promoting and supporting lateral transfers as a valuable career move, companies continue to overemphasize the "onward and upward" trajectory, which just creates more organizational layers. Moreover, the lack of substantive differentiation in performance bonuses discourages the stars and overcompensates the weak links. Costs rise, but not the cream of the talent pool.

4. *Structure:* Structure—the "lines and boxes" on the organizational chart—gets the lion's share of the attention in most restructurings, as the name would suggest. However, our research indicates that structure should be defined last, after the key organization roles and decision rights are defined. Structure-based solutions are still necessary and valuable. Companies should eliminate excessive organizational layers and increase managers' spans of control (i.e., more direct reports) to speed decision making, clarify accountabilities, and remove costs. Executives should reassess their primary and secondary organizational axes to align their cost

reduction efforts with their strategic priorities. They should also central-ize scattered and fragmented functions where such centralization would increase efficiency without sacrificing effectiveness.

3. Talent

The success of an organization ultimately rises or falls with its people. As you redesign your organization, think through the talent implications, too. For example, what are the critical roles in the organization, and what sort of competencies do you require in these roles to enable the transformation and build differentiating capabilities? Do you home-grow your talent or do you hire from the outside? If you do grow your talent, what methods do you use to develop them (e.g., mentoring, rotations, and development roles)? Do you value deep functional expertise or broad general management and leadership skills?

An organizational restructuring provides the perfect opportunity to refresh the talent in critical roles. This is the right time to take calculated risks to "ventilate the organization" and give stretch opportunities to the rising stars who have been "blocked" by long-tenured but mediocre senior and middle managers. Sometimes such changes are necessary—the old guard may be unwilling or unable to adapt to the new normal.

4. Management Processes

Management processes for developing strategy, prioritizing differentiating capabilities, designing accurate budgets and forecasts, and tracking business performance—all are critical elements of your organization. Are your long-term and short-term planning processes dynamically aligning capital and resources with priority opportunities? Do you have the right forums and debates so that big ideas are funded and the right investment trade-offs are made?

* * *

Getting these four elements in place is critical to laying a strong foundation for growth, but perhaps more important in sustaining the gains of a cost transformation and institutionalizing new behaviors in the organization.

Enable Change and Cultural Evolution

Change on the scale of a Fit for Growth transformation must be grounded in the organization's culture. Those on the front line and in the back office have to embrace and enable the change, and the only way that will happen is if you leverage what works in your company's culture. The Fit for Growth journey is an arduous one and will require many if not most of your people to change not only what they do, but also how they behave day to day. That is a considerable ask, and it will go unanswered unless you put your culture to work.

Any corporate transformation—whether it's to encourage collaboration, unleash innovation, or improve productivity—requires people to alter their methods of working in big ways and small. But a cost restructuring is potentially the most dislocating and treacherous of transformations. You are asking some people to leave the company entirely, others to relinquish staff and perquisites, and still others to step into new roles or relocate to new cities or even countries. To get people to come on board and stay on board with the new normal, you have to enlist your culture—that intangible collection of instinctive, repetitive habits and emotional cues and responses that determine what people feel, think, and believe about their work.

You can't copy a culture. You can't even pin it down easily. So how do you enlist it or, indeed, exert *any* influence on it? Not easily, we admit. Formal efforts to change a culture or replace it with something new and different inevitably fail because they never reach their target: the hearts and minds of employees.

These initiatives start with a false premise: that you can swap out an established culture with a different one that you prefer. You cannot simply replace a culture like an old machine—if you could, it would not be your culture in the first place! But you can align some of its more useful cogs. Make use of what you cannot change by appealing to the positive elements and emotional forces in your existing culture to align it with the change you want to see happen. You work with and within your culture, rather than fighting it.

So, we recommend that change management campaigns focus on behaviors—the few most critical behaviors. Over time, as you shift these behaviors, they become embedded in the culture and influence mindsets, motivating employees, for example, to spend every dollar as if it was their own. We will discuss how you can influence these few critical behaviors and, by extension, your culture in Chapter 16.

Continuous Cost-Fitness Renewal

As any out-of-shape person looking to take and keep weight off will tell you, there is no quick or easy fix. The road to fitness requires discipline and perseverance, and often the journey must be undertaken under difficult conditions—earnings pressures, supply chain disruptions, and organizational resistance, to name a few.

As it should, the fitness regimen we recommend starts with strategy—identifying and redeploying resources to those capabilities that give you a right to win in your chosen market—and ends with organization and culture—pulling the levers that will ensure your people and business make the transition and sustain the gains. In between is a programmatic and multifaceted approach to building a lean and thoughtful cost structure that will position your company for long-term growth.

But "starts" and "ends" are misleading terms. The secret to true fitness is continuous improvement. Fit for Growth companies are always honing their capabilities and cost structure so they don't have to undertake large programs every several years. They monitor and adjust their growth priorities and their resource deployment as an ongoing activity to help the company reach its performance aspirations year after year (see "What a Fit for Growth Company Looks Like").

Being Fit for Growth may seem like an onerous task. But it can also be the beginning of a new virtuous cycle. As resources move from nonessential to critical capabilities, your company can put more capital into growth strategies. The cost side of your ledger will read less like a list of burdens and more like a register of enabling choices, with a direct link between the money you spend and your prowess in the marketplace.

What a Fit for Growth Company Looks Like

Although every company is different, our Fit for Growth Index analysis revealed a set of common characteristics that distinguish the "fittest" companies across the three pillars of our framework.

Clear capabilities-driven strategy: At Fit for Growth companies, strategic priorities are specific, actionable, and—most critically—widely understood at all levels of the company. Leaders make clear

(continued)

(*continued*)

choices, striving for "best-in-class" prowess only in the distinctive capabilities that create sustainable competitive advantage, and accepting "good enough" in other areas. Through rigorous, forward-looking review processes, they are able to keep their strategies relevant, sensing and rapidly adapting to market changes. They're quicker to innovate, are willing to make calculated big bets, and feel no qualms about killing investments that aren't paying off.

Cost alignment: In the area of resource alignment, Fit for Growth companies employ a disciplined process that ensures adequate funding for high-growth core activities. Clear and objective investment criteria prevent department rivalries and other parochial concerns from interfering with allocation of funds to top corporate priorities. These companies manage spending strategically, making rigorous trade-offs based on cost transparency and a deep understanding of where money is actually made. Acquisitions are made only if they advance the company's strategic positioning, and never if the target won't be a good cultural fit.

Organization that enables growth: Fit for Growth companies are organizationally efficient, flexible, and lean. They align their power structures and allocate decision rights in ways that best serve strategic priorities and business realities, rather than aligning them with historical legacies or individual agendas. They create nimble mechanisms for governance and collaboration across business units. Talent-management practices support key capabilities by moving the most highly skilled people into pivotal roles. A coherent culture sets norms and expectations that reflect the requirements for success in the marketplace. An ethos of excellence and continuous improvement prevails, reinforced by systems that reward performance.

Cultural evolution that enables and sustains the gains: Fit for Growth companies enlist their culture to get fit and stay fit. Cultural norms reinforce a company's focus on its cost efficiency and ways to compete (and win) in the market. Their people are energized to be a part of the company and are motivated to do their best for their customers, communities, and colleagues. When change is needed, the leaders catalyze it by appealing to the positive elements and emotional forces in the existing culture to align it with the change they want to see happen.

3

The Leader's Role

Aligning Costs with Strategy

In working with senior industry leaders in dozens of organizations implementing sweeping Fit for Growth transformation programs, we have seen some succeed spectacularly and others stumble. But whatever the circumstance or outcome, certain consistent leadership lessons emerge on how to achieve the promise of a large-scale restructuring while avoiding the pitfalls.

Most of the leaders we work with are experienced corporate practitioners—they've been through their share of change initiatives (and likely endured many that failed earlier in their careers). They know that success is rarely a matter of applying the latest breakthrough methodology or jargon-laden formula; rather, it's an exercise in common sense, the common sense that comes with experience.

Unfortunately, the faith and ability to apply that common sense—especially in a large-scale cost restructuring—is all too rare. Why is it so difficult to keep a sharp focus on the basic priorities that any CEO knows are important? We believe that the uncertainty of the process is partly why. Any transformation aimed at altering an organization's basic way of operating disrupts business as usual and requires individuals to change long-established behaviors—starting at the top with the CEO. This requires everyone else to take a collective leap of faith. They must adjust their habits and adopt new structures, working practices, and guidelines without a clear line of sight on the outcome of all these efforts. The need for change may be pressing and the targets clearly conveyed, but the way the journey will unfold is unknown. Much of it cannot be known.

This uncertainty is unsettling and means that contradictory messages will filter back to the top leadership. Juxtaposed with signs proclaiming real progress will be frantic feedback that "we can't work this way!" To make the journey of transformation, leaders must have the conviction—along with the humility—to press forward, even when the route to their destination isn't fully mapped out.

How Do You Know When It's Time?

What is clear and what ultimately motivates leaders to take the first steps on a Fit for Growth journey is the discomfort of staying where they are. Perhaps your company is facing one of these situations:

- An activist investor is demanding a step-change reduction in your cost structure—or in your lead competitor's cost structure, and you're next.
- Your costs have been growing faster than revenues and you cannot stem the tide.
- You need to invest in new capabilities, but legacy processes continue to absorb resources and you cannot find the funds to invest in new capabilities.
- Competitors are challenging your fundamental business model, and you need to adapt quickly.
- You're divesting a business and don't want stranded costs.
- Or you just see the writing on the wall and know that you need to transform your business before the market does it for you. (By the way, that's the way to be: proactive in staying Fit for Growth.)

Whether the underlying issue is one of market competitiveness or your own financial stability, there are any number of reasons to embark on a Fit for Growth program, and even strong and stable companies are candidates. What will vary—depending on the company's market competitiveness and financial strength—is the relative emphasis of the program. Is your company

THE FIT FOR GROWTH JOURNEY DEPENDS ON YOUR STARTING POINT

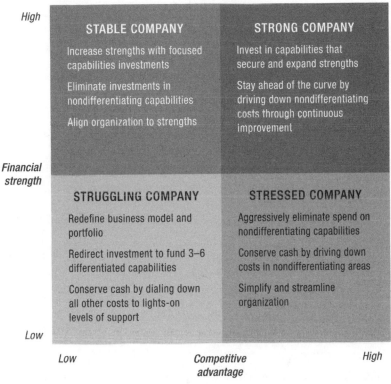

STABLE COMPANY

Increase strengths with focused capabilities investments

Eliminate investments in nondifferentiating capabilities

Align organization to strengths

STRONG COMPANY

Invest in capabilities that secure and expand strengths

Stay ahead of the curve by driving down nondifferentiating costs through continuous improvement

STRUGGLING COMPANY

Redefine business model and portfolio

Redirect investment to fund 3–6 differentiated capabilities

Conserve cash by dialing down all other costs to lights-on levels of support

STRESSED COMPANY

Aggressively eliminate spend on nondifferentiating capabilities

Conserve cash by driving down costs in nondifferentiating areas

Simplify and streamline organization

High / *Low* — *Financial strength*

Low — *Competitive advantage* — *High*

Source: PwC Strategy&

Figure 3.1

stressed, struggling, stable, or strong (see Figure 3.1)? In the lower left quadrant, you have a struggling company trying to shed costs as quickly as possible to survive; in the upper right is a strong company looking to invest in key capabilities to stay ahead of its industry.

In our experience, the agenda of a typical Fit for Growth transformation is 80/20—80 percent weighted toward cost reduction and 20 percent toward building capabilities. In some cases, it may reach 70/30, but rarely 60/40. Our strong and persistent advice to clients is to establish more of a balance between cutting costs and growing stronger. And we are seeing especially prescient companies doing just that.

The Three Core Questions Leaders Ask

So, knowing that many of the steps along the journey are uncertain and disruptive, and that most companies embark on the journey from a reactive rather than proactive posture, what advice do we offer leaders as they design and execute major cost-restructuring programs? Over the years, we have found that CEOs and other top leaders have three core questions:

1. How do I energize my organization for transformation?
2. How do I achieve cost fitness while also enabling growth?
3. How do I actually manage the transformation and make it enduring?

We have distilled a set of 10 leadership principles that provide answers to these questions. These combine the first principles of strategic cost reduction and reallocation with the "new normal" mandate dictated by increasingly activist investors and shareholders demanding accelerated value creation. In the following sections we review each question in turn, along with the principles that address them:

Question 1: How Do I Energize My Organization for Transformation?

CEOs succeed in compelling and accelerating implementation of large-scale, complex change by starting at the top. They look in the mirror and ask, "How do I lay out a case for change that will stir my senior team into action and allow us to speak with one voice to the entire organization?" The CEO's challenge is to engage personally with his or her colleagues who run the company's business units and functions, and work to bring them on board until they share his or her sense of passion and urgency for executing the chosen strategy. Until the entire leadership team feels that sense of personal accountability, the organization cannot make the required leap forward.

Principle 1: Make the case for change. Most people understand that business conditions are tough. A highly competitive marketplace will affect companies in unpredictable and often punishing ways. As a result, they are prepared to accept and even support a large-scale change effort if they are convinced it is necessary. But for this to happen, the CEO must personally make the case, starting with a compelling and candid analysis of the business climate and the company's (faltering) position within it. He or she needs to make bracingly clear why the organization must make major changes.

As one CEO we worked with said, "If you're the leader, you've got to define the problem, no matter how brutal, and you've got to use honest and unambiguous language. Your staff can't do it. Your senior managers can't do it. Only *you* can tell people about the reality your company is facing. If you don't, they'll never accept it."

This analysis must be done from a *market back* perspective: it must demonstrate a clear connection with the needs of the company's customers, and it must accurately depict the competitors. It must articulate the company's differentiating capabilities and underline the importance of redirecting investment to them. The analysis should be forward looking as well, providing a compelling picture of what the organization can become.

The CEO need not map out details, but he or she must make clear the magnitude of the challenge, and the commitment to a new aspiration must remain unswerving as the particulars develop. He or she must maintain a sense of urgency by continuing to press and elaborate on the case for change throughout its implementation. Meanwhile, the executive team needs to purposefully reinforce that message by articulating the goals and the value of becoming a more focused, growth-oriented company and modeling the behaviors expected.

Often a CEO is reluctant to make the case before hammering out all the details. Even with a "burning platform" (a clear and credible picture of the dire fate that looms if the organization doesn't change), leaders are often unwilling to present a plan that does not feel complete. Yet not only is a detailed road map unnecessary at the start; it can actually be counter-productive. Presenting too much detail gets people focused on particulars rather than on the larger purpose, which is nothing less than a new way of operating in the marketplace. In addition, even if it were possible to offer a fleshed-out plan, doing so would leave no room for people to participate in its development, a process that is vital both for generating fresh ideas and for ensuring that people feel committed to the outcome.

Of course, nothing commits the organization to the cost savings goal more emphatically than communicating it to the outside world, particularly shareholders. Publicly committing to the financial impact of the cost-restructuring program at its outset (e.g., on analyst calls) reinforces its strategic importance and serves as a powerful deterrent to backsliding.

Principle 2: Align the top. The senior management team must invest in the case for change first. They must be unified, aligned, and committed to taking the steps necessary to achieve the targets articulated. That's not always easy. The more revolutionary the change, the more likely it is that those with power and status in the old regime will resist it. Some members of the incumbent management team will lack the capabilities, mindset, and willpower to execute the program. For that reason, one of the early actions in any transformation should be facilitating those executives' alignment—or their departure—swiftly and discreetly. Don't hang skeptics publicly; bring them in for a one-on-one fireside chat to let them know that the transformation is not going away. Recognize that many "squeaky wheels" care deeply about the organization. Securing their cooperation for the collective journey is worth the effort because, once they see the light, they often become the most effective and passionate advocates for change.

Every individual on the leadership team needs to have a stake in the *whole* transformation, not just that piece related to his or her business or function. As one CEO put it, "Everyone has to own the problem, even if they don't like doing so. They've got to understand it, believe it, suck it up, and move ahead." This particular leader brought his senior team together on a retreat early in the process, laid out the case for change, and then asked each one of them to put into words exactly why he or she was personally committed to the transformation. By requiring them all to thoughtfully articulate ownership, he was able to create genuine consensus around a difficult undertaking.

Aligning the top often requires moving people out of traditional silos, at least temporarily, so they can broaden their perspective beyond execution of their day-to-day responsibilities. For example, one CEO we know of had his general counsel take charge of the company's emerging-markets growth strategy during a transformation. You also need to put incentives in place to provide team leaders with a clear stake in the ultimate success of the change effort. Financial incentives are necessary but not enough. Public recognition is another motivator. One CEO we worked with put the executive most skeptical about centralization in charge of the initiative to centralize—visibly identifying her with its success or failure and compelling her to wear the company hat instead of the mantle of her division. It worked!

Principle 3: Declare a "new day" and grant amnesty for the past. While it's important to make clear the burning platform you are running *from*, it's even more essential that you paint a compelling picture of the promising destination you are headed *to*. You have to anchor the disruptive change you are launching in a positive, strategic vision of the future and your company's prospects for growth in it—a vision that will actually inspire and attract people to commit.

There are winners and losers in any major change initiative. In designating some capabilities or businesses nonstrategic, you will be threatening established fiefdoms with entrenched supporters. Bring these controversial decisions and thorny issues to light in an inclusive, constructive way, one that focuses on the future, not the past—what you hope and expect to accomplish rather than on the threats and tough times ahead. Encourage teams to speak openly, without censoring themselves, when they present ideas to the leadership. Every vested interest that is cut should be linked to an opportunity for doing something great in the future.

Start by granting amnesty for the past. There is nothing to be gained from looking backward and blaming past administrations or decisions. To appeal to hope and that positive vision of the future, explicitly rule out censure and sanctions for past actions. It's a new day. By granting amnesty, you also communicate that traditional roadblocks and excuses—such as "We've always done it that way"—no longer apply. Managers will reconsider priorities and trade-offs that were previously inconceivable. That said, amnesty is not a license to perpetuate bad behavior. Employees, even leaders, who resist or undermine the journey ahead should be given the option, indeed the invitation, to disembark.

In everything you do, avoid putting people on the defensive. If your mandate appears to be simply reducing headcount, the only emotion you will stimulate is fear. And fear does not embrace change. Fear hunkers down and defends its turf. This is why a positive view of the post-transformation future is so important. Indeed, many renowned business leaders, including Jack Welch and Steve Jobs, have built thriving enterprises based on early and aggressive cost transformation. If people perceive that they will end up working in a less bureaucratic company poised for growth, they will sign on.

Principle 4: Showcase quick wins. To build confidence and accelerate momentum, identify and showcase quick wins early in the transformation process. These are cuts that generate significant savings rapidly with relatively minor transition costs. These early "trophies" communicate that the company is serious about tackling nonessential, nonstrategic costs to free up funds for its truly differentiating capabilities.

These quick wins encompass more than the low-hanging fruit captured in any standard round of cost cutting. They can be found in three principal areas.

1. *Discretionary spending:* Tighten your belt by doubling down on "nice to have" expenses. Fully enforce your spending policies, lower expense approval thresholds, and eliminate perks for those who go "above and beyond" on matters unrelated to your strategy. Dial down support services. You might reduce the number of custom reports or analyses that the finance staff is required to produce and adopt self-service or standard reports instead. Or you might redesign travel policies with tighter approvals for long-distance trips.

2. *External spending:* Aggressively negotiate prices with suppliers. Seek outright concessions in certain categories while negotiating contracts with more favorable pricing (in return for higher volume or longer terms) in others.

3. *Management hierarchy:* Examine your middle and senior manager ranks and assess their spans of control (i.e., number of direct reports). Seek opportunities to consolidate management positions or increase their spans. Challenge the seniority and salary-grade creep of your middle management, and consider a one-time releveling of salary bands.

Question 2: How Do I Achieve Cost Fitness While Enabling Growth?

A Fit for Growth effort ideally follows a thoughtful sequence: focus on capabilities, align the cost structure, and organize for growth, with an underlying base of enabling change and cultural evolution, as noted in Chapter 2. Costs are often the red flag summoning immediate attention, particularly when a company's financial situation is dire. The balance sheet may be listing under the weight of unfunded liabilities or the organizational structure may be out of whack. However, you should not set about aligning your cost structure until you know what you are aligning it to—your differentiating capabilities. That is the only way to enable growth while cutting costs.

Principle 5: Put everything on the table. To be credible, you have to put absolutely everything on the table, even seemingly "sacred cow" expenses such as the business or the function the CEO used to run or the one he or she just acquired. Everything should be under consideration: the company jet, the executive dining room, corporate giving, even employee benefits. This sends a powerful signal to the organization that "we're all in this together." If the CEO's pet project is on the chopping block, the urgency of change becomes clear, and managers will be more reluctant to buttonhole their sponsor on the executive committee to apply for special exemptions.

To demonstrate that indeed everything was on the table, a media company recently eliminated all executive frills, starting with the corporate headquarters building—a crown jewel, but located in a different part of town than the company's other offices. Moving the senior executives into the same building with everyone else made a strong statement to shareholders and the public—but it was just a start. The company went on to recast its expense policies and evolve its corporate culture to be more egalitarian. Some of the changes might have been merely symbolic; executives shed their suits, and everyone began coming to work in jeans and T-shirts with the company logo, for example. But those changes accompanied other, more substantive shifts, including an open seating plan and perks that were more evenly distributed through the company.

This example raises an important point: the value of democratizing the process of identifying potential cost savings. The top team and transformation team may not recognize all the opportunities by themselves. Involve people throughout the company in assessing your cost structure dispassionately, while looking toward the future. Encourage them to suggest ideas, and give them the cover and support they need to speak openly, without fear of reprisal.

Principle 6: Challenge the what, how, and how well. To compel the nature and magnitude of change you are seeking, you need to address the root causes of high costs rather than just the symptoms. Don't just look at *how* or *how well* you do something, but also *what* you do in the first place—that determines your cost structure. Carefully assess the businesses in your portfolio, the products and services you deliver, the customers and markets you serve, the capabilities you invest in, and your operations and administrative footprint. Look at where you have located your operations and support functions. Without taking a good look at these structural questions in light of your strategy, you will only be nibbling at your cost base, rather than taking a big bite.

Assess these elements of your cost structure objectively, with an eye toward the future and a stronger foundation for growth. Jettison the businesses and products that do not build on your distinctive capabilities. Relinquish the customers who don't produce sufficient margins, or reorganize your operations to serve them at an appropriate cost.

Don't try to be world-class at everything—that's a recipe for waste. If the function, process, or activity is not integral to delivering on your strategy or enhancing a capability that truly differentiates you in the market, settle for being good enough. Apply this fresh lens to your entire business and look for step-change shifts in costs, even if it means substantially reducing head count, IT investment, or whole processes.

Principle 7: Balance cost cuts with capabilities investments. The prospect of working hard to build something competitively distinguishing is highly motivating for most employees; the prospect of cutting costs is not. Therefore, efforts to significantly change the cost structure of an organization must always be framed within the positive context of building unique, distinctive, and powerful capabilities.

The bottom-line impact of a cost transformation is quantifiable and appealing to certain audiences, such as shareholders, which is why many CEOs lead with it in their rallying cries. But articulating a clear and coincident commitment to investing in the company's differentiating capabilities is equally important, and enlists even broader support, including the support of the employees charged with making the transformation happen.

One of our clients was particularly clear and compelling in casting its cost reduction initiative in terms of the key capabilities it would need to move forward: nontraditional marketing expertise, a facility for managing outsourcing relationships, and sharp brand focus. By deftly describing these capabilities and how they served the larger strategic vision, the CEO was able not only to set a new course for revenue growth, but also to convince employees that the transformation offered them a chance to build their own experience and skills. This helped people embrace the change.

The mistake we see all too often is that senior leaders defer capabilities building until the cost savings have been captured. They figure they will have the time and energy to focus on their growth agenda later. But you can't effect step-change transformation without fueling your growth engine. If you don't identify, articulate, and nurture your differentiating capabilities, you will stunt your new, slimmed-down organization.

Question 3: How Do I Manage the Transformation and Make It Enduring?

The magnitude and nature of the change you're undertaking inevitably creates a unique risk profile along each step of the change process. What is the best way to mitigate those risks? Depending on the company's culture and the magnitude of the effort ahead, the solution tends to fall along a spectrum, but we recommend a programmatic approach. That can range from a small executive steering committee charged with overseeing the cost reduction effort, to a fully staffed and empowered program management office (PMO), run by a lead transformation executive with multiple work-streams designing and executing changes across the company. The more the effort is embedded in the culture of the company, the more likely it will take root and endure.

Principle 8: Set up a parallel organization to change the business. Cost transformation is not business as usual, but you need to run your business as usual while you design and enact the necessary changes across your organization. The best way to accomplish this is to establish a dedicated PMO to oversee implementation of a single, cohesive transformation program—rather than a collection of separate and decentralized expense-reduction projects. Led by a highly credible and widely admired senior leader, this is a cross-functional team of the company's most creative and talented managers and staff who are dedicated to the transformation. The PMO is charged with achieving program goals and working with the executive team to deliver results.

The central task of the PMO is to guide the complex, often disruptive change process and to align the many cross-functional working teams that will drive the transformation. These teams will essentially be designing the future of the organization, so staff them with "the best and brightest," and give them the information and authority they need to make the necessary trade-offs and execute decisions once approved. Each team should be tasked with clear targets and deliverables. The PMO tracks progress in a standard ized way tied to the bottom line, and schedules frequent reviews with senior management to assess that progress, make decisions, and report ongoing results. Last, the PMO helps the organization adopt a continuous-improvement approach so it can keep capturing gains after the formal transformation program ends.

Principle 9: Communicate before, during, and after. As noted by one CEO who skillfully built support for a wholesale transformation of his company, "If you want to motivate people to do something big, you must use clear language. People deal with reality better than with ambiguity." Communicating early and often is an article of faith in these massive change campaigns—it's almost trite—but very few companies manage to deliver on the promise, caught up as they are in the day-to-day tumult of a transformation program.

Major change will not happen, and it definitely won't stick, if employees don't have a clear idea of what the future holds. Skillful internal and external communication tied to a strong strategic vision is a must. Internally, the CEO must make the case for change in blunt, realistic, lucid terms. All the communications that cascade from that should be consistent, yet adapted to the specific issues and concerns of each business unit or function. It's important to recognize that the most important internal audience, necessarily, will be the survivors—those who will remain part of the company after the cost restructuring. And in a networked environment in which e-mail communication is common, and forwarding messages is as easy as a mouse click, communicators must accept that anything they write for an internal audience will make its way to analysts, reporters, or competitors.

External communications to Wall Street analysts and the media should be proactive, clear, and consistent as to the goals of the transformation, addressing specifically how it benefits the business in the short and long term. Sometimes, approaching analysts early with a strong, market-based rationale is extremely effective in getting investors to understand and support the changes. Communications to the board of directors should frame every objective within the larger strategic vision and new operating model.

The most common mistake we see in communications occurs when leaders wait too long before explaining the logic behind the transformation strategy. This hesitation generally arises because the CEO doesn't have all the answers yet and fears announcing anything before a detailed plan is in place. But waiting too long dilutes urgency and undermines the market-based case for change. It also creates a vacuum in which rumors run rampant, putting senior managers in the position of responding to their staff rather than leading them.

Principle 10: Keep the weight off. A cost transformation is more than an exercise in reconfiguring costs and strategy—in fact, it's doomed to failure if that's all it purports to be. The true transformation is in the behaviors and practices of the people who comprise the organization. If these don't change, the change will not stick.

During the course of any major change effort, new practices for achieving accountability, distributing benefits, allocating incentives, and tracking results are introduced. These should remain in place even after financial targets are met. Another common mistake we see is when leadership declares victory at the finish line yet fails to follow through on signals that parts of the business are reverting back to the old operating procedures.

To avoid that setback, don't dismantle the PMO too soon—it can help institutionalize new ways of working, budgets, and incentives.

As anyone who has successfully lost weight can attest, it requires vigilance and discipline to keep from slipping back into old habits. Leaders must continue to enforce new policies, procedures, and resource allocations to ensure that differentiating capabilities continue to receive disproportionate investment, while other expenses are tightly managed.

What Makes the Fit for Growth Approach Different

These 10 principles represent our best advice based on decades of working with companies to reduce their cost structures—often radically. It's this experience and the lessons learned from our work that informed the development of the Fit for Growth approach. Fit for Growth is not only about cutting costs—it starts from a fundamentally different premise than classic cost cutting. It's about enabling growth. And you have only to look as far as your front yard to understand that the best way to encourage growth in the direction you want is to prune, sometimes severely. You need to eliminate the dead wood and errant limbs that divert resources from the core and thriving parts of the plant.

The Fit for Growth approach differs from conventional cost reduction in terms of philosophy, methodology, organization linkage, change management and sustainability, as Figure 3.2 shows. We will explore these further, particularly in Part III.

In essence, the Fit for Growth approach differs from conventional cost reduction in its perspective. It starts with strategy—with a focus on what to keep, rather than what to cut. All spending is investment. Every cost is a choice. The secret to unlocking growth through cost reduction is to make deliberate choices not only about what to cut, but also about where to invest.

In our view, the right choices are those that close the gap between strategy and execution. This means investing in differentiating capabilities— the combinations of processes, tools, knowledge, skills, and organization that consistently deliver value for you and that set your company apart from others. You compete on the basis of your differentiating capabilities. They

KEY DIFFERENCES OF THE
FIT FOR GROWTH APPROACH

Cost Reduction Approach		Fit for Growth Approach
Benchmark-driven approach focused on matching competition	PHILOSOPHY	Strategy-back approach that protects "good costs" (differentiating capabilities) and reduces "bad costs"
Applies a broad suite of cost reduction levers across all cost pools uniformly	METHODOLOGY	Prioritizes capabilities, segments costs, and applies reduction levers at tailored intensities
Focuses on structure—"lines and boxes" and "spans and layers"	ORGANIZATION LINKAGE	Views holistic organization design as key to transforming and sustaining the new cost structure
Pushes for a top-down cascade of leadership alignment and communications	CHANGE MANAGEMENT	Advocates culture-led change focused on scaling a critical few behaviors and leveraging employee "pride builders"
Addresses sustainability during implementation	SUSTAINABILITY	Includes organization, process, talent, and cultural enablers of enduring cost management from Day 1

Source: PwC Strategy&

Figure 3.2

are complicated and expensive enough to require most of your time, money, and attention—but without them, you are just like every other company.

In the new normal—a world of global competition, market share erosion, and margin compression—being like every other company is just not good enough.

PART II

How to Cut Costs and Grow Stronger

A Manager's Guide

4

Levers of Cost Reduction

What, Where, and How

From reading Part I of our book, you should understand the hallmarks of a Fit for Growth organization: a relentless focus on differentiating capabilities, an omnipresent discipline to optimize costs, and an aligned and supportive organization to enable growth. Fitness is an ongoing exercise, comparable to what an athlete does by training methodically and regularly. It is not, in other words, a one-time activity. Unfortunately, like the patient who doesn't change his habits except in response to a doctor's dire warning, most companies do not think about fitness until they have a problem—until their profitability, market share, or stock price suffers. At that point a company must act quickly to get back in shape, and rather than a well-intentioned goal toward which everyone works gradually, cost reduction becomes an urgent sprint to survive.

Part II of our book is dedicated to helping companies understand the tools they have at their disposal—the *levers* they can pull—to cut costs. To focus on each of these levers and explain them in detail, we will show how they work in a major, programmatic Fit for Growth transformation initiative. To be sure, the same cost-reduction levers can be, and often are, used in less comprehensive circumstances—when healthy companies are trying to improve an already high level of performance, redeploy their resources to carry out new strategies, or maintain and increase their fitness level after a transformation is complete. The levers we discuss in this part of the book will be familiar to these high-performing companies and may well explain some of their success in the first place.

Any well-run Fit for Growth transformation initiative has three major elements:

1. *Setting the objective*—a target for overall financial savings and a timeframe for achieving it.
2. *Identifying differentiating capabilities* that define your company—these will highlight areas that must be preserved and, if possible, strengthened while you are cutting elsewhere.
3. *Selecting the levers* you will use to transform the cost structure and free up funds—either to take them straight to the bottom line or reinvest them in your differentiating capabilities.

Setting the Objective

Every cost transformation program needs to put a stake in the ground in the form of a stretch target that quantifies the program's expected benefits. The target represents a macro-level financial goal and serves two purposes. First, it crystalizes the challenge for the company—namely, whether the company is facing a temporary hurdle (a small, short-term earnings shortfall), an existential challenge (imminent bankruptcy), or something in between. Second, the target stimulates the organization to break free from existing modes of operation and think aggressively and creatively about what it can change. If the target calls for a 20 percent expense reduction, everyone understands that business as usual and incremental remedies won't be sufficient, and that a radically new approach is needed.

The cost-reduction target is determined top down by senior leaders, and is informed by the company's objectives, external benchmarks, and investor expectations. Multiple methods are typically used to "triangulate" the target: each method provides a point estimate or a range of savings, and collectively these estimates provide senior leaders a stretch target. Improvements in share price, EBIT margin, and cost as a percentage of revenue are typical goals and methods to triangulate the target. Metrics from a direct competitor are often used as a yardstick.

For example, a group of activist investors had acquired a significant stake in a major technology company that had fallen on tough times. The company's EBIT margin lagged its major competitor's margin by about a third, and the activists challenged management to address the gap.

Before setting out on a transformation effort, the management team deliberated what margin improvement was needed and, consequently, what type of effort was needed. As the first step in their performance improvement journey, they set a margin improvement target using four estimates:

1. They targeted the top quartile of EBIT margin among their peer set, which would generate a $350 million improvement;
2. They evaluated investors' earnings expectations, which suggested a $400 million improvement;
3. They benchmarked their operations and costs and sized a $325 million gap with similar organizations; and last,
4. The management team included their own "gut sense" margin improvement estimate: $300 million.

Based on these estimates, the management set a $300 million to $375 million margin improvement target, with a $400 million stretch target (see Figure 4.1).

ESTIMATING THE MARGIN IMPROVEMENT TARGET

Source: PwC Strategy&

Figure 4.1

This sort of exercise is immensely valuable. It helps companies set savings targets that are aggressive yet credible, covering enough funds to achieve financial objectives and reinvest in growth, while providing a cushion if everything does not go as planned.

Along with the magnitude of the target, management needs to decide how quickly they want to cut costs. Our experience suggests that accelerated transformations—those done in two years or less—do best. The more aggressive timeline spurs the organization to think creatively, keeps management focused, and staves off organizational fatigue.

Identifying Differentiating Capabilities

A Fit for Growth transformation is different from a typical cost reduction effort due to its focus on preserving and strengthening a company's differentiating capabilities. The cost reductions cannot be arbitrary, implemented across the board, or done without regard for differentiating capabilities. On the contrary, this is one situation where executives not only can, but absolutely must play favorites—they must make deliberate choices about where to cut aggressively, where to cut more thoughtfully, and where they might even want to spend more. As we noted in Chapter 2, the aggressive cutting should focus on lights-on and table-stakes capabilities. The more thoughtful cutting (only to ensure efficient execution) should be in differentiating capabilities.

A *capability* is a combination of processes, tools, knowledge, skills, and organization. In our lexicon, a *differentiating* capability is one that enables a company to outperform; it is something you do well that customers value and competitors cannot beat. When three to six mutually reinforcing capabilities come together in a differentiating capabilities *system*, a company gains a competitive advantage and a right to win over its competitors.

Since so much of a company's success hinges on these three to six differentiating capabilities, they must be preserved, and in fact strengthened, during a Fit for Growth transformation. This means that at the start of the transformation, the executives should explicitly identify and agree upon the differentiating capabilities.

There are a few challenges to doing this. First, companies sometimes define their differentiating capabilities so broadly that it is unclear whether they truly understand what they do that's distinctive. For instance, a consumer healthcare company could say that "product development" and "marketing" are two of its differentiating capabilities. But are those descriptions specific enough to be useful? In the days when Pfizer had a consumer healthcare division, it defined two of its capabilities in a much more nuanced way. One capability was claims-based marketing around a specific health benefit; another was the ability to influence regulatory management and government policy. These were core components of Pfizer Consumer Healthcare's capabilities system; they gave it a significant edge in the market and helped it sell its products in a wide number of countries.[1]

Second, executives naturally think of differentiating capabilities from their own vantage point: for an R&D leader, it might be some aspect of innovation; for an operations leader, it might be a highly flexible set of manufacturing processes; and for a sales leader, it might be the sales team's ability to build and maintain relationships with key customers.

Third, executives struggle to narrow down the list of differentiating capabilities to a few (3–6) that truly *differentiate* the company. To many, everything they do is special, and not selecting something as a differentiating capability implies they (or one of their peers) is not good at what they do.

If the differentiating capabilities are not articulated appropriately and agreed to, executives risk cutting or overinvesting in the wrong places. But how do you articulate your differentiating capabilities?

The best way to get agreement about your differentiating capabilities is through another triangulation. An internal self-assessment is the first step. What does your executive team believe your company does especially well? Why is this decisive in the marketplace? Second is a validation of your internal perspective through an external customer assessment. Do your customers choose you for the reasons you think and value the same capabilities that you do? This provides an important unbiased perspective. And the third step is an additional calibration through benchmarking your capabilities against the competition. This requires an objective assessment of what you and your rivals do well, and which capabilities you excel at and perform better than they do. Benchmarking can also offer insights into the question of what you should be doing with a capability—should you build it out more if it can be a true point of differentiation, or build out different capabilities if there is a white space in the market that you can better serve? In this triangulation exercise, executives must shed their biases and force-rank three to six top capabilities that provide the company with a right to win over competitors.

Selecting the Cost-Reduction Levers

Once the executive leadership team has set a stretch target and identified differentiating capabilities, it is time to think about how to free up the funds. Fit for Growth companies don't boast of their ability to do more with less, as the cliché goes. Their filter of differentiating capabilities allows them to do more in the areas that matter more, even after making cuts. To accomplish this and reach their target, in every other area, they understand they *must do less with less*.

In our client work, we use a Fit for Growth Cost Reduction framework that organizes various cost reduction levers (see Figures 4.2 and 4.3). The framework challenges companies to reevaluate basic tenets of their business by asking three questions: "What do we do?" "Where do we do it?" and "How (and how well) do we do it?"

"What" Do We Do? Business Portfolio and Capability Choices

These are the investments and costs that are most fundamental to what a company has chosen to do: what products and services does the company sell, to which customers, in what markets, and through which channels. What are the differentiating capabilities versus the table-stakes and lights-on capabilities? Even the seemingly core costs associated with differentiating capabilities merit scrutiny. A company might decide to simplify its operational complexity by divesting pieces of its business portfolio, ceasing to serve unprofitable customers, or exiting a geographic market. The two levers that can be applied to the "What do we do?" question are:

1. *Portfolio rationalization:* Evaluates the net margin contribution and strategic coherence of products, customers, geographies, and entire business units, and decides which ones are central to the company's strategy and way to play.
2. *Zero-basing:* Evaluates the existing set of capabilities and makes choices on what to dial down or simply eliminate. Zero-basing is predicated on the

FIT FOR GROWTH COST REDUCTION FRAMEWORK

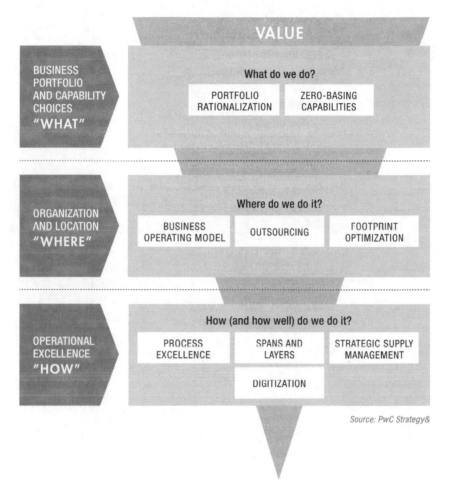

Figure 4.2

concept of a blank sheet and the idea that it's what one is keeping, not what one is cutting, that needs to be justified.

"Where" Do We Do It? Organization and Location

Decisions involving the operating model define how a company organizes its operations and support, how it delivers those services, and where it locates

SAVINGS POTENTIAL BY TARGETED COST LEVER

Cost reduction lever category	Lever	Time needed	Savings potential of addressed spend
BUSINESS PORTFOLIO AND CAPABILITY CHOICES	Portfolio rationalization	~1 year	20%–30%
	Zero-basing capabilities	6–18 months	20%–35%
OPERATING MODEL	Business operating model	12–24 months	15%–25%
	Outsourcing*	6–18 months	5%–50%
	Footprint optimization	12–24 months	15%–20%
OPERATIONAL EXCELLENCE	Process excellence	3–15 months	10%–20%
	Spans and layers	3–4 months	10%–15%
	Strategic supply management	6–12 months	5%–10%
	Digitization	1–3 years	20%–25%

*Outsourcing manufacturing, transportation, and warehousing can result in savings of 5%–10%.
Outsourcing IT and back-office business processes can generate savings of 30%–50%.
Source: PwC Strategy&

Figure 4.3

them. These decisions may imply standardizing and consolidating work across lines of business or geographies in shared service centers, moving operations and support work to low-cost countries, or simply outsourcing select processes to a vendor.

The three levers in this category are:

1. *Business operating model:* Redefines how roles, responsibilities, and decision rights are distributed between headquarters, business units, and shared service organizations. These decisions will influence the level of centralization and standardization in the organization.

2. *Outsourcing:* Evaluates whether some internal capabilities are better performed by a vendor. Outsourcing can cover the vast majority of a company's value chain, including manufacturing, supply chain, R&D, and support services such as IT or finance.
3. *Footprint optimization:* Restructures the physical footprint of a company's manufacturing plants, distribution centers, and R&D and administrative offices. The sites can be consolidated or moved to low-cost locations to reduce costs and improve effectiveness.

"How" and "How Well" Do We Do It? Operational Excellence

Operational excellence levers make it possible to execute existing work more efficiently. These levers include optimizing processes, delayering the organization and increasing management spans of control, deriving benefits from strategic sourcing, and digitizing processes. In many cases, these are areas companies regularly evaluate, versus just giving them attention during enterprise-wide transformations.

Operational excellence levers include:

- *Process excellence:* Optimizes processes for greater efficiency and effectiveness by using Lean, Six Sigma, and other approaches.
- *Spans and layers:* Increases direct reports and reduces management layers to decrease management overhead and flatten the organization.
- *Strategic supply management:* Improves the efficacy of an organization's direct and indirect material spend.
- *Digitization:* Evaluates existing processes, customer channels, and partner interactions for opportunities to use technology to automate manual work and replace manual interactions with digital ones.

Selecting which levers will be used and how is a pivotal moment in any transformation program. These decisions will determine how much savings you produce, the degree of change your organization needs to manage, and how well you are positioned for future growth. Considerable synergies can be achieved by applying multiple levers concurrently across multiple functions and business units. For example, business-portfolio decisions frequently give rise to footprint and operating model questions. Process excellence is much more powerful when combined with digitization. And zero-basing is inherent in levers such as process excellence, strategic supply management, and outsourcing, all of which are about discontinuing low-value work and making lights-on capabilities much more efficient.

Over the next nine chapters, we will dive deeply into each of the levers—what they entail, when and how to execute them, and the best practices for applying them successfully.

5

Portfolio Rationalization

Decide What Business You Should Be In

Strategic clarity and coherence set successful companies apart from their competitors. Coherent companies offer products and services that fit seamlessly with their value proposition and leverage the company's differentiating capabilities. At the corporate level, this often means disinvesting in—or exiting entirely—businesses that don't fit their chosen identity. This strategy is supported by the economic concept known as the *conglomerate discount,* which argues that managing a diverse set of businesses hampers focus, creates complexity, and makes it difficult to scale winning capabilities. As a result, conglomerates often generate lower returns than more focused companies.

The same logic applies throughout the company's portfolios of products, services, markets, and sales and distribution channels. As the portfolios become more diverse, complexity rises, driving up costs and creating ineffectiveness. *Portfolio complexity* usually increases as companies seek growth—as they look for new ways to satisfy customers, expand into new customer segments or geographies, address more specific consumer or customer needs and wants, or provide differentiated levels of service. As we noted in Chapter 4, decisions about the portfolio are fundamental to "what the company does" and cascade throughout the organization, making them a key element in the cost reduction framework. Rationalizing the portfolio is thus a powerful lever for cutting costs and refocusing the company on its differentiating capabilities, making it central to the Fit for Growth transformation framework.

What Is Portfolio Rationalization?

In the pursuit of growth, many organizations tend to add complexity by expanding or diversifying the portfolio with, for example, new customers, products, services, or channels. Figure 5.1 shows the relationship between

TRADE-OFFS BETWEEN VALUE AND COMPLEXITY

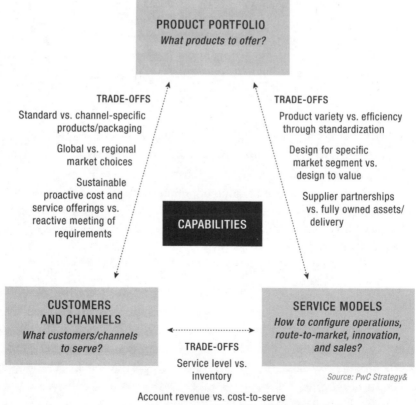

PRODUCT PORTFOLIO
What products to offer?

TRADE-OFFS
Standard vs. channel-specific products/packaging

Global vs. regional market choices

Sustainable proactive cost and service offerings vs. reactive meeting of requirements

TRADE-OFFS
Product variety vs. efficiency through standardization

Design for specific market segment vs. design to value

Supplier partnerships vs. fully owned assets/delivery

CAPABILITIES

CUSTOMERS AND CHANNELS
What customers/channels to serve?

TRADE-OFFS
Service level vs. inventory

SERVICE MODELS
How to configure operations, route-to-market, innovation, and sales?

Source: PwC Strategy&

Account revenue vs. cost-to-serve

Traditional vs. omni-channel fulfillment

Figure 5.1

complexity and value as companies make decisions about the products they offer; the ways they configure their operations and go-to-market, innovation, and sales strategies; and the customers and channels they serve. In most cases, these decisions involve trade-offs, and organizations have a tendency to gradually add complexity over time as they negotiate these trade-offs—often without realizing it.

Portfolio complexity shows itself in two ways. The first is in diminishing returns: each dollar of revenue added comes at a higher cost, since it is more expensive to do many things if they are not at scale or don't line up with the company's capabilities. The second is in collaboration disadvantage: complexity across the portfolio forces management to spend more time coordinating internally. Again, costs rise disproportionately as a result.

Portfolio complexity can take many forms:

- *Category complexity:* Having a diverse set of product or service categories to cater to different customer needs or segments drives supply chain costs, sales costs, and design and innovation costs higher. These inefficiencies also ripple across the organization in higher overhead costs.
- *Product complexity:* A high number of stock-keeping units (SKUs) can drive high inventory or production costs per unit for manufacturers, due to small production runs, small package sizes, and the inefficient logistics and warehousing needs that the disparate products require. For service providers, too large a portfolio of product or service offerings, as well as too much customization of different offerings, can create inefficiency and drive costs as well.
- *Customer and channel complexity:* Serving many customers can drive up cost-to-serve due to the various service needs and service-level requirements of customers, or the variety of trade terms that need to be administered
- *Geography complexity:* As companies expand into new markets, especially in new countries, complexity rises as they need to manage additional distribution channels, dedicated local teams, transportation and logistics, product localization and local rules, regulations, and taxes. Serving small-revenue countries, even if the goal is to eventually grow there, can create large costs.

Case Study: An Overly Complex Commercial-Products Business

A \$1 billion commercial products division of a globally diversified company recently found itself struggling to defend its market position, find growth, and boost its bottom-line performance. Leadership realized that portfolio complexity had spiraled out of control, due in part to a history of loosely integrated acquisitions in which overlapping or similar brands and products were acquired. The company had dozens of brands, product categories, facilities, P&Ls, and ERP systems, more than 1,500 suppliers, and hundreds of thousands of SKUs, but less than 15 percent of the portfolio delivered more than three-quarters of sales. A portfolio optimization program analyzed the brand and product portfolios, searching for commonality and duplication in such areas as brand positioning, applications, channels, delivery models, production, and sales approaches. Each product was assessed in terms of its contribution to the portfolio and the trade-off among costs, value contribution, and strategic importance. The effort ultimately reduced the number of product lines by almost 50 percent, and total savings for the company resulted in a 7 percent improvement in EBIT.

Portfolio rationalization systematically analyzes the profitability of categories, products, customers, channels, and geographies to identify where complexity is driving high costs, understand the root causes, and take out both the costs and the underlying drivers of complexity. The goal is to reduce complexity that is not differentiated or adding value, while building a capability to manage the "good complexity" that is driving profits.

Not all complexity is bad, of course. Complexity is good when the balance between added value and added costs is right—and when managers are able to limit the rate at which costs go up. A company can create competitive advantage when it knows how to add complexity in the pursuit of growth that's based on its differentiating capabilities—creating offerings that competitors can't match without being overwhelmed by operational cost or organizational gridlock (see Figure 5.2).

STRATEGIES TO BALANCE REVENUE AND COMPLEXITY COSTS TO MAXIMIZE VALUE

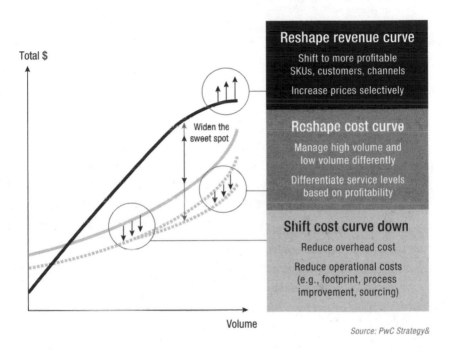

Figure 5.2

Portfolio Rationalization Myths Debunked

Complexity is bad; companies should have a more streamlined or simplified portfolio. The key is to strike the right balance between rewarded and unrewarded complexity, accepting or even adding complexity where the company's capabilities can actually drive profitable growth. The combination of products, customers, propositions, channels, and geographies should be optimized to maximize the spread between the cost of complexity and the value.

(continued)

> *(continued)*
>
> *I'm in a fixed-cost business and need to maintain my unprofitable customers to cover my fixed costs.* Given sufficient time, there are no fixed costs. Companies should treat as many cost line-items as possible as intrinsically variable and seek opportunities to scale them according to sales. Overhead structures and other typically "fixed" costs should be scaled according to projections and continuously scrutinized. Instead of allowing portfolio complexity to increase just to cover fixed costs, other cost levers can be used to keep variable costs low or to reduce overhead costs.
>
> *I need to maintain a broad portfolio—including the unprofitable tail—or risk losing my customers altogether.* The customer base and customer preferences are often less correlated than they appear. Customers may very well buy products or projects independently. And a full product range of high, medium, and low offerings may not be necessary for each channel or each customer. The incremental sales and incremental cost need to be evaluated on a case-by-case basis.

When to Use Portfolio Rationalization

Many companies recognize that portfolio complexity is an issue, especially in dire situations such as the case of the commercial products business discussed earlier. Many others, however, fail to see an underlying portfolio complexity problem. Some companies may even mistake the problem for a virtue. They may see their diverse set of product and service categories as proof that they're diversifying market risks, or feel their sprawling and diverse catalog of products and large numbers of customers is evidence they're serving their customers well—all the while ignoring the growing complexity that's undermining their bottom line. Many others find they have created a portfolio complexity problem as they try to react to changes in their marketplace, as in this next case.

Companies that aren't sure if portfolio complexity is an issue should look for a variety of symptoms. Ask yourself these six questions:

1. Is our time to market much slower than the competition's? Are we too slow to respond to changes in the market, or are we sometimes failing to respond at all?
2. Have we been trying to reduce costs across all products, SKUs, or market segments without much success? Do we need to take a more structural approach in our go-to-market and product segmentation approaches?
3. Are we justifying activities and products because we are labeling customers or products as "strategic," even when we know or sense that profitability is not optimal?
4. Are activities fragmented? Are we doing many different things, but none or few at scale?
5. Are too many products or customers generating diminishing returns as sales increase?
6. Does decision making take too long, with multiple iterations? Are we spending more and more time aligning the organization instead of focusing on customers or products?

Answering "yes" to any of these questions suggests that portfolio complexity should be analyzed.

Case Study: Failing to See a Complexity Problem

An industrial services company that maintains large machinery was under pressure from falling demand and increasing competition. Thinking that the drop in the market would be temporary, management lowered prices to stabilize volume and market share in order to cover its fixed costs and avoid layoffs. The new projects the company acquired, however, were typically for smaller machines and generated less revenue per unit than the bigger, higher-value projects they used to do, even though these projects required the same level of customization, spare-parts inventory, and service. As a result, their margin was hit twice: once by lower prices in a more competitive market, and again by much higher complexity costs per unit of revenue.

After a year, as profitability tanked, the management team accepted that the previous market volume and price levels would

(continued)

(*continued*)

not return. Only at that point did they analyze true project profitability (including fully allocated costs) to understand how bad the situation was. As a result, the company refocused on the bigger projects and dropped the smaller ones. This forced them to close a number of workshops and lay off workers as well as reduce overhead and sales force—essentially a reset of their entire business to operate profitably at 30 percent lower revenue.

How to Rationalize the Portfolio

Rationalizing the portfolio follows a three-step process, and it is essential that the transformation team involve all stakeholders from all functions in the analysis and decision making. As noted in the discussion about trade-offs, unless portfolio decisions are made on a collaborative, cross-functional basis, it is easy for decisions made to reduce complexity in one area and to create additional complexity elsewhere (see Figure 5.3).

Step 1: Understand Portfolio Complexity

The first step in portfolio rationalization is to analyze the true, integral profitability of categories, products, markets, channels, and customers.

BUSINESS PORTFOLIO OPTIMIZATION APPROACH

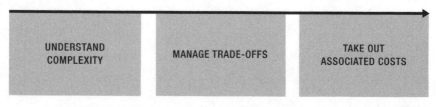

Source: PwC Strategy&

Figure 5.3

Unfortunately, many companies don't have this information readily available. To develop it, they need to perform an analysis that can be likened to activity-based costing. This traditional method of allocating indirect costs, based on a good proxy of how much indirect cost each element consumes, can provide a directionally correct picture of profitability—but it is complex and time consuming. So it pays to first define hypotheses on where the problem might be and to focus the analysis on the expected problem areas, rather than for every product or customer category.

Performance analyses often provide revealing insights—and instantly show where money is being lost. They also enable you to see the underlying problem clearly—for instance, that a small customer or low-volume SKU carries some of the exact same costs in terms of support activities as a large customer or high-volume SKU. For example, at the industrial services company we discussed earlier, nearly 40 percent of projects did not deliver the 15 percent margin required to cover indirect costs, and 20 percent of projects did not make any profit at all, even before cost allocations. A long tail of projects that are not profitable or are below target profitability is not atypical, although in this example it had materially worsened over a short period.

The analysis for categories, markets, channels, or customers is similar to the methodology for products, but applies different lenses. For customer or channel profitability, for example, you would look at the integral cost-to-serve at the current service levels, and at customer profitability. Customer segmentation can be a powerful tool in such an analysis. We often see companies that are spending significant time and resources on customers that are not generating high margins. However, even clients that are generating apparently healthy margins may in fact be unprofitable if they are accounting for a disproportionate share of unallocated costs. In the following case study, such an analysis revealed that the company was devoting too many resources to high-revenue but unprofitable customers, while spending too little on smaller customers with greater profit potential.

These kinds of portfolio analyses can help managers drive a richer conversation—away from the symptoms ("My costs are too high") to the underlying drivers ("Can we afford to serve all these customers in a high-touch model? Do we really need to carry all these products in stock?").

Case Study: Client Segmentation in Business Services

Leaders at a global business services provider were consolidating operations following a merger that had increased the product and services portfolio and moved the firm into a leading industry position. However, costs were rising and competition was intensifying in its most profitable business segment. The company's cost structure was too fixed and underleveraged, eroding margins, and client satisfaction in key areas was low. Leadership launched a transformation to rebuild profitability and set the stage for continued growth. One focus area was improving client services management. Goals included integrating one management approach across services, better managing client demand, recovering "at risk" clients, and managing costs.

The company created metrics to segment clients by cost-to-serve and revenue potential, which provided a realistic view of challenges in the client portfolio and revealed that many large clients were unprofitable (see Figure 5.4). The company had created ad hoc, short-term modifications for several unprofitable clients that increased complexity without adding perceived client benefits. The analysis also revealed that the company was underinvesting in growing the base of smaller, profitable clients. By isolating "good costs" from "bad costs," the segmentation analysis enabled the company to direct resources toward these more profitable clients, and to invest in developing new solutions and entering new markets and more profitable segments.

The result was a 20 percent reduction in direct costs over 18 months, with 20 percent of the cost savings reinvested to create new capabilities. Customer retention and satisfaction improved significantly, with "at risk" clients declining by 30 percent.

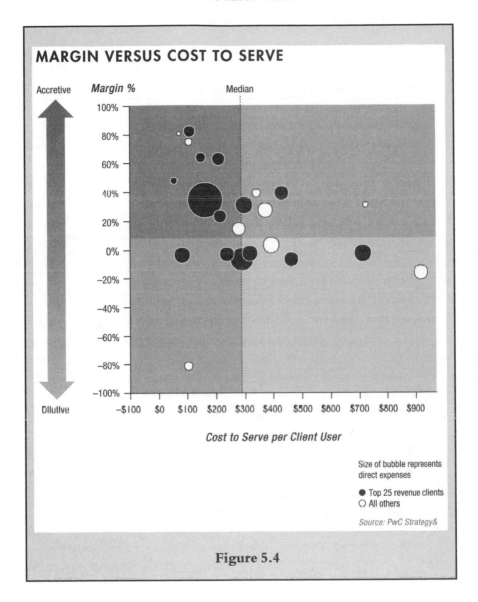

Figure 5.4

Step 2: Manage the Trade-offs

Once the complexity costs and their underlying drivers are identified, the next step is to determine how to solve the problem. There is obviously no single right answer, but some examples will illustrate the actions you can take—as well as the trade-offs that need to be understood to prevent mistakes by making hasty decisions based solely on the analytics.

If low-volume products or SKUs are unprofitable, for example, the questions become: What happens if I stop producing or selling these products? Can I migrate the customer to another product? Will I lose a customer who also buys other, profitable SKUs, once the unprofitable SKUs are no longer available? To answer these questions, you need to link the customers who are buying the products and consider how much of your total revenue the unprofitable product represents. If, for example, three-quarters of such unprofitable products are sold to customers who are otherwise very profitable, the losses may be an acceptable cost to retain the profitable customers.

If a customer is unprofitable, you should test whether the cost-to-serve that customer can be reduced by leveraging multiple methods such as reducing service levels, reducing high-touch/high-cost services, or moving the customer to lower cost support (such as largely self-serve). However, if these options are exhausted, not feasible, or would be suboptimal for the more profitable customers, then portfolio rationalization might be the right decision. In a manufacturing business this might mean simply terminating those contracts or no longer serving these customers. In a project business it might mean no longer accepting projects under a certain projected profitability threshold.

Since the goal of rationalization is to reduce complexity across the company's overall portfolio, leaders must understand and accept trade-offs that are hard for any one department to make. Instead, you need to expand the governance of the rationalization program, and unite the key departments (sales, customer service and operations, marketing, and manufacturing) to make these decisions in light of "what's best for the enterprise."

Step 3: Take Out Associated Costs

It often seems counterintuitive to significantly rationalize a portfolio. Taking out a significant part of unprofitable revenue only eliminates the variable costs. Stranded fixed costs, applied to a lower revenue base, will initially make the problem look worse. And, if new—and profitable—volume cannot be found in the short term, the company will have to take out fixed costs as well. Indeed, this is exactly what needs to happen. The organization has built up significant costs to support the complexity.

Only by taking out these associated costs will portfolio rationalization truly pay off—and many of the levers that can be used to do this are discussed in the following eight chapters.

Portfolio Rationalization Best Practices

Assume that there is portfolio complexity and that it can be rationalized. Start looking for the symptoms and you will likely find significant opportunity.

Be pragmatic. Avoid "boiling the ocean." Learn to recognize the symptoms and start digging into the true costs only where you anticipate you will find the problem. Otherwise portfolio rationalization risks becoming a very extensive cost-allocation exercise with no immediate purpose or impact.

Don't label a product or customer as "strategic" too easily. In most cases, a radical reduction of the unprofitable tail will lead to few collateral losses, and those losses can mostly be justified by the upside efficiency and profitability gains of the portfolio rationalization.

Immediately take out the associated fixed costs and support infrastructure. If not, the benefit will be limited, and complexity will creep back quickly as your managers find ways to remain active and generate new work and complexity.

Make portfolio rationalization a routine and a capability. Most companies only look when they have a problem. Best-practice companies monitor and clean up their portfolio continuously.

6 | Zero-Basing

Justify What to Keep, Not What to Kill

Zero-basing is an essential tool for any company pursuing a Fit for Growth transformation. More than a cost management lever, zero-basing is an overarching, holistic method of examining all business activities to distinguish the differentiating capabilities that create sustainable competitive advantage from the table-stakes capabilities needed to compete in the marketplace and the lights-on capabilities needed to operate any business. Zero-basing is a repeatable process for rigorously scrutinizing every dollar in a company's budget and instilling a culture of cost management across the organization. A well-executed zero-basing program yields sustainable cost reductions, fosters a mindset of questioning the need for every activity, and releases funds to invest in differentiating capabilities.

What Is Zero-Basing?

Zero-basing examines the costs of all activities, based on their strategic priority, value added, and business necessity, rather than budgetary precedent. Nothing is funded just because it was in last year's budget. Instead, zero-basing demands that a strong case be made for every expenditure. A decision-tree analysis based on five questions separates costs that support differentiating capabilities from those that support table-stakes and lights-on capabilities:

1. *What do we need to absolutely keep this business or function going?* What is the bare minimum we need to do? Not all non-differentiating activities can be eliminated. Some are necessary to operate as a business or meet legal and regulatory requirements—to keep the lights on.
2. *Which non-lights on capabilities drive true competitive differentiation and support our right to win?* These are the activities that underpin your three to six truly differentiating capabilities.
3. *Of the capabilities that are not differentiating or lights-on, which ones do we think we can cut altogether?* After scrutinizing various activities in light of budgetary limitations, you may decide your company can do without many things previously considered table stakes.
4. *Of the capabilities we want to preserve, is there a more economical way of deploying them?* The performance and efficiency of many capabilities can be improved using the levers discussed elsewhere in this book.
5. *What risks would the business run if it made the cuts and changes we're considering?* Evaluate the risk through the lens of a business case. Ensure risk-mitigation expenditures generate an acceptable return on investment in light of the likelihood and magnitude of the risks.

Answering these questions enables a company to realign spending priorities to reflect the importance of each capability to competitive differentiation, and to channel resources to critical capabilities while cutting back elsewhere. After assigning each activity to the three capability categories—differentiating, table stakes, and lights on—a company can realign its cost structure to reflect its strategic priorities (see Figure 6.1).

A comprehensive zero-basing can reset the cost structure drastically (assuming no similar recent pruning exercise). A large portion of the savings results from simply eliminating or dialing down spend in non–lights-on activities, through tough choices about where to spend the company's limited funds. In addition, across all capabilities, including lights-on, costs are optimized by applying the cost levers discussed elsewhere in this book, such as portfolio rationalization, outsourcing, business process optimization, and digitization.

A CAPABILITIES-BASED COST STRUCTURE

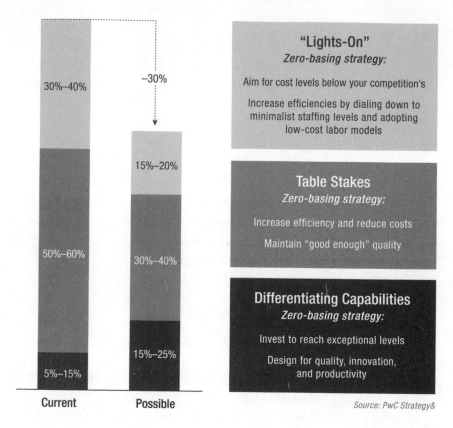

Figure 6.1

For example, the information technology department of a large consumer packaged-goods company reduced internal costs by a total of 39 percent by combining a zero-basing approach with a segmented service model (which systematically restricted and prioritized demand and delivered much of the service through a low-cost outsourcing partner). The most important business units and business applications received the lion's share of dedicated discretionary resources, such as system enhancements and projects to build new features. Even service levels for activities that were previously considered lights-on, such as resolving application-user service tickets, were scrutinized and further segmented based on the criticality of an application to the business. Break-fix tickets for mission-critical applications were addressed right away, while low-priority tickets for applications that did not affect revenue were resolved days or weeks later. Such practices let the department spread demand and reduce the total amount of resources needed at any point in time. This move, in combination with a highly outsourced delivery model, allowed the organization to treat the number of resources as variable and to better match supply of IT resources with prioritized demand.

As a result, costs for differentiating capabilities were trimmed by a modest 10 percent—enabled by better-matched supply and demand, and access to a wide pool of talent through strategic suppliers. Table-stakes activities were cut by 30 percent by right-sizing service levels per application-segment and reducing the number of duplicate applications. Lights-on activities were slashed 60 percent, benefiting significantly from an investment in virtualization and an outsourced delivery model, as well as from offshoring routine applications and infrastructure maintenance services (see Figure 6.2).

A Versatile, Holistic Cost Lever

Zero-basing is a versatile tool that can be used narrowly to optimize a single function, or broadly across a group of functions, a business unit, or the entire organization simultaneously. This comprehensive approach maximizes efficiency throughout the company by putting the entire cost structure on the table and enabling trade-offs on where to dial down and where to invest. In addition, when departments collaborate, they break down the silo mentality and deliver cross-organizational savings that can far exceed the benefits of optimizing individual units.

Internal customers of IT, finance, or HR functions cause unnecessary spending when they ask for more services, or "higher-touch" services than they truly need. This may result from a lack of transparency into the cost to deliver a service, or from functional leaders' desire to pursue excellence initiatives that do not support a company's differentiating capabilities. In such scenarios there are opportunities to rationalize demand for high-touch services, such as superfluous financial reports, unnecessary training sessions, nice-to-have IT projects, and redundant market studies, and to generate significant savings by reducing service levels.

ZERO-BASING AN INFORMATION TECHNOLOGY FUNCTION

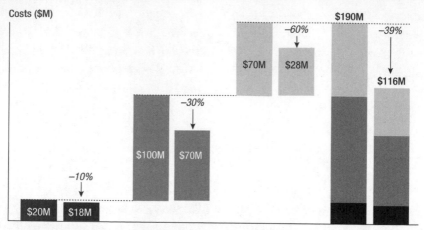

Differentiating Capabilities	Table Stakes	"Lights-On"	Total

Differentiating Capabilities

Invest in sales analytics tools that facilitate user self-service

Establish strategic suppliers to get access to skills in emerging technologies

Outsource development work for strategic projects

Table Stakes

Rationalize business applications to reduce redundant functionality

Offshore routine maintenance activities (e.g., change request, break/fix tickets, upgrades) for all applications including strategic

Match service levels for mission-critical applications to business need—reduce response and resolution times for medium- and low-priority requests

Implement limits around ad hoc analytics and reporting requests

Establish governance around which projects and change requests are prioritized and worked on

Reduce/eliminate use of software vendor consulting services unless mission critical

"Lights-On"

Virtualize physical servers to achieve 80%+ level of virtualization

Offshore helpdesk support to achieve 50%+ savings

Reduce service levels to applications that are not critical to running the business (e.g., ERP)

Transition to a remote user support model versus having dedicated IT personnel in each facility

Source: PwC Strategy& client experience

Figure 6.2

Zero-Basing Myths Debunked

Before delving deeper into zero-basing, we'll dispel some common misconceptions about the process.

Zero-basing only works on discretionary, non-labor sales, general, and administrative (SG&A) expenses. Any expense, whether in labor or nonlabor SG&A (overhead costs that typically include sales, marketing, finance, HR, IT, and other headquarters activities), or in cost of goods sold (direct costs associated with manufacturing and distributing products, including supply chain, warehousing, and distribution) can and should be eliminated when it adds too little value and isn't necessary to meet operational or legal requirements. In addition, zero-basing drives efficiency in both discretionary and nondiscretionary activities.

Zero-basing reduces resource levels to the bare lights-on minimum. This is only partially true. Zero-basing determines the lights-on spending baseline, but it also provides a framework for deciding what additional activities to fund, and how much to spend above baseline. For some activities, bare lights-on spending may be the right amount.

Zero-basing consumes enormous amounts of time and overwhelms an organization. In our experience, a dedicated team can complete an initial zero-basing exercise in two to three months, and then conduct periodic reevaluations that take only a few weeks.

Zero-basing is for companies with falling revenues and profits. Zero-basing applies to all companies. For fast-growing companies, zero-basing ensures that resources are allocated in line with growth priorities.

When Should You Zero-Base Your Capabilities?

Companies often turn to zero-basing at times of crisis or dramatic change—such as an imminent bankruptcy—when they need rapid and significant cost reduction. More recently, however, zero-basing has become a go-to method for executives under pressure from activist investors demanding rapid improvement in margins and shareholder returns.

While zero-basing works well as an emergency cost-reduction lever, it is also a powerful tool for companies that need to realign cost structures with a new business strategy. If any of the following statements describe your company, consider zero-basing your cost structure:

- Substantial cost cuts are needed in a short time.
- The company needs to redeploy investments across its capabilities in light of changes in its customer base, competitive landscape, or strategy.
- Multiple large-scale capability-building initiatives across the company are vying for scarce funds, causing many initiatives to stall.
- The company has not evaluated its expenses and priorities thoroughly in several years.
- Management wants to challenge the status quo and change ingrained habits across the organization.

How to Zero-Base Your Capabilities

Zero-basing is a multistage process of evaluating cost structures throughout your organization, establishing spending targets based on your company's particular needs and strategy, and restructuring costs to meet those targets. In a zero-basing exercise, all capabilities and associated costs are categorized as lights on, table stakes, or differentiating, and their costs are challenged. For lights-on costs, a "clean-sheet" view of the lowest-cost model is created, along with associated risks. For table-stakes costs, capabilities are prioritized based on the value they create, with some capabilities cut back and all reviewed for opportunities to improve efficiency. Last, differentiating capabilities are also prioritized based on value, and the company considers possible investments and efficiency-improvement opportunities for each capability (see Figure 6.3).

ZERO-BASING APPROACH

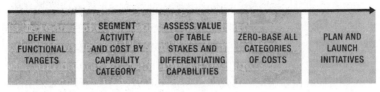

| DEFINE FUNCTIONAL TARGETS | SEGMENT ACTIVITY AND COST BY CAPABILITY CATEGORY | ASSESS VALUE OF TABLE STAKES AND DIFFERENTIATING CAPABILITIES | ZERO-BASE ALL CATEGORIES OF COSTS | PLAN AND LAUNCH INITIATIVES |

Source: PwC Strategy&

Figure 6.3

Step 1: Define Functional Targets

Just as a Fit for Growth transformation starts by setting an enterprise savings target, a zero-basing exercise begins by establishing top-down savings goals for each capability, function, or business unit included in the exercise—much like the target-setting exercise for the overall transformation described in Chapter 4. These top-down targets are critical to achieving savings goals, because they push the organization to question what activities are truly necessary versus merely "nice to have." Without an aggressive top-down target, companies often fall into the trap of defending existing cost structures, preserving the current organization, and seeking only incremental improvements, instead of exploring ways to eliminate and/or reduce costs.

In addition to setting overall functional targets, set targets by capability category, too. We suggest setting low savings targets for capabilities identified as differentiating, while setting aggressive ones for table-stakes and lights-on capabilities. As a result, functions that deliver multiple differentiating capabilities will be asked to deliver far less savings than functions that provide only lights-on capabilities. When a single differentiating capability happens to be delivered by multiple functions, it is important to ensure that no function can decimate the differentiating capability in an attempt to meet its savings target.

Step 2: Segment Activity and Costs by Capability Category

Effective zero-basing requires a deep understanding of your processes, particularly the allocation of time and money across capabilities. Gather cost information with activity surveys in each function. Responses will reveal how people spend their time, enabling you to segment activities in each function that fall into the categories of lights on, table stakes, and differentiating. Your goal is to account for 100 percent of the time and cost associated with every capability and activity, including external expenditures and temporary resources. This will build your understanding of the work performed and its cost for eventual zero-basing. However, the mere allocation of functional resources across functional activities—while necessary—is insufficient. Also critical is the need to categorize the full suite of functional activities into lights-on, table-stakes, and differentiating capabilities to make transparent how much cost and effort is directed toward activities that enable you to win against competitors (differentiating) versus activities that are necessary to keep you in the game (table stakes and lights on). The best surveys leverage standard industry-process taxonomies that enable comparisons with external benchmarks, but are customized enough to reflect the terminology and processes used by the organization.

Step 3: Assess the Value of Each Capability Category

Once you have a baseline of activities and corresponding costs, determine the value of each cost category. First, set aside any costs and activities that support lights-on capabilities—activities that are necessary for operation or are legally required. These category of activities will be evaluated later to see how they can be performed more efficiently.

Once lights-on activities are filtered out, ask functional leaders responsible for providing a service to value the importance of activities supporting differentiating and table-stakes capabilities. To assess their contribution to strategic priorities and the bottom line, you might ask, "To what extent does this activity drive margin, cost control, or growth?" "To what extent does this activity drive differentiation by supporting a key capability pillar?" or "How does this process help the function effectively and successfully deliver service?"

At the same time, determine how much value internal customers get from various services. Ask them such questions as, "How does this activity help you deliver value to external customers?" or "How well does this activity enable your mission?" or, more to the point, "What are the risks to your business if this activity was discontinued?" Often, we see a big gap between what functional providers of services deem valuable and what the internal customers receiving those services actually find valuable. To make the discussions with internal customers most productive, table-stakes and differentiating activities are bundled into "decision packages"—clusters of table-stakes or differentiating activities that can be logically grouped to make a decision about the associated activities. For example, can the activities in the package be delivered more economically? Can the level of service be minimized? Or can an activity be entirely discontinued and, if so, what is the associated impact on costs, service levels, and business risks?

Aggregating the provider and customer scoring for each decision package enables you to identify the groups of activities that comprise each capability, prioritize those necessary to stay in business, and create a list ranking the importance of all other functional activities, along with associated costs from Step 1 (see Figure 6.4).

Step 4: Zero-Base Current State

Actual decisions about what work to dial down or optimize happen in formal "challenge" sessions. These sessions are designed to help executive leaders understand the work being performed, why it's performed, who is generating the request, the resources consumed, and the value generated by the work, as well as the risks of eliminating it. Armed with such information, executives can make key decisions and trade-offs about which activities must be funded to remain competitive, while also ensuring such retained activities are optimally efficient. Challenge sessions work best when they are conducted on a single day and organized by function and/or process area. Participants should include the leader whose group is being analyzed, the overall transformation lead, business and functional subject-matter experts, and key customers of the function.

To kick off the challenge sessions, the leadership team should revisit corporate strategy and the differentiating capabilities required to support that strategy. This strategic review enables decision makers to generally assess the appropriate level of spending for each company function, based on the strategic importance of the capabilities it supports. After making these broader determinations, leaders should look across functions at a macro

DECISION PACKAGE ANALYSIS FOR TABLE-STAKES ACTIVITIES

REPORTING DECISION PACKAGE

Activities	Cost ($MM)	"Lights-On" Scenario	Cost ($MM)	"Lights-On Plus"	Cost ($MM)	"Full Scope"	Cost ($MM)
Basic SAP reporting	3	X	3	X	3	X	3
BI analytical reporting	2.5		0	X *low-cost location*	1.5	X *low-cost location*	1.5
BU or product-specific reporting	5		0	X *major brands only*	0	X *major brands only*	2
Shared standard analytics	5		0		5	X *small brands only*	5
Dedicated analytics support	3		0		1	X *major brands only*	1
Total	18.5		3		10.5		12.5

FORECASTING DECISION PACKAGE

Activities	Cost ($MM)	"Lights-On" Scenario	Cost ($MM)	"Lights-On Plus"	Cost ($MM)	"Full Scope"	Cost ($MM)
Obtain key inputs	5	X	2	X	3	X	4
Forecast P&L by BU	3	X	3	X	3	X	3
Forecast P&L by product line	6					X *top products only*	2
Forecast P&L by brand	2			X *major brands only*	1	X *major brands only*	1
Forecast cost of goods sold	2					X *by SKU from shared service*	2
Forecast SG&A and sales comp	1			X	1	X *via shared service*	
Total	19		5		8		12

Notes: BI = Business Intelligence; BU = Business Unit

Source: PwC Strategy&

Figure 6.4

level to determine where they may want to be as lights on as possible to fund differentiating activities in revenue-generating functions. For example, this process led a consumer packaged goods manufacturer to decide to be lights on in IT and HR, dialing down capabilities in IT innovation, digital transformation, talent analytics, and high-touch HR business partnering to fund more investment in product innovation and brand-building capabilities.

Once the decision team has made macro-level resource allocation decisions by function, they move into individual functional discussions. They start with a blank sheet, assuming no spend in the function. To build the functional spend, they begin by reviewing the lights-on work and spending, to ensure that these activities are truly lights on and fully optimized. This involves challenging whether more commoditized lights-on costs such as IT infrastructure, accounting operations, HR administration, and back-office processing operations can be delivered more economically by embracing lower-cost models or outsourcing. It also means defining—in as clean-sheet a manner as possible—the "bare minimum" of expertise necessary to satisfy the company's legal, regulatory, and fiduciary obligations. Companies' risk-tolerance policies for such work is often needlessly overengineered.

Next, they compare the bare-minimum total lights-on costs with the functional affordability constraint, which is the new target functional budget. If there is room left in the functional budget after the lights-on work is funded, then select table-stakes and differentiating capabilities can be "added back" based on the relative return on investment each activity will provide, up to the top-down target set for the function. At this point the team should rank-order differentiating and table-stakes capabilities by decision package, and through an iterative process determine what to stop doing, do less of it, or do it cheaper by decision package, to make new cost structures and processes sustainable. All other activities that do not fit into the budget should be eliminated, and corresponding risks evaluated and acknowledged.

One of the most challenging issues we see in this phase is the tendency to overestimate what constitutes a lights-on activity. Highly regulated or expertise areas like tax, legal, quality assurance, risk management, or compliance often argue that everything they do is lights on. However, closer scrutiny may reveal that many activities aren't legally required, but reflect risk mitigation strategies that are business decisions.

Resolve sometimes weakens at this point, as executives shrink from the tough calls required to prioritize only the most essential activities. It can be hard to accept the painful reality that much of the lights-on work must be performed at very lean levels and that even some table-stakes capabilities may have to be cut back to fully support key strategic priorities. Executives confronting these decisions need to keep in mind that winning strategies aren't built on across-the-board excellence, but on deliberate choices to invest in distinctive capabilities in a few key areas while cutting back everywhere else.

Step 5: Plan and Launch Initiatives

After senior stakeholders make their decisions, teams develop implementation plans. These plans establish an overall structure for the implementation, establish a timetable for each step, and assemble teams to carry the initiative forward.

Implementation plans must address the behavior changes needed to achieve program goals, and establish mechanisms and governance structures for rejecting wasteful expenditures and for monitoring resource allocation. The teams must brace themselves for some fallout the first few times they decline to meet a request, and leaders must be there to support their teams and reinforce the value-trade-off decisions that were made. Remember that effective cost transformation requires changes in organizational behavior and long-term vigilance. An officially defunded activity will continue consuming resources if internal customers keep asking for it and providers keep saying yes.

Any company aiming to reduce costs without losing its competitive edge can benefit from zero-basing. This systematic approach illuminates the true drivers of cost, enabling organizations to root out unnecessary expenditures and enhance efficiency in all activities. Unlike traditional short-term cost-cutting tactics, zero-basing generates structural trade-offs and cost reductions that are sustainable over the long term. These fundamental improvements drive down overall spending while bolstering distinctive capabilities in line with a Fit for Growth cost transformation.

Zero-Basing Best Practices

Commitment from the top and cross-functional cultural change. Senior leadership drives change by demonstrating a willingness to challenge the value of all work, explore new ways of working across all functions, and modeling a new attitude toward spending. This inspires cultural and behavioral changes that drive more value than short-term cost savings.

Fit-for-purpose stretch goals. Zero-base your activities based on the cost structure needed to achieve your target profit margins, seeking best-in-class performance only where it's necessary to deliver on your way to play. Use zero-basing not as a bottom-up method of identifying savings opportunities, but as a tool to meet the top-down savings target established for the program.

New ways of working. A successful zero-basing program changes the way a company works by prioritizing activities that drive competitive differentiation, cutting back or eliminating others, and optimizing efficiency everywhere.

Ongoing discipline. To sustain the benefits of zero-basing, revise planning, resource allocation, and business-performance review processes. A full zero-basing exercise is too much work to do annually. Instead, put in place a process to look at new or incremental costs through the zero-basing lens every year, and do the full cost segmentation every three years or so.

Do no harm. An effective zero-basing initiative drives efficiency and cultural change without impeding growth. It generates funds for investment in differentiating capabilities by targeting lights-on and table-stakes activities for greater savings, rather than butter-spreading cuts across all areas in equal amounts.

Effective messaging and transparency. The right messaging tone intrigues and engages key audiences, while the wrong one merely annoys. Frequent, comprehensive progress reports—with the right level of transparency—build support by demonstrating concrete benefits from zero-basing, without sending unnecessary shock waves through the organization.

The right people at the table. Input from the people directly responsible for processes and budgets under scrutiny improves decision making and fosters commitment to the zero-basing agenda. But don't delegate zero-basing decisions to lower-level managers; senior leaders of various functions should make the calls.

Pitfalls to Avoid

Aiming low. Focusing on individual expenditures at too granular a level obscures opportunities to transform costs more dramatically through structural changes, such as exiting markets, discontinuing product lines, and eliminating capabilities.

Stopping short. When companies eliminate only discretionary work, they miss the chance to save more by optimizing all their costs. Lights-on work should not receive "blanket amnesty" as it can be made more efficient as well.

Waiting for perfection. A zero-basing program will never get out of the gate if leaders insist on having pristine data before making decisions. Most decisions can be based on "directionally correct" data.

Deferring to providers. Those who perform an activity often consider it differentiating and essential to the business. Accepting their assessment without giving due weight to customer scoring will protect activities that should be tested rigorously.

Avoiding tough calls. If the cost reductions and savings target are perceived as voluntary, decision makers will often forego savings because they can't bring themselves to take the difficult steps needed to rationalize cost structures.

7

Aligning the Operating Model

Redefine Where Critical Work Gets Done

A company's operating model defines where critical work is done in the organization, and how resources should be organized to deliver that work. It reflects a series of choices about the roles and structure of each major organizational unit, determining the respective roles of corporate headquarters and business units, the boundaries of each line of business, how people work together within and across those boundaries, and how global functions and shared services support the business units. These choices shape key characteristics of the company that affect baseline cost levels: how the company faces off to customers and competitors, the number of business units, what work is shared across the organization or dedicated to individual businesses or functions, and the degree of standardization versus customization and centralization versus decentralization of various business processes, and the number of locations. Therefore, changing the operating model can have a big impact on both a company's relationship with its customers and its cost structure. A key step in a Fit for Growth cost transformation is to ensure the operating model aligns with the company's strategy and supports its differentiating capabilities—and if that is not the case, acting quickly to adjust the operating model. Too often, companies embark on cost-reduction programs without taking a hard look at their inherent operating model and organization, then find themselves weakening critical capabilities as they try to drive down costs.

Operating Model Elements and Archetypes

At most companies, the primary building blocks of the operating model are the corporate core, the business units, and a shared services organization that provides company-wide support services (see Figure 7.1). The corporate core sets overall vision and strategy, governs the enterprise, and ensures

OPERATING MODEL FRAMEWORK

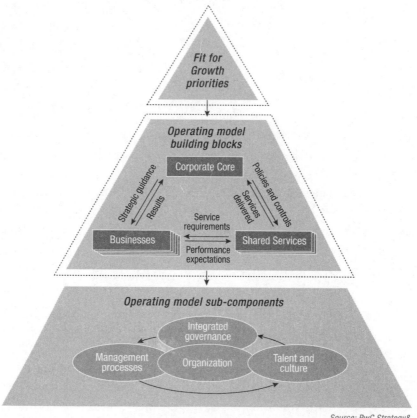

Source: PwC Strategy&

Figure 7.1

compliance with legal and fiduciary requirements. Business units focus on delivering value to customers in a competitive marketplace, making day-to-day operational decisions and any strategic calls delegated by the corporate core. Shared services provide common services such as information technology, customer call centers, accounts payable, and benefits administration to business units and the core. In some companies, shared services are part of the corporate core and are not a standalone unit. Supporting the primary building blocks are the operating-model's subcomponents that define governance, organization, business management processes, and talent and culture.

There are four basic operating-model archetypes, or *models*, for the roles and relationships of the company's organizational units (see Figure 7.2). These range from a holding company with no operational role for the corporate core (Model 1), to centralized management under an operationally involved core (Model 4). Most companies fall in the middle, with the corporate core either focused on strategy and oversight (Model 2) or engaging in active management (Model 3). These differences reflect fundamentally distinct philosophies about how and where in the company value is created. Models 1 and 4 are most dependent on the "great person" theory—that a few highly skilled and intelligent people can add enormous value by being able to look across the business, have a strategic vision, and align and motivate resources to that vision. Models 2 and 3—the strategy and oversight structure and the active management structure, respectively—depend on individuals who create value by leading rather than doing.

Model 1, Holding Company, embodies the minimalist approach. The holding company manages the businesses as a portfolio, giving them considerable autonomy to set their own strategies and make their own operational decisions. This decentralized model limits the corporate core to establishing and monitoring financial targets and other fundamental organizational objectives. Holding companies believe that economies of scale are not particularly important because there is relatively little overlap between their businesses, or because the costs of administering scale would overwhelm any savings. When corporate scale is justified, holding companies achieve it through networks rather than through a formal hierarchy. Business units are standalone entities supported by a full suite of overhead functions, technology, and infrastructure. A costly side effect of all this autonomy is underleveraged scale across the organization.

OPERATING MODEL ARCHETYPES

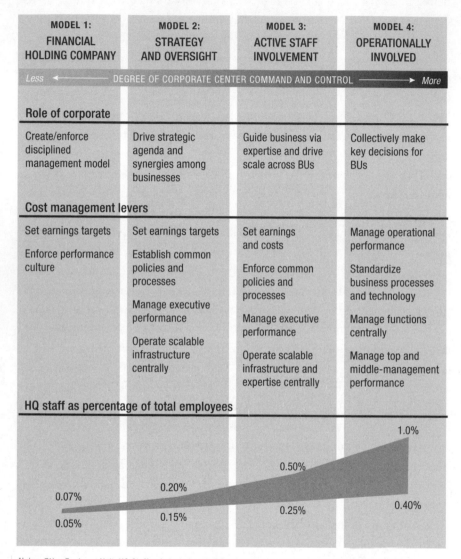

MODEL 1: FINANCIAL HOLDING COMPANY	MODEL 2: STRATEGY AND OVERSIGHT	MODEL 3: ACTIVE STAFF INVOLVEMENT	MODEL 4: OPERATIONALLY INVOLVED
Less ← DEGREE OF CORPORATE CENTER COMMAND AND CONTROL → More			
Role of corporate			
Create/enforce disciplined management model	Drive strategic agenda and synergies among businesses	Guide business via expertise and drive scale across BUs	Collectively make key decisions for BUs
Cost management levers			
Set earnings targets Enforce performance culture	Set earnings targets Establish common policies and processes Manage executive performance Operate scalable infrastructure centrally	Set earnings and costs Enforce common policies and processes Manage executive performance Operate scalable infrastructure and expertise centrally	Manage operational performance Standardize business processes and technology Manage functions centrally Manage top and middle-management performance
HQ staff as percentage of total employees			
0.07% 0.05%	0.20% 0.15%	0.50% 0.25%	1.0% 0.40%

Notes: BU = Business Unit; HQ Staff only includes traditional corporate core functions, excludes corporate shared services

Source: PwC Strategy&

Figure 7.2

Model 2, Strategy and Oversight, is based on the philosophy that value is created in two places: at the business units closest to the customers, and at the corporate level, through linkages between business units. In this model, the corporate core is small (e.g., only 100–150 people for a $20 billion company), performing only a few well-defined roles. The corporate core sets corporate strategy and policy, identifies ways to create value above and beyond the business units' individual contributions (such as by sharing best practices, creating new businesses, or incubating enterprise-wide capabilities), and creates and enforces a disciplined business-performance management model. Consolidating and sharing work across the business units is limited to the few most scale-sensitive processes such as transactional back office services.

Model 3, Active Management, is a more centralized approach with a strong role for the corporate core. Leaders of companies operating in this model believe they create significant synergies by closely linking their business units to go to market together, and by sharing as much of their support services as possible. This approach works best when business units have similar products or serve similar customers, and need the same (or very similar) support services from the center. In this model, senior corporate leaders help business units develop their strategies and annual plans, and make calls on how to allocate capital to the business units. While the business units retain some core processes, much of the transactional and expertise-based support services, such as technology and finance, are shared across businesses.

Model 4, Operationally Involved, establishes the broadest role for the corporate core. Strategy, planning, policies, and even major operational decisions cascade down from the top. Business units exist primarily to carry out directives from corporate. This highly centralized approach consolidates most key processes at headquarters, which controls all overhead, sales and marketing, and operations functions. Likewise, this model integrates technology across the company and may even operate on a single platform. Even when the work itself isn't consolidated, powerful functional organizations direct activities, manage functional budgets, and allocate resources among business units.

There is no single "right" model that applies to every company, but there are guidelines that suggest which model works for a company based on its situation. Generally, companies move toward Model 4 or Model 3 when there are natural strong linkages among its business units (such as similar products, customer bases, competitors, or assets), when the strategic agenda calls for a "one company" model for leveraging the entire enterprise, when the talent bench is much stronger in the corporate core than in the business units, and when the CEO has a more hands-on management style. Absent these conditions, companies move toward Model 2 or even Model 1.

Along with defining the role of the corporate core, companies also need to organize their business units. There are many options for organizing business units to fit with the company's strategy (see Figure 7.3). Specific solutions depend on the dynamics of the industry (e.g., the importance of customer intimacy and customer diversity, and the pace of change in the market) and the characteristics of the particular company (e.g., the product or service complexity and level of coordination needed, talent bench strength, and need to leverage scale). Capabilities play a big role here—the organizing principle of a company's business units should support its most important capabilities. For example, if responsiveness to local environmental and market demands is critical to a global company, it may organize its business units geographically. Similarly, if a single customer interface and effective coordination across geographies, products, and functions is imperative, then a customer-based structure may be the right solution.

The next choice in the operating model is how support services are organized and delivered. Many companies adopt the "shared services" model, combining and consolidating services from headquarters and business units into a distinct, market-efficient entity. Shared services acts as a kind of business unit for support services.

Shared services should not be confused with traditional centralized corporate staff. Shared services seek to simulate the supply and demand interaction of an open market, while leveraging the entire organization's scale for support services. In a shared services model, internal customers—the business units—specify their service needs and evaluate the performance of internal providers with measurable, market-based criteria. Providers—shared services—must meet those requirements and prove their ability to compete vigorously with outside vendors. Business units that must respond to the demands of the marketplace deserve support services on par with the best available in the market. Structured in this way, shared services becomes another business unit, perceived and managed as an outside vendor, with no choice but to be price competitive.

BUSINESS UNIT CONFIGURATION OPTIONS

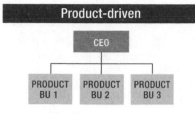

Product-driven

Advantages

Focuses on innovating and integrating products to serve customers

Adaptable to fast-changing external environment

Disadvantages

High-cost structure due to low economies of scale

Conflicts between product and customer strategy

Challenges with cross-selling

Function-driven

Advantages

Maximizes economies of scale

Builds functional competencies and skills

Enables deployment of talent on a global basis

Disadvantages

No P&L accountability except at CEO

Easy to fall into a silo mentality

Risk of internal focus and loss of market/customer responsiveness

Geography-driven

Advantages

Effectively deliver on regional differences in customer demands

Increased speed in responding to geographical issues

Increased ability for local talent sourcing and management

Disadvantages

Challenges coordinating functions across regions

Potentially excessive layers between HQ/Int'l/Region/Cluster/Country

Tension between products/brands and regions in tailoring products to local markets

Customer-driven

Advantages

Encourages customer intimacy and responsiveness

Able to respond to market/customer change

Disadvantages

High-cost structure due to low economies of scale

Challenges in coordinating with products, channels, and markets

Over-rotating on customer satisfaction could drive high cost-to-serve

Note: BU = Business Unit   *Source: PwC Strategy&*

Figure 7.3

The final step in structuring an operating model is defining the linkages that hold the company together. Linkages range from vision and values to specific management processes. A well-defined system for developing strategy, setting goals, delegating authority, planning and budgeting, measuring performance, and rewarding results is absolutely critical to the enterprise. To be Fit for Growth, companies must have well-oiled processes that articulate their strategies and differentiating capabilities, redirect resources toward those differentiating capabilities, measure their business and individual performances, and identify and reward high-performing talent commensurate with their performance and potential.

When to Redesign Your Operating Model

Sometimes it's obvious that you need to adjust your operating model; maybe you've changed strategy, completed a major acquisition, or embarked on a Fit for Growth transformation. At other times it's less clear. If you're wondering whether a full or partial redesign is in order, ask yourself these questions:

- Do execution breakdowns keep you from realizing your strategic ambitions?
- Is your company organized to capture its biggest growth opportunities?
- Are fast-growing business units held back because they have to fight with troubled businesses for resources?
- Do you make and execute decisions fast enough to outmaneuver competitors?
- Are your business units agile and responsive to markets?
- Do you have trouble sharing information and transferring best practices across organizational lines?
- Has the corporate headquarters staff remained stubbornly large while the rest of the organization has become leaner?
- Are redundant service organizations scattered across your business units?

If the answers to a number of these questions cause concern, your operating model may not be fulfilling its essential role as a sturdy bridge between your strategic goals and execution.

How to Redesign Your Operating Model

Operating models take many different forms across the corporate landscape. Each company must follow its own path to the optimal design, based on its strategic priorities, business and asset portfolio, geographic footprint, and other unique characteristics. But the design process always requires fundamental decisions about the roles and structure of the three major organizational units. First, however, you'll need to answer four basic questions:

1. Where are my resources and costs, and are they in the right places? Examine cost levels in areas such as HR, IT, finance, sales, R&D, and marketing, and ask yourself if spending corresponds with strategic priorities.
2. What approaches will yield the greatest savings? Look for opportunities to build economies of scale through consolidation, drive efficiency by standardizing processes, reduce labor costs through automation and wage arbitrage, and cut spending by managing internal demand for various services.
3. What corporate operating model will best enable cost savings and capture growth opportunities? Perhaps a slimmed-down Strategy and Oversight Model with empowered business units and a multifunctional shared services organization will deliver the benefits you seek. Or maybe an Active Management Model with strong corporate functions charged with driving global functional synergies is a better way of capturing those gains.
4. How do we rewire the organization to support the new operating model? Determine which elements of the legacy organization should be retained in the new model. Consider possible changes in structure and decision rights, and how to reshape management processes to reinforce the new structure.

Based on your answers to these questions, define your major organizational units—the business units, corporate core, and shared services. While every operating model redesign process is different, most move through four major phases: understanding value creation levers, framing options to accelerate value creation, developing a new organizational architecture, and implementing the new design (see Figure 7.4).

OPERATING MODEL APPROACH

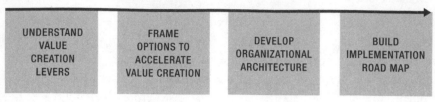

Source: PwC Strategy&

Figure 7.4

Step 1: Understand Value Creation Levers

Operating model redesign starts with a hard look at your current operating model. Review what the organization looks like today, how it got there, and the strategic intent behind the current design. Determine if the strategic considerations that shaped your present model are still relevant. To understand the current operating model, examine the basic building blocks and how they are organized. For example, natural business units may be organized by product lines, geography, or function. Review what work is shared and standardized across the organization, and what role the corporate core plays. Look beyond formal roles and structures to tease out how decisions are made, who makes them, and how well information flows across the organization. This inquiry will reveal more than the org chart about how your operating model actually works.

As you develop a picture of the operating model, seek to understand its variations (e.g., all support functions are consolidated except for one business unit) and the reasons for those variations (perhaps that business unit is slated for divestment). In addition, gather basic cost and headcount data by function, role, and location to build an organizational resource baseline. Then take a step back to assess the purposes of your current operating model. How was it meant to help your company execute its strategy effectively?

Case Study: A Global Auto Supplier Centralizes Shared Services

With sales sliding and profits shrinking, a global automotive supplier decided to cut sales, general, and administrative (SG&A) costs dramatically. The first step was to locate major sources of SG&A expense across a multi-matrixed organization. The company was organized around several product-led divisions, four primary geographic regions (North America, Europe, Latin America, and Asia-Pacific), and large automotive OEM customers such as Ford and General Motors. Each leg of the matrix had staff supporting matrix requirements, while additional overhead spending emanated from corporate core housing functions such as IT, finance, HR, facilities management, and real estate. Although divestitures of unprofitable product lines had reduced revenue by more than 20 percent, headquarters was unable to right-size itself and was saddled with stranded costs.

Leaders of various units rushed to defend their organizations when the CEO called for SG&A reductions. Most argued that they had already cut SG&A to the bone, and urged the CEO to look elsewhere for savings. An examination of the cost structure highlighted that SG&A costs were concentrated in the product divisions—which had big budgets for sales, marketing, finance, procurement, and divisional management—and the corporate core. Dissatisfaction with corporate support services also added overhead, as business units seeking better service created their own duplicative support groups. Regional and customer organizations spent relatively little on SG&A, but undermined effectiveness by slowing decision-making and blurring accountability.

The company identified three key changes that would improve efficiency: reducing services and seniority levels at the corporate core to fit the needs of a smaller organization, consolidating back office services globally and managing them along "factory-like" principles for the lowest possible cost, and flattening a hierarchical "command and control" organization. Pushing aside internal resistance, the CEO established a global shared services organization to handle most of the

(continued)

(continued)

company's transactional SG&A processes. A global shared service leader was charged with driving 40 percent reductions in IT activities, sales contract administration, transactional finance processes, transactional HR, and facilities management, through consolidation, outsourcing, and Lean process management.

In addition to creating a global shared services organization, the company made other significant changes in the operating model to enable cost savings, including:

- Redefining the mission of corporate headquarters to focus on strategy and performance management, rather than business unit operations and functional excellence across the organization. This redefinition led to a dramatic reduction of corporate HQ staff that had been built up to closely monitor the businesses or drive unaffordable, unnecessary functional programs.
- Focusing on a core set of business lines grouped into "natural" product business units (PBUs) and eliminating a layer of divisional managers who served mainly as "span breakers." Within the PBUs, resources were aligned and P&L authority established.
- Eliminating regional organizations, and moving leaders of product-based business units from North America to the regions where those business lines were most dominant.
- Rationalizing service levels in finance, HR, and IT by substituting a fit-for-purpose set of self-serve, call center, and in-person services for the high-touch "concierge" services that support functions housed in the business units had been providing.

The CEO got the results he was hoping for, and then some. SG&A costs declined 50 percent in activities turned over to the global shared services organization, far exceeding the original goal. The total number of staff required to provide support services decreased by nearly 1,000 or 25 percent of original size. Global shared services contributed two-thirds of the benefits from a broader cost transformation program, while consistently meeting service level requirements.

Once you understand the current operating model, you can look for ways to improve it. Interview senior managers to identify pain points and the root causes of flaws in the current operating model. Such pain points and root causes take many forms:

- Significant overhead costs arising from excessive decentralization and suboptimal shared services,
- Highly customized and complex business processes rooted in weak functional governance,
- Heavy middle-management structures resulting from an over-matrixed organization that requires excessive management to coordinate headquarters and natural business units,
- Too many value-adding layers that diffuse accountability and slow down decision making, or
- Measures and motivators too focused on short-term objectives, which in turn inhibit prudent risk taking and stifle innovation.

Early interviews often reveal pain points and help form an overarching hypothesis for improvements, while later interviews serve to diagnose the effectiveness of the operating model and zero in on specific improvement opportunities. Later interviews also help identify common capabilities that could be leveraged across the business, and determine which functions should be owned and executed centrally, regionally, or at a local level.

Based on this input, decide where performance accountability should reside, and how to define governance and decision rights to support those who are accountable. Last, understand which organizational costs support your strategic differentiation, and make sure your operating model is fit for strategy.

These conversations also will illuminate the differing perspectives of managers in various business units, functions, and locations. Their insights shed light on organizational effectiveness, opportunities to improve, and how well your current operating model supports building and deploying differentiating capabilities. By the end of Step 1, you'll know where your costs are, where decision rights lie, and what challenges a new operating model must address.

Step 2: Frame Options to Accelerate Value Creation

Step 1 gives you a firm grasp of the major themes behind your operating model and strategic aspirations, current pain points, future state requirements, and desired culture. Now it is time to translate these themes into guiding principles and corresponding success measures that will serve as the North Star of your redesign effort and help establish criteria for choosing a new operating model. Your guiding principles should express overarching goals such as "enable cross-category collaboration," "encourage prudent risk taking and enhance breakthrough innovation," "enable the organization to move faster," or "leverage back-office scale across the organization to drive efficiencies." As you focus on this future vision, also keep your sights on major inefficiencies identified in Step 1. Articulate these improvement opportunities in terms such as "sub-scale processes," "misaligned incentives," or "ineffective decision rights." These clearly defined objectives and challenges will inform your trade-offs as you define alternative operating model options.

In developing operating model options, consider multiple parameters that define how the organization is structured, where work is done, and how various alternatives would advance your guiding principles and resolve existing pain points. Operating model options should address the respective roles and decision rights of corporate headquarters and businesses units, establish the business unit orientation (whether they are organized by product, customer segment, or geography), determine which processes should be handled by business units and which should be shared, and assign P&L ownership, along with corresponding decision rights and governance. (See Figure 7.5.)

Evaluate each operating model trade-off independently and create a number of scenarios for the future operating model. The best redesign programs test "aggressive," "moderate," and "passive" scenarios. Each scenario should describe the changes required, in terms of functional roles, decision rights, major business processes, and costs. These definitions enable company leaders, often in the form of a steering committee, to select the best operating model.

Step 3: Develop Organizational Architecture

With feedback from senior leaders, you can define the operating model in detail and build organizational consensus. Start by outlining the basic organizational building blocks: the role and organizational axes of business

OPERATING MODEL OPTIONS

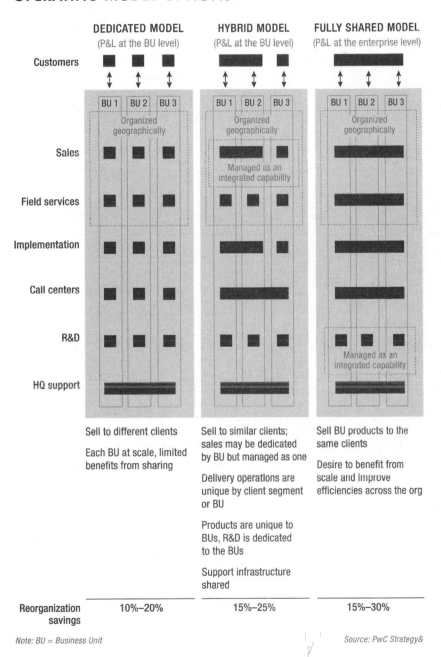

Figure 7.5

units, the level of sharing, centralization, and standardization of support functions, and the role of the corporate core. Then add more detail to this foundation: determine which functions will be centralized or decentralized in the business units, the level of outsourcing to employ, and major changes to the organization footprint. Next, assign decision rights for major business processes, and define the new interactions between the business units, support functions, and corporate core. As you complete the design, be sure to quantify the cost implications of these decisions and work them into the budgeting process.

Once you have defined the future operating model, consider organization and workforce transition plans. Identify and define significant shifts in executive roles, day-to-day responsibilities by function, implications for decision making, and any geographic people moves that may be required. Last, ensure that the changes are executed by revising performance metrics and your overall performance management architecture to support the new operating model.

Step 4: Build an Implementation Road Map

Successful operating model change requires a detailed road map that reshapes the organization quickly without disrupting ongoing business operations. A good map lays out a clear timeline and a sequence of organizational changes that are aligned with each other, and with your ongoing business calendar and other major change initiatives. Implementation plans typically identify five to 10 major work streams, often associated with a function or an end-to-end process, and assign each to an owner who will be accountable for executing the changes.

Plans often start with tactical changes such as new reporting structures, new job titles and role descriptions, geographic moves, and executive management staffing and selection. Later, they address the longer-term challenges of capability gaps in talent, processes, or technology. This approach builds momentum and locks in some quick wins, while helping people understand the new operating model and behavioral expectations.

Support the implementation plan with well-developed change impact assessment, communication, and change management programs to target those who are most affected by the changes and educate people across the broader organization on the "what, why, and when" of the new model. Simultaneously, roll out a performance dashboard that will track key performance indicators for the new operating model and highlight opportunities to refine the model as it takes shape.

A strong governance process to clear away roadblocks and deflect the all-too-common internal resistance to organizational change is essential. Frequent communication, faithful adherence to your success measures, and vigilant monitoring of results will help ease internal anxieties and ensure your new operating model delivers the expected benefits.

Operating Model Best Practices

Holistic design. A good operating model design not only saves money, but also fits the company's enterprise strategy, differentiating capabilities, unique product- and customer-specific processes, and geographic profile.

Checks and balances. To prevent any part of the organization from wielding too much power, an operating model should establish checks and balances, such as a requirement that annual plans be approved by both the corporate core and the business units.

Strong business cases. Well-executed organizational redesign programs overcome internal resistance by laying out a sound business case for every decision to move an activity from one part of the organization to another.

Clear road maps. Companies with effective operating models do more than draw new organizational structures and order people to change their ways. They explain how the new system will work, outlining clear roles, responsibilities, and accountabilities throughout the organization. They spell out how decisions will be made, how decision makers will get the information they need, and how the organization will motivate people to adopt new behaviors.

Pitfalls to Avoid

Strategic myopia. Organizational design choices driven by short-term factors undermine longer-term efforts to build structures that support differentiating capabilities.

Obsession with efficiency. Effectiveness is just as important. An operating model optimized only for cost reduction won't help a company execute its strategy.

Stopping with lines and boxes. Too many CEOs merely redraw the organization structure, expecting people across the company to know how to adjust to the new operating model. The operating model definition must go beyond lines and boxes to explicitly define the roles, accountabilities, and decision rights of each organizational element, introduce new performance measures and metrics, and establish new governance, planning, and performance management processes.

Same old ways. The best operating model redesign won't help if people don't align their behavior with the new structural framework.

Copying a competitor's operating model. Market analysis and benchmarking competition is a valuable tool to help evaluate operating model options and challenge the status quo. But an operating model that is not tailored to your specific strategies, priorities, and differentiating capabilities is doomed to backfire.

8

Outsourcing

Let External Providers Generate Value for You

Outsourcing is an important tool for companies seeking to transform cost structures. It can reduce costs, improve service levels, and guarantee annual productivity gains by enabling a company to hand off necessary but non-differentiating business processes to external service providers with specialized expertise in a wide range of processes. Providers offer services for back-office functions such as the IT help desk, accounts payable, and payroll; operational activities including transportation and warehousing; and customer-facing processes like sales and call center operations. They deliver value through leveraging their technical platforms, process expertise and standardization, continuous improvement, economies of scale, and labor-cost arbitrage by moving work to lower-cost locations. Outsourcing also serves the primary objective of a Fit for Growth cost transformation: freeing up time and resources so that companies can focus on capabilities that support their unique way to play.

What Is Outsourcing?

What comes to mind when you think of outsourcing? Vast call centers in southern India where customer service agents earning a fraction of Western wages field inquiries from consumers in North America and Europe? Massive contract-manufacturing complexes in China churning out gadgets for multinational consumer electronics companies? Both impressions are accurate examples of outsourcing, but neither captures the full picture.

Before going deeper, let's define outsourcing and clarify the difference between outsourcing and offshoring. *Outsourcing* is a contractual relationship in which a company pays an external service provider to perform activities it would otherwise handle in house. The provider could be anywhere—a remote offshore locale, a neighboring country, or even right next door. *Offshoring*, on the other hand, moves work overseas, usually in search of lower labor costs, either managing it internally through a global in-house center or using an outsourcing provider with facilities overseas. The discussion in this chapter will focus on outsourcing, regardless of location.

The power of outsourcing stems in part from its broad scope. You can outsource just about any link in the corporate value chain, from research and development to manufacturing, supply chain, sales, and back-office activities (see Figure 8.1). Major targets for outsourcing are processes that contain many rule-based, repetitive tasks that can be performed remotely and that also have a very mature, sophisticated external provider base. Examples include selling, general, and administrative (SG&A) functions (which can include accounting, benefits administration, and IT) to take advantage of labor arbitrage and best practices; manufacturing and warehousing operations, where specialized providers have advantaged scale and low-cost labor; or even sales force organizations for nonstrategic customers, with which brokers are able to achieve a lower cost to serve without compromising customer service.

Outsourcing creates value in three primary ways:

1. Turning fixed labor costs into variable expenses that rise and fall with fluctuating business volumes;
2. Driving efficiencies through the provider's highly competitive labor costs, expertise, scale, and platforms; and
3. Transforming processes through the provider's investments in automation and other technologies that spur continuous improvement and year-over-year productivity gains.

Over the typical five-year life of an outsourcing contract, external service providers can generate savings of 30 to 35 percent on sales and

PROCESSES OFTEN OUTSOURCED
BY MANUFACTURING COMPANIES

FUNCTIONAL AREA	PROCESSES	FUNCTIONAL AREA	PROCESSES
Product Development	Market analysis and verification Product prototyping Preproduction Product data management	Finance	Cost/Plant/Accounting T&E Accounting General Accounting Accounts Payables Accounts Receivable Fixed Assets Payroll Standard Financial Reporting
Sourcing and Procurement	Sourcing Spend management Procurement support Supplier administration Order management	HR	Training Benefits Administration Comp Admin Pension Admin Relocation/ Expat. Admin Recruiting Admin Employee Record Keeping
Supply-Chain Planning & Execution	Inventory management Warehousing Inbound and outbound logistics Reverse logistics Facilities maintenance Supply chain analytics		
Manufacturing	Plant maintenance Contract manufacturing	IT	Networks Data Centers Help Desk Desktop Support Infrastructure maintenance Development and Applications Maintenance
Marketing	Analytics Call centers		
Sales and Service	Order fulfillment Outside sales	Legal	Contracts Litigation Arbitration Mergers and Acquisitions

Source: PwC Strategy&

Figure 8.1

marketing costs; 5 to 10 percent on manufacturing, transportation, and warehousing costs; 35 to 45 percent on information technology costs; and 30 to 50 percent for back-office business processes such as accounts payable and receivable (see Figure 8.2).

TYPICAL BREAKDOWN OF SAVINGS FROM
BUSINESS PROCESS OUTSOURCING (BPO),* BY SOURCE

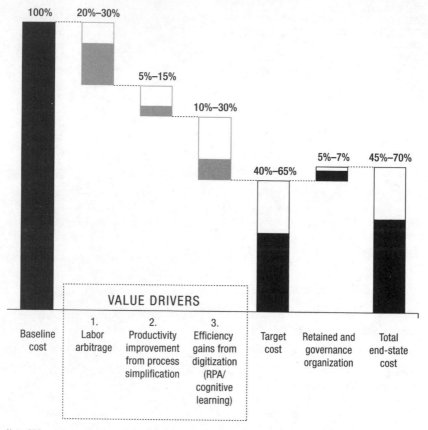

Note: BPO represents processes in Finance, Human Resources, Sales Back Office, and Customer Service

Source: PwC Strategy&

Figure 8.2

Outsourcing Myths Debunked

Despite the proven benefits, some companies still hesitate to out-source. Resistance often stems from a few common misconceptions:

Nobody can do it better than we can. Executives sometimes believe their own people are best qualified to handle their company's processes.

> But an external service provider that specializes in a particular process will always do it better than nonspecialists.
>
> *We'll lose control of outsourced processes.* Companies worry about what will happen if they lose direct control of essential business operations. Well-designed outsourcing arrangements are centered around service-level agreements, performance measures, and issue resolution and escalation processes. Together these safeguards ensure the company still retains control over the outcomes of a process while handing execution to a provider.
>
> *People won't want to work here if we outsource jobs.* Some fret that talented employees will avoid companies that outsource noncore processes. On the contrary, the best employees prefer companies that allow them to focus on key strategic activities.
>
> *Employee morale and community relations will suffer.* While anti-outsourcing backlash can't be ignored, it can be mitigated through strong communication and assistance for displaced employees.
>
> *Outsourcing is only a labor-arbitrage play.* Some still doubt outsourcing generates meaningful benefits beyond labor-cost savings. But the largest benefits of outsourcing are from productivity gains and process transformation, along with functional, operational, and technology benefits.

When to Outsource

Companies outsource for many different reasons. Large companies tend to view outsourcing as a way to maximize efficiency in high-volume, commoditized business activities such as order entry or travel and expense processing. Smaller companies, however, may not have sufficient transaction volumes to benefit from incremental savings on commoditized activities. But they can nevertheless use outsourcing as a tool for growth as well as cost savings. External service providers offer capabilities a small company may lack, such as advanced R&D, product design, or data analytics. And the emergence of cloud-based, "as a service" external service providers has enabled small companies to tap some of the benefits larger organizations get from outsourcing, such as process standardization, market-leading capabilities, and application support.

In our experience, companies often turn to outsourcing when they face one of these common business challenges:

They need the scalability and flexibility of resources an external vendor can provide;

They perform important but nondifferentiating work that bogs down senior management, or need differentiated capabilities that the company does not have yet;

They need quick access to an external provider's expertise and diverse talent pool;

They are unable to invest in capital and talent required to generate efficiencies in their nonstrategic operations; or

Outsourcing vendors can perform the same work at lower cost.

The best candidates for outsourcing are standardized, well-documented processes with clearly defined inputs and measurable outputs. Stable technology is also important—don't ask an outsourcer to manage processes scattered across myriad IT systems riddled with bugs and other shortcomings that compromise data accuracy and undermine service quality. You should also avoid the temptation to outsource overly complex, nonstandardized processes involving customized activities and variable outputs, or those requiring frequent judgment calls by front-line workers with deep understanding of the business. Broken or flawed processes should not be outsourced unless you have a clear plan to fix them with an external provider that has the expertise and a reputation for operational excellence in the specific process. Last, outsource only when viable external providers with relevant experience are available and willing to take on your processes in a way that will serve your transformation objectives. In cases where you have to rely on a third party to deliver a differentiated capability, make sure that you either have a plan to build the capability internally or lock in the vendor into a long-term agreement.

The Outsourcing Process: How It Works

Ready to outsource? Fortunately for you, two-plus decades of predecessors have marked a clear path to follow (see Figure 8.3). While this approach is designed for back-office and information technology, it can also work, with

OUTSOURCING APPROACH

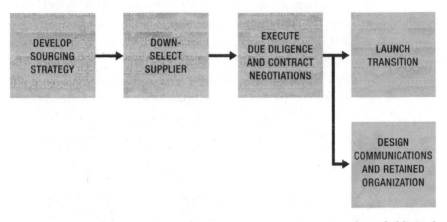

Source: PwC Strategy&

Figure 8.3

some tailoring, for manufacturing, supply chain, R&D, and other parts of the value chain that may benefit from outsourcing. First, you need a sourcing strategy that establishes a framework, rationale, and processes for deciding what to outsource, picking service providers, identifying risks, estimating costs, and defining the benefits you expect from outsourcing. Next comes supplier selection, with requests for proposals circulated to prospective candidates, and an evaluation process based on their responses. After narrowing the field to a few contenders, conduct financial and operational due diligence and choose a finalist. Contract development and negotiations proceed in parallel with transition planning, leading to a final agreement with a service provider. The process requires a wide array of expertise, including subject-matter experts who understand the scope of the project, procurement experts familiar with vendors, pricing benchmarks and other marketplace factors, and lawyers who know how to negotiate outsourcing contracts.

Step 1: Develop Sourcing Strategy

A well-developed sourcing strategy is the cornerstone of smart outsourcing. It lays out screening criteria and other guidelines for critical decisions about which processes to outsource and how. Your strategy should articulate the specifics of what you are trying to accomplish, the geographies, functions, and processes to be sourced, insource-outsource scenarios, associated economics and risks, and transition strategies. From this you can find the best partners, know what market pricing and terms are required to implement the solution, and define a plan for execution against the business case. You are also well positioned to articulate and undertake the necessary change management within your organization. These decisions require a thorough understanding of your company's requirements for each business activity, and a willingness to at least consider outsourcing every process.

You forfeit potential value when you don't question preconceptions about which processes an outside provider can or cannot perform. No process should be exempt from outsourcing unless a rigorous, objective analysis reveals compelling reasons to keep it in house. Nor should any process be outsourced unless such an analysis shows the move would create more value than handling it internally. To ensure a meaningful comparison, the outsourcing scenario should not be compared to the "as-is," in-house process performance, but to the "to-be" process performance, where identified improvements are factored into the performance of the in-house process.

The best outsourcing candidates are uniform, well-documented processes that produce standardized outputs in a repeatable, measurable way and require little or no interpretation by staff. Maximize potential cost savings by focusing on processes that employ significant numbers of employees—at least 20 to 30 full-time-equivalent employees (FTEs). Assess the supplier base to ensure that large, proven service providers are available to ramp up quickly and meet your needs. Also assess the risks before pulling the trigger. Outsource only processes that can be handed off without jeopardizing intellectual property, customer relationships, or regulatory compliance.

Don't let departmental boundaries confine your outsourcing program. Many end-to-end business processes span several groups within a company. The spectrum of activities involved in receiving and processing customer sales, for example, covers various sales and finance processes, while the "hire to retire" HR lifecycle encompasses human resources and finance. You can't hold an external provider accountable for end-to-end performance if half the process stays in house. Bundle all interrelated activities in a single, comprehensive outsourcing contract.

After "what" comes "how." For each process you intend to outsource, choose a service model that serves your objectives and fits the requirements and operational characteristics of the process. The primary models are offshore, onshore, and nearshore outsourcing. When choosing, weigh factors such as savings, security, regional stability, cultural compatibility, language proficiency, and ease of access to outsourcing centers.

Offshore outsourcing offers the most potential savings. It's a good choice for companies seeking maximum cost benefits on highly standardized processes that tap widely available skill sets. Drawbacks include cultural challenges and shortages of specialized talent, and potential negative publicity and even government scrutiny in some industries.

Companies often choose onshore outsourcing when regulatory barriers restrict overseas knowledge transfers, or when they need easy access, time zone compatibility, and home-market language skills. Onshore outsourcing centers also may offer more-sophisticated talent, but yield less cost savings. Nearshore outsourcing sits somewhere between the two, offering greater savings than onshoring, along with synchronous time zones, relatively easy access, and a degree of cultural affinity with customers.

Step 2: Down-Select Suppliers

When you have determined scope and delivery model, it is time to assess potential suppliers. Use sourcing experts and analysts' reports to identify potential candidates with relevant experience and capabilities, capacity to meet your volume requirements, and stable businesses. Then engage three to five of the most promising providers in a rigorous competitive-bidding process to secure the best possible pricing and service commitments.

We discourage sending broad requests for information (RFIs) to a large number of providers. These time-consuming "open auditions" produce little information that isn't available from industry reports. Even worse, a scatter-shot RFI signals that you don't understand the market and lack clear objectives, which may lead providers to steer you toward solutions that serve their needs better than yours. We recommend having a clear perspective on your scope and moving straight to a request for proposal (RFP) with three to five top providers.

Your RFP should be prescriptive, requiring vendors to answer specific questions directly related to your needs. Their answers will allow a team of internal stakeholders to review RFP responses side by side and evaluate bidders on objective criteria across five dimensions:

1. *Basic qualifications.* These include an external service provider's experience and capabilities, financial strength, and capacity to handle the work you plan to outsource, including future growth.
2. *Proposed solution.* Compare the bidders' plans for performing the work, service level and productivity commitments, and track records with outsourcing transitions. Also assess how well each provider understands your specific process needs, the challenges and objectives of the assignment, and its role in your broader transformation agenda.
3. *The team.* Size up each bidder's team. Is senior management committed to your work? How many staffers would they dedicate to your account? How good are their workers? Look past sales teams and their polished presentations to scrutinize staffing models, and insist on meeting the operational experts who would oversee your work daily.
4. *Fit.* Pay attention to "soft" factors such as a provider's culture and alignment with your organizational values. Preexisting relationships between key players at your company and the external service provider may provide comfort in this area. Look for flexibility and the creativity needed to devise innovative solutions to unique challenges that may arise during the assignment.
5. *Pricing.* Understand the cost assumptions underlying each bidder's price estimates, including the estimated number of FTEs assigned to your work, the mix between offshore and onshore FTEs, and projected increases in worker productivity.

Step 3: Execute Due Diligence and Contract Negotiations

After scoring bidders, invite the top two or three contenders to intensive joint-solution design sessions, where you will clarify the solution and sources of value you expect to tap. Define the respective roles, responsibilities, and decision rights of each party to the relationship, and lay out a clear timeline and cost-allocation regime for the transition phase. These daylong sessions with the subject-matter experts who would work on your account are your best opportunity to gauge a vendor's ability to deliver on its promises and drive buy-in from your organization for the outsourcing initiative. Spending a day with them also allows you to evaluate their expertise and assess how well they fit with your company culture. By the end, you should secure agreement from all finalists on key deal terms, building in contractual incentives for the supplier to achieve your goals (see Figure 8.4).

While a clear favorite may emerge from these discussions, don't limit your options until contracts are finalized. Companies that commit to a favorite vendor too early may tip their hands, sacrificing negotiating leverage they might have retained if the vendor thought they were still negotiating with a competitor, and possibly missing out on favorable contract terms they otherwise might have secured.

Contract negotiations are critical to the long-term value of the outsourcing relationship. Negotiate in parallel with at least two of the strongest candidates until scope, price, and other major terms are nailed down. Take a balanced approach: to avoid prolonging negotiations unnecessarily, acquiesce quickly on terms that are less important to you, but don't let time pressures force you into unfavorable concessions on terms that really matter.

Step 4: Launch Transition

When a contract has been signed, the delicate work of shifting internal processes to an external provider begins. This transition phase is critical, setting in motion relationships, expectations, and patterns of behavior that can make or break the outsourcing initiative's ultimate success. Transitions are managed by a joint transition team with members from the client and external service provider. Each side appoints an overall transition leader and joint managers for every process to be outsourced. The team establishes a timeline and key milestones for the transition. Team leaders monitor progress, identify potential obstacles, and resolve issues escalated by the process managers.

With a team in place, the outsourcer staffs up to handle the work, either by hiring and training new workers, or by reassigning and retraining existing employees. After staffing is complete, process-knowledge transfer begins. The external service provider learns the process by sending representatives to shadow incumbent company workers. Then the work shifts to the outsourcer in a controlled transfer, under the supervision of company

SERVICE PROVIDER DUE DILIGENCE CRITERIA

TECHNOLOGY SERVICE PROVIDER ASSESSMENT

	Question to discuss	Example	Relative perception of vendor: 1	2
FLEXIBILITY VS. DISCIPLINE	Do I want a supplier that instills discipline in my operations at the expense of losing flexibility?	Adherence to strict production protocols and schedules	◑	◐
CULTURAL FIT	How easy is to work, interact, and communicate with the supplier?	IT delivery team located overseas, with layers of processes to establish personal contact	◑	◑
PROACTIVITY AND INNOVATION	Will the supplier proactively bring new ideas to improve my operations and business?	Improved virtualization products that allow more instances in virtual machines	◑	◐
BUSINESS UNDERSTANDING	Will the supplier understand and adapt to my complex business?	Workload in summer period and increasing regulatory requirements in finance	●	●
COMMITMENT TO CORPORATE GOALS	Will the supplier care long term about my business? Long-term or short-term relationship?	Technology road map is designed to evolve with the business	◑	◑
PRICE	What are the one time costs? What are ongoing costs?	Service rates and investment into the account	●	◔

◔ Meets minimal requirements
◑ Meets partial requirements
● Meets all requirements

Source: PwC Strategy&

Figure 8.4

representatives who "reverse shadow" the external service provider's workers as they perform the process.

Last, the transition moves into the pilot phase, in which the external service provider handles a limited amount of work without direct client supervision. If the external service provider meets required service levels during the pilot phase, full-scale implementation of the contract can begin.

Step 5: Design Communications and Retained Organization

Outsourcing frequently triggers anxiety within an organization. Setting realistic expectations among those affected is essential to success. Yet too many companies neglect to define updated organizational roles and responsibilities or communicate them properly, leaving important stakeholders uninformed and wary. Successful outsourcing programs proactively address the fact that an outsourced organization operates and manages very differently than one that is not. Remaining employees will have to focus on managing the vendor instead of executing the services themselves. That means they will have new responsibilities and need new skills. These changes in how and where work is done must be engrained in the organization through continuous, targeted communication.

Case Study: Outsourcing Drives Savings, Performance, and Competitive Advantage at P&G

Consumer products giant Procter & Gamble (P&G) consolidated many processes in the late 1990s, creating a global business services organization that supported business units under a shared services model. But by the mid-2000s, the company was looking for new ways to improve shareholder returns while still delivering best-in-class service to business units.

P&G turned to outsourcing, forming strategic supplier relationships that tapped the strengths of external partners to improve service levels, reduce cost-to-serve, and provide greater access to innovation. After assessing back-office processes on the basis of several financial,

(continued)

(*continued*)

market, and strategic factors, P&G identified a broad range of processes in five distinct areas that appeared ripe for outsourcing: (1) IT Infrastructure, desktops, application development, and maintenance (2,000-plus FTEs); (2) facilities management (600-plus FTEs); (3) HR and employee services (800-plus FTEs); (4) transactional finance processes (2,000-plus FTEs); and (5) consumer relations. Because of the project's wide scope, P&G chose a best-of-breed vendor strategy to engage the best providers for each process and mitigate the risk of underperformance. P&G also visited prospective suppliers to confirm their capabilities and cultural compatibility. On these visits, company executives met highly educated and experienced workers who were committed to continuous improvement and innovation.

In the end, P&G entered into five outsourcing contracts ranging in duration from 5 to 10 years, with total expected billings of more than $4 billion. The contracts not only generated more than $1 billion in operational savings, but also improved service levels and productivity, turned fixed expenses into variable costs, created seasonal staffing flexibility, and gave P&G "follow the sun" capabilities. Strategic partnerships with external service providers also help P&G integrate acquisitions faster and at lower cost. P&G sees outsourcing and its strategic partnerships as a competitive advantage that makes the company stronger in key back-office functions, freeing up the organization to focus on the consumer.

Outsourcing Best Practices

Organizational buy-in and commitment from the top. Like the broader Fit for Growth transformation, an outsourcing program needs buy-in at all levels. This starts with a commitment from top leaders to move quickly and make the right choices for the company. Strong leaders push aside organizational resistance to outsourcing, making it clear that "not doing this" isn't an option. They base decisions on clear business reasons, and make sure the organization understands their rationale.

Clearly defined objectives, scope, and measures. Companies that outsource successfully understand their own internal costs and performance levels, and the trade-offs inherent in their suppliers' cost structures and delivery models. They outsource processes only when performance is measurable and an external provider can be held fully accountable for achieving clearly defined objectives. Undeterred by the complexity of managing multiple vendors, they distribute processes among best-of-breed providers when it will generate more value.

A case to beat. Strong outsourcing programs start by determining the best result the company could achieve by transforming a process internally, assuming access to the best technology and other transformation tools. This "internal case to beat" establishes a baseline for outsourcing decisions and negotiations with service providers.

Effective transaction management. Pace and timing matter a great deal in outsourcing. The best-managed programs allow enough time to define project scope and select a provider, but don't drag out decision making. They maintain momentum by sticking to a strict timetable—usually three to six months for defining scope, choosing a provider, and signing a contract.

Good advice. Outside expertise can add considerable value, especially for companies unfamiliar with outsourcing. Legal counsel with outsourcing experience can help companies manage their contractual liability while building in the flexibility to terminate outsourcing relationships when necessary.

Win win contracts. A good outsourcing agreement is fair to both parties. It ensures reasonable profits for the external service provider and competitive market prices and service levels for the company. The best contracts include incentives such as gain-sharing to encourage innovation, and penalties for failure to meet agreed-upon service levels. While 7- to 10-year IT and business-process outsourcing deals have been common, we see a recent trend toward shorter deals that provide more flexibility and the ability to test the competitive market sooner.

Ongoing involvement. Outsourcing isn't abdication. You still own the overall results, so you need to actively manage your external service providers. Successful companies establish robust vendor management offices to oversee outsourcing relationships and monitor service quality. They also retain critical knowledge of outsourced processes, so they can manage external providers effectively. Yet they balance rigor and flexibility, avoiding micromanagement of service providers without "handing over the keys." Focused on results, they give providers leeway to propose creative solutions, and rely on service level agreements and metrics to evaluate performance.

Pitfalls to Avoid

Outsourcing broken processes. It's tempting to ask somebody else to clean up your mess. Don't outsource a broken process without a plan to fix it.

Focusing only on cost. Companies that focus only on unit cost savings blind themselves to the broader benefits of outsourcing. In their zeal for short-term savings, they sacrifice the greater value to be reaped from true process optimization.

Underestimating internal challenges. It takes time and concerted effort to overcome internal opposition to outsourcing. Companies sometimes fail to confront the misconception that "outsourcing won't work here," or allow managers to protect their organizations without putting forward a business case for keeping the function in house.

9 | Footprint Optimization

Rethink Your Operations and Overhead Locations

A company's footprint is made up of all the locations where it has manufacturing plants, distribution centers, service points, R&D centers, and administrative and support offices, and it drives a large part of a company's cost structure. Optimizing the footprint involves analyzing and making changes to these locations. Footprint optimization is among the most powerful levers within the Fit for Growth transformation framework, both for reducing costs—by as much as 15 to 20 percent over 12 to 24 months, in our experience—and for providing a solid but flexible foundation for future growth that takes service levels and customer proximity into account.

What Is Footprint Optimization?

Footprint optimization involves systematically analyzing—and improving—how effectively the company's locations work together, how cost-effective they are, how well they support the company's strategy, and how adaptable they are to changing markets and customer requirements. The decisions companies make about their footprint cut across their entire value chain.

In the past, many companies—especially manufacturers—were slow to change their footprints. Many achieved great success with vertically integrated business models that afforded end-to-end control of product quality, and they were able to leverage economies of scale to use all production assets and drive down unit costs. Today, improvements in logistics, digitization, and communications, more streamlined supply chains, and the emergence of low-cost country sourcing afford companies more options—and advantages—for challenging preconceptions about where different business activities should take place.

Depending on their specific requirements, including cost structure, flexibility needs, product life cycles, technology intensity, value density of products, and sales markets, most companies use variations on one of four "network" archetypes:

1. *World factory*, where one or a very few sites supply multiple markets to capture the benefits of production scale;
2. *Hub and spoke*, where upstream production processes are concentrated at one or a few sites, and downstream productions processes are carried out at local sites;
3. *Low-cost manufacturing*, where the lead production site is located near R&D facilities and volume production is located in low-cost countries (LCCs); or
4. *Local for local*, where demand is served by local sites with little or no interaction between them.

Although these examples describe manufacturing organizations, the same principles apply to other functions, such as R&D or back-office support (see Figure 9.1).

In manufacturing industries, company footprints greatly conform to locations of manufacturing assets, both those they own and those of contract manufacturers. This in turn influences the location of distribution facilities, and to some extent of engineering, R&D, sales, operations, and administration facilities.

Many companies in developed markets have moved much of their manufacturing to offshore LCCs to access lower labor rates. For many other manufacturers, however, the primary decision of where to locate production facilities depends not only on the labor rates, but also on their ability to get their product to key markets quickly and the associated supply chain costs,

FOUR "NETWORK" ARCHETYPES

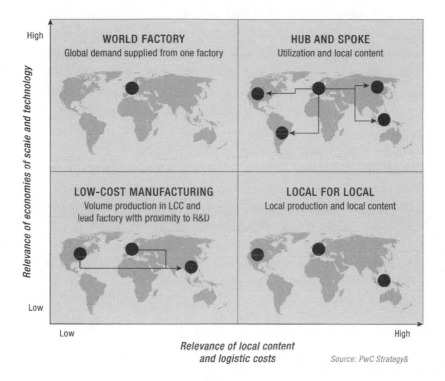

Figure 9.1

including for transportation and carrying inventory. For example, a company with a large U.S. distribution network may want a small number of highly efficient warehousing and distribution facilities in lower-cost locations near its major regions—but a larger number of smaller facilities, dispersed nationally near major cities, will allow faster delivery times.

In service-heavy industries like retailing, banking, insurance, and health care, the footprint includes customer-facing locations and operations processing centers, along with SG&A support offices. All companies have general and administrative (G&A) activities. These are much less visible to customers, and customer and market considerations take a back seat to internal optimization considerations, including labor rates, access to talent pools, infrastructure quality, and tax incentives. In these G&A processes, many companies follow a hub-and-spoke footprint model. Optimizing the transactional processes of this model's footprint (such as accounts payable, general ledger transactions, employee data management, and IT applications maintenance) requires different considerations from its expertise processes (e.g., budgeting, investment analytics, compensation design, data modeling).

For scale-sensitive transactional processes, leading-edge companies consolidate the work in one global center, or two to three regional centers, located in LCCs with sufficient access to talent. These offshore global in-house centers (GICs), also commonly referred to as captive centers, offer significant operational and cost advantages—sometimes yielding savings of as much as 65 percent. For processes requiring more skill and internal-customer proximity-sensitive expertise, companies locate some of their staff in smaller offices, closer to internal customers, and the rest in the GIC.

Beyond reducing labor costs, setting up a GIC can yield strategic and other benefits, including the following:

- Access to comparable or better-quality talent
- Ability to build or enhance critical capabilities such as R&D and analytics
- "Follow-the-sun" 24/7 coverage
- Tax advantages
- A platform from which to expand in emerging markets
- Breakthrough innovation and faster time to market

Large companies often choose a hub-and-spoke model for their GICs, which enables them to optimize the advantages that different locations offer. One global insurance company, for example, established its two largest GICs in India to perform IT, HR, facilities and administrative services, claims processing, and actuarial and marketing analytics, because of industry maturity, low costs, and a large and growing labor pool. The insurer also established smaller offices in Ireland (for software development, data modeling, and UK and European contact center capabilities), the Czech Republic (to supplement high-end data analytics capacity for the India location), the Philippines (for call centers, due to its low costs and accent-neutral labor pool), and Costa Rica and Canada (for time-zone-related call-center work) (see Figure 9.2).

The R&D footprint also involves trade-offs. In some cases, companies may want to locate dispersed R&D facilities near their key production facilities to facilitate collaboration. In other cases, the more important consideration may be to concentrate a smaller number of R&D sites where specific talent is most readily available. For technology companies and technology-intensive manufacturing and service firms, that may mean

GIC HUB-AND-SPOKE FOOTPRINT
FOR A GLOBAL INSURANCE COMPANY

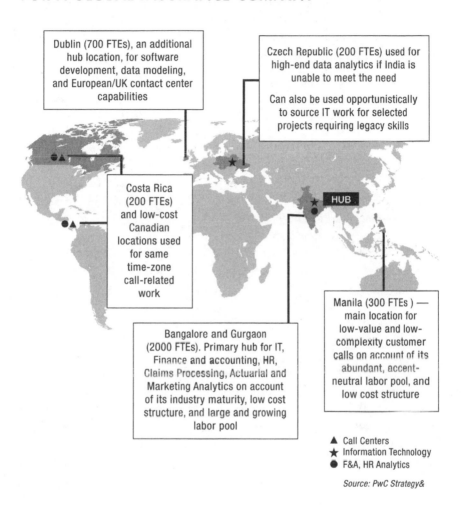

Dublin (700 FTEs), an additional hub location, for software development, data modeling, and European/UK contact center capabilities

Czech Republic (200 FTEs) used for high-end data analytics if India is unable to meet the need

Can also be used opportunistically to source IT work for selected projects requiring legacy skills

Costa Rica (200 FTEs) and low-cost Canadian locations used for same time-zone call-related work

HUB

Manila (300 FTEs) — main location for low-value and low-complexity customer calls on account of its abundant, accent-neutral labor pool, and low cost structure

Bangalore and Gurgaon (2000 FTEs). Primary hub for IT, Finance and accounting, HR, Claims Processing, Actuarial and Marketing Analytics on account of its industry maturity, low cost structure, and large and growing labor pool

▲ Call Centers
★ Information Technology
● F&A, HR Analytics

Source: PwC Strategy&

Figure 9.2

locating R&D in Silicon Valley or another global tech hub. For specialized businesses such as pharmaceuticals or optical products, R&D locations may need to be near major research universities.

When to Use Footprint Optimization

Footprint optimization is an essential part of a Fit for Growth transformation initiative due to its impact across the company's value chain, but it is also an exercise that companies should undergo every few years. Markets today are changing much more rapidly than most companies do, and footprints risk becoming outdated. Companies must ensure their footprint remains aligned with the overall business strategy, customers and suppliers, talent needs, and cost structure. Indicators for considering footprint optimization include the following:

- *Subpar operational results:* Your manufacturing footprint is no longer cost competitive. The distribution network is underserving your most important customers and overserving others. Innovations take too long to get to market, and are difficult to pull back when they underperform. Overhead costs are generally higher than those of competitors. As a result, your company is unable to adapt to and serve new growth markets, and competitors with more advantaged footprints are gaining market share.

- *Shifting industry dynamics:* Changes in the industry structure that affect your supply base and demand base can affect your footprint. Suppliers may be moving. Fluctuations in sales volume among regions may suggest ways to optimize your manufacturing locations and supply-and-distribution chains.

- *Wage arbitrage opportunities:* Changes in regional wage rates may offer an opportunity to realign the footprint. Wages in global locations that were low-cost in the past may be rising relative to wages in other locations.

- *Collaboration and integration opportunities:* Sometimes companies operate in many locations due to choices made in the past to leave acquired businesses as stand-alone, or to set up business units or specific functions in their own locations, to enable a specific objective. Consolidating them may improve efficiency and collaboration.

- *Economic and tax-incentive opportunities:* If your company has large number of employees at a single office or campus where a lease will expire in the next several years, reassessing the footprint can unlock significant potential gains.

Case Study: A New Footprint for an Aircraft Engine Production and Maintenance Company

Several years ago, MTU Aero Engines—a $4.5 billion company headquartered in Germany, with operations in Europe, North America, and Asia—realized it needed to rethink its global footprint to support an ambitious growth plan that envisioned long-term participation in some of the key global airline engine programs. MTU's business is the design, development, manufacture, marketing, and support of commercial and military aircraft engines, and it partners with all the industry's leading players, including GE, Pratt & Whitney, and Rolls-Royce. In the commercial maintenance, repair, and overhaul (MRO) sector, the company ranks among the top five service providers for commercial aircraft engines and industrial gas turbines.

Developing and manufacturing aircraft engines requires very long-term commitments that only pay off over 20- to 30-year delivery time spans. It is therefore crucial to qualify for engine programs at their inception and participate throughout their life span by meeting strict criteria for competency and competitiveness. MTU's challenge in manufacturing and engineering was to manage costs to compete effectively for future engine programs, and its challenge in MRO services was to enable anticipated growth, balance uneven utilization at some of its existing sites, and increase efficiency and cost competitiveness.

MTU developed a global structural-site concept to address these challenges that included creating a new best-cost location in Poland for manufacturing, engineering, and MRO service capabilities and capacities. The concept was a step change for a quality-conservative industry, made possible by Poland's excellent infrastructure and people resources, as well as MTU's measured, structured approach to building and ramping up the new location with a series of sequential upgrades. It also required a major change-management effort within the company. MTU was able to manage the typical issues that arise in Germany (and Europe) due to worker's council involvement via a structured, cooperative process.

The resulting balanced global footprint has been highly successful, yielding a significant competitive advantage for all areas in engineering, production, and MRO, and has enabled MTU to participate in some of the most prestigious and growing long-term aero engine programs currently running.

Footprint Optimization: How It Works

In designing an optimized footprint, the transformation team should link the footprint design to the company's competitive strategy. It needs to recognize the footprint's central role in enabling top-line growth while driving improvements in bottom line performance, and it must integrate footprint needs into the company's go-to-market and product strategies, while accounting for industry dynamics. Leaders should strive for a holistic solution, understanding that the entire operating model is a critical component in realizing the value of the footprint. Processes, decision rights, tools and IT, and metrics all need to be aligned to fit the new footprint—when you change the footprint, you may also have to change the wiring of the business to match. We suggest a five-step process for footprint design (see Figure 9.3).

Step 1: Identify Business Requirements

Footprint optimization should start with understanding the customer requirements you need to meet and win. This macro view of what is happening with your organization, the industry, and the market is meant to provide a clear overall picture of the company's present and future competitive needs, and to identify where your footprint is not aligned with your differentiating capabilities. Key areas to investigate and understand include:

- The company's market and demand scenarios;
- The planned product and portfolio strategy, and its development over the next several years;

FOOTPRINT OPTIMIZATION APPROACH

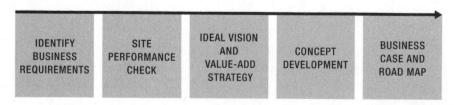

Source: PwC Strategy&

Figure 9.3

- The current state of production technology and key performance indicators for plants;
- Customer service levels and quality requirements;
- Constraints on operations, such as contracts and general agreements; and
- A financial review of cost structures, headcount, and working capital.

These factors should help you understand where you may have too much presence, versus not enough. For example, you may not want to reduce your sales footprint in a growth market where face-to-face interaction is the norm.

Case Study: Footprint in Food Manufacturing

A North American food company facing rising cost pressure and slow growth looked to its manufacturing footprint as a key to future market success. A new footprint was reconfigured "market-back" and underpinned by a lower cost structure to address evolving consumer demands. Within just three years, the client established its position as the innovation leader in new categories, funding investments therein with the cost savings the footprint optimization achieved in its core business.

The client's initial challenges stemmed from a continued shift in consumer preferences away from traditional products toward new categories. Because the original network had been built for stable demand in core products, declining volumes wreaked havoc on the cost structure. Making matters worse, consumers were demonstrating more price sensitivity toward these same categories, putting additional pressure on margins, and a number of smaller, more agile players innovating their way into the market were capturing growth and more favorable pricing in new categories. Taken together, the client was left with an underperforming product portfolio and manufacturing capabilities too outdated to capitalize on the market shift.

Re-architecting the footprint had become an economic and strategic imperative. Reversing the company's fortunes would first require

(continued)

(*continued*)

dramatically improving its cost position relative to its competition for its core volume. More important, the company had to prudently add new capabilities to innovate for growth and provide a path to future success.

Resetting costs required understanding what the market demanded, in terms of price and service, and aligning production assets accordingly. By understanding the fundamental economics of manufacturing and squaring these with market demands, the client was able to determine the cost position they needed to achieve for advantage and the levers they needed to pull to do so. The lowest cost of goods sold could be reduced significantly through structural changes: consolidating similar assets to maximize manufacturing scale and usage, leveraging a regional footprint to reduce logistics costs, and capitalizing on lower labor costs.

Fixing the growth problem proved more challenging because it required placing bets on new capabilities in advance of a proven market need. Initial consumer research provided a glimpse of such new capabilities, but the resulting innovation pipeline was filled with smaller and more numerous projects than before. This new level of variety necessitated looking at the innovation pipeline more holistically to find ways to aggregate new products based on similar capabilities and build scale where possible. For the remaining innovations that held potential, capabilities could be outsourced to a third party, minimizing the initial investment risk.

The final key to the new footprint was to establish a Lean manufacturing support team that could scale with evolving business needs. Over time, portfolio complexity had increased support costs; each new product had brought with it an incremental level of support in the form of planning, production management, quality, and engineering. This support resided within each of the respective plants, creating pockets of knowledge and a support structure that was inflexible to market demand. The new footprint leveraged centers of excellence focused on capabilities rather than locations to build and share technical knowledge. To keep associated overhead costs as low as possible, plants were to be managed as smaller regional clusters. Multiple plants in geographic proximity would be managed by a regional team that better leveraged support resources and drove best-practice sharing across plants.

The results of the footprint transformation were rapid and dramatic. Margins improved almost immediately as supply chain costs were cut by more than 15 percent. Growth also rose sharply as the new footprint drove more than 10 percent of total revenue from new products. As a final confirmation of the strategy's success, return on invested capital rose dramatically.

Step 2: Site Performance Check

This step is a bottom-up objective assessment of your existing footprint. The footprint is tested for alignment with the corporate strategy, benchmarked against best practices, and compared across the company's network, focusing on productivity, utilization, and costs of headcount and operations. Current facilities can then be compared with a structured framework of attractiveness and competitiveness that weighs factors such as efficiency of scale, availability of talent, labor rates, and tax implications. This step identifies which locations add the most value to your business and which should be candidates for scaling back, closure, or divestment. It also helps determine how competitive your current footprint is and could be, by framing some of the big choices and making the footprint optimization exercise more manageable.

Step 3: Ideal Vision and Value-Add Strategy

At this step you should have a good understanding of the external and internal factors influencing your decisions and target areas. Now, overlay your operational strategies, including trade-offs such as flexibility, agility, operational versus capital investment, and go-to market strategies. You can then make decisions that will help you exploit economies of scale, leverage your technology investment, and be close enough to the customer while staying flexible, especially locally. These decisions will help you decide more easily what functions to perform yourself versus leveraging partners to do them without incurring unreasonable sunk costs. They also help you determine the best network archetype for your organization, as illustrated earlier in this chapter.

Step 4: Concept Development and Evaluation

As the concept and implementation plan is developed, the team needs to identify the key cost drivers and their importance for each option. Opportunities will range from the current state to the ideal; the team's next step is to identify and evaluate the scenarios in between. Each scenario should incrementally exploit key leverage points, but remain grounded in the realities of implementation, investment, timing, risk, and interdependencies. Scenarios should range from incremental (such as consolidation within existing plants) to very aggressive (the unconstrained ideal). Each will be developed and tested against strategic criteria, taking account of the implications of key cost drivers. The decision framework that companies use typically includes these six criteria:

1. *Proximity to customers and suppliers:* Many manufacturing companies want to locate their production facilities close to their most important markets, which has implications for their distribution and supply chain footprints.
2. *Key wage rates:* Labor costs are a key cost driver in many industries, and the large variability of wage rates across global regions, and in different regions within countries, offers significant labor arbitrage opportunities.
3. *Access to talent:* Workforce characteristics are important in any footprint decision, and may be the most important criteria for specific activities like R&D, customer-support call centers, or advanced manufacturing. When companies need to bring in expatriates, quality-of-life issues (housing, schools, and cultural institutions) can be an important consideration for having the right talent.
4. *Infrastructure:* Good highway systems, port facilities, and airports are important for businesses that ship physical goods. Reliable utilities, such as electricity and high-speed Internet access, are essential for companies locating back-office functions.
5. *Economic and tax incentives:* Many countries, as well as state and local governments in the United States, offer economic incentives and tax abatements that can provide significant financial benefits.
6. *Political, legal, and regulatory stability:* Some locations are obviously unsuitable for business activities, but others may be in more of a gray area that requires analysis.

This is the stage where you analyze trade-offs while developing options for the new footprint. For example: Which is more important for your organization—maintaining service levels for customers, or incurring low inventory costs? Labor competency or strike risk? Local supply-base opportunities or delivery time? Tax considerations or public image?

Given the complexity of adjusting the footprint, the amount of analysis involved, and the number of trade-offs and potential outcomes, it's important to avoid trying to get the perfect answer right away. We recommend a "funnel" approach, where you start with a high-level solution anchored in technical fit segmentation and clustering. Then narrow the options, first with a rough evaluation, and further narrow the list with detailed evaluations and bottom-up analyses, until you're ready to zero in on a final list.

Be aware: Evaluating each of these scenarios requires an initial estimate of implementation timing and investment. Once you have aligned on the key scenario, you have a starting point for more refined investment estimates and implementation timing.

Step 5: Business Case and Road Map

This step happens iteratively and in parallel with Step 4, as the final options are evaluated and a business case and transition plan are developed to reach the target state, including timelines, milestones, metrics, and implementation costs. The business case needs to be sophisticated enough to consider all costs (one time and ongoing) while anticipating environmental and legal implications and any tax benefits. You also need to consider the implications to your business—for example, if you reduce the number of warehouses or centralize customer service globally, do you risk lost sales?

Footprint Optimization Best Practices

Start with a market-back approach. Focus on customer demand and service level expectations.

Analyze scale and complexity effects. Balance lower cost per unit that comes with greater scale, but is potentially offset by rising complexity costs (e.g., locate all support functions in one global hub, but manage the complexity arising from the hub's scope and the needs of internal customers).

Understand labor–automation trade-off. Recognize that automation choices will vary based on volume (low vs. high) and the local labor rate.

Incorporate the total costs and implications of a new footprint. Include all costs (labor, transportation, inventory, facilities) along with additional risks and support requirements.

Use hypotheses to drive optimal network scenarios. It is not practical to evaluate all potential network changes, so use a hypothesis-driven approach to identify key scenarios and focus on those.

Pitfalls to Avoid

Underestimating the transition costs. Footprint changes require significant one-time investments to set up new facilities, but the transition costs are also measurable (e.g., redundant capital, closing costs, productivity ramp-up costs, expatriate compensation).

Failing to recognize current productivity and service levels. Understand the productivity potential of the new footprint, something that can likely be achieved with little capital, before making a footprint decision.

Missing the product mix difference. Don't overgeneralize to generate an answer that is correct for a nonexistent average product; understand the big differences in terms of labor content, shipping density, and material.

Failing to plan for "new ways of working." These may be required with a new footprint.

Underestimating the people elements. Plan for a dip in productivity in the closed or consolidated facilities as employee morale dips. Also, plan to capture deep reservoirs of experience and transfer this knowledge to the new facilities.

10 | Process Excellence

Simplify Work and Minimize Bureaucracy

Process excellence advances a Fit for Growth transformation by optimizing processes to achieve sustainable efficiency and effectiveness while supporting differentiating capabilities. It takes a market-back view to identify the real sources of customer value in a product or service, determines which processes create that value, and simplifies or eliminates other processes. Process excellence improvements often leverage tools such as Lean, Six Sigma, and others, but the approach differs from these familiar continuous-improvement methods in important ways. Traditional methods work within existing structures to foster incremental, evolutionary improvement from the bottom up, independent of what the rest of the business may be doing. By contrast, process excellence applies a market-driven perspective to create a blueprint of the four macro business processes found in every company—innovation, sales and marketing, delivery, and support—and how they interact to deliver the targeted customer-value proposition (see Figure 10.1).

Then it takes a "fit for purpose" approach to select the right mix of techniques, and optimize and re-base the remaining sub-processes. This unique approach to simplifying entire parts of the business and core operations often releases sufficient cash savings to help self-fund the creation of new capabilities.

MACRO PROCESSES

EXAMPLE

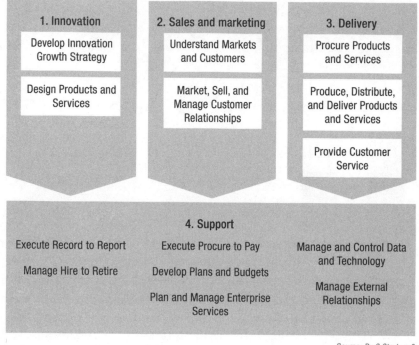

Source: PwC Strategy&

Figure 10.1

What Is Process Excellence?

Process excellence is an approach to optimizing how a company brings goods or services to market. It employs a range of tools and techniques to make processes more coherent, aligning them with the company's strategy so that they work together to consistently produce desired outcomes. The goal is not simply to reduce costs, but instead to reshape processes to fulfill customer needs at cost and service levels that meet organizational objectives. By doing that, it offers a solution to one of the most vexing concerns for today's corporate leaders: how to do more for the customer, for less. Respondents to the PwC 2015 Global Operations Survey reaffirmed that understanding customer value, having the flexibility to change direction, and managing complexity and costs are the top challenges companies face (see Figure 10.2). Process excellence enables leading firms to achieve these multiple objectives.

TODAY'S OPERATIONAL CHALLENGES

Percent of COOs responding to an issue as most,
second-most, or third-most challenging

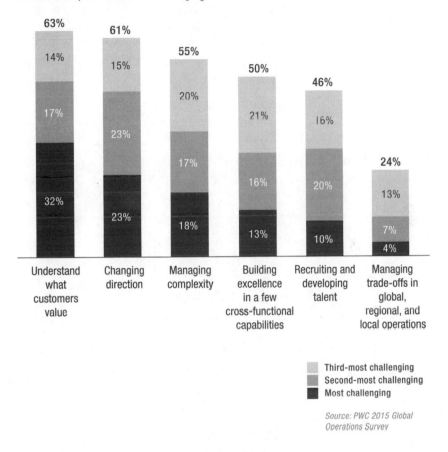

	Third-most challenging
	Second-most challenging
	Most challenging

*Source: PWC 2015 Global
Operations Survey*

Figure 10.2

Case Study: Process Excellence in the Mining Industry

Resource companies compete in cyclical industries. To win requires capabilities that allow them to manage both economies of scale and flexibility. This case refers to one of the leading resource excavation companies during the 2008–2009 financial crisis. Shifting market forces drove significant reductions in demand and intense cost pressures. Executives realized that dramatic action was necessary to keep the

(continued)

(*continued*)

company afloat. They decided to use process excellence to reduce costs and position the company to compete in a shrinking market. Focusing on its biggest spend areas—delivery and support processes— the company decided to re-base all its core processes. They launched a mine-by-mine process excellence effort aimed at increasing output by 20 percent while re-basing the core cost structure.

A market-back view clarified a dual objective for the mines: excavating as much as possible without compromising safety while reducing the cost structure by billions of dollars. Support activities handled by individual mines such as sales, planning, and transportation were centralized into a single center, which fostered coherence and effectiveness. Decision making began to reflect the strategic aims of the company as a whole, rather than the priorities of each mine. Reducing the number of moving parts enabled the company to be more flexible and effective.

Next, the company defined the key customer and product bundles and realigned its entire operating model to serve them. They also created a new performance excellence team, which embedded controls and best practices into delivery processes facility by facility and measured expected improvements. Within six months, the savings each mine achieved had generated enough funds to improve additional facilities and develop new capabilities in pricing analytics and management reporting. Within 18 months, the process excellence effort provided the company with the leading cost structure in the industry.

Change initiatives seeking the optimal balance of cost and customer value usually need to untangle a web of complex processes spanning multiple cost centers and departments. Most companies lack a clear understanding of their customers' true expectations, making it harder to focus, scope, and be more aggressive on process improvement efforts. Executives often start with the obvious: applying improvement tools to known process problems, or standardizing to a single model. But moving too quickly, while satisfying at first, often saps energy and creates distractions from core improvement opportunities. In addition, traditional process improvement methods often compete with—or are not coherent with—other on-going improvement initiatives such as digitization, outsourcing, and footprint optimization. Process excellence, by contrast, aligns with these transformation efforts and generates greater benefits and flexibility.

Process excellence advances transformation goals in four distinct ways: reducing process costs; improving quality; boosting revenue, either by creating new capabilities within existing cost structures, or improving products or the customer experience; and strengthening the balance sheet by reducing the capital levels required to run the business.

Reducing costs: Process improvements save money by reducing the labor and materials required for each step in a process. Typically this involves improving the efficiency of labor and assets by reducing the activity in a process, or by finding new sources of materials and labor (as described in Chapters 8, "Outsourcing," and 12, "Strategic Supply Management"). Taking a market-back, macro-process view allows companies to re-base costs more quickly by leveraging multiple improvement levers (including simplification, automation, predictability, and quality improvements) across more cost areas.

Improving quality: Quality improves as a company eliminates process flaws and unnecessary complexity that may result in subpar products or services, or require costly manual workarounds that invariably fail to meet rising customer expectations and the demands of a growing business. Interestingly, the highest-quality processes often have the lowest costs.

Boosting revenue: Process excellence efforts free up time and resources that enable companies to invest in the products and features that customers value. Defining that sweet spot requires a fact-based, customer-back analysis, using one or a combination of many tools and methods available, to understand what customers truly value.

Strengthening the balance sheet: As processes become more efficient, working-capital needs decline for accounts receivable, accounts payable, and inventory, freeing up funds to pay for future phases of the transformation. Improvements in supply chain design, procurement processes, and manufacturing flow drive these savings. At the same time, optimized processes can reduce capital spending budgets by enabling a company to produce more without adding capacity, while generating resources for investment in additional improvements.

Process excellence operates at two levels—fostering better interplay among macro processes, while improving the key individual business processes within each category that support differentiating capabilities. The goal is to improve and align all processes to deliver broader benefits for the enterprise, by envisioning a master blueprint that shows how the four macro processes work in concert toward future-state objectives of the transformation. In contrast, typical process improvement techniques target discrete steps in individual processes or sub-processes, often in isolation.

Rebalancing an Operating Model with Process Excellence

An agile, customer-driven innovation process was fueling rapid growth at a manufacturer of recreational vehicles. Unfortunately, its macro processes for delivery, marketing, and staff support couldn't keep pace with innovation, which rolled out new products in market-beating time and delivered "facelifts" to existing products faster than competitors.

The delivery macro process was emerging as a particular source of delay. The sourcing process within delivery couldn't meet its twin goals of capturing sustainable savings while ensuring adequate supply for the continuous stream of new products and facelifts flowing from the innovation machine. Although the company was working with suppliers to drive incremental improvements in strategic sourcing on a year-by-year basis, it hadn't taken on the bigger challenge of building a world-class delivery process. The time was ripe for a process excellence initiative to bring the delivery macro process up to the level of innovation.

Focusing on sourcing processes, the company built the capabilities necessary to feed innovation throughout the product lifecycle, while also accelerating material cost savings. A benchmarking exercise identified opportunities for "step-change" improvement in materials costs, which the company captured through internal cost-reduction initiatives and leveraging its scale with strategic suppliers. The company also fostered closer integration of delivery and innovation processes. Involving strategic sourcing earlier in product development gave it more lead time to deliver needed supplies, while cost modeling and supply economics analysis gave both innovation and sourcing teams a deeper understanding of product costs.

Process excellence enabled the company to deliver high-ROI results in the near term, while creating the conditions for sustained capabilities improvement and material cost savings. The broader macro process of delivery became more agile and responsive to changing customer requirements. Closer links between delivery and innovation enabled a reexamination of product features from a cost perspective, and triggered joint analysis to ensure market-back customer acceptance for cost-driven changes.

Ultimately, the company's delivery processes encompassed a sustainable end-to-end suite of capabilities, from the strategic to the transactional.

When to Use Process Excellence

Companies may turn to process excellence when they need a step change in process efficiency that they cannot achieve with traditional continuous-improvement tools. But how can you tell if your company needs such sweeping change? In our experience, process excellence delivers superior results in five common scenarios:

1. *When quality and customer satisfaction are not competitive.* The ultimate outputs of efficient processes are higher-value interactions with customers, happier employees who aren't burdened by wasteful activities, and confidence in delivering value every day.
2. *When processes are overly complex.* Process excellence rationalizes and simplifies multiple complex processes comprising numerous functions, many business units, and large numbers of people.
3. *When data pose a challenge.* Process excellence identifies the data required for each process, and addresses the challenges of delivering that information when and where it's needed.
4. *When significant technology initiatives don't deliver the expected value in business operations.* Process excellence is a precursor to digitization and the use of tools like robotic process automation; often, companies turn to technology before prioritizing, rationalizing, and improving processes.
5. *When permanent, radical change is needed.* By fundamentally transforming processes, process excellence drives strategic change that lasts for years.

Process Excellence Myths Debunked

Several widespread misconceptions can cause companies to reject process excellence altogether or capture less than full value from a process excellence initiative.

Process excellence is for manufacturers, not service companies. Every business delivers value to customers through a series of processes that can be analyzed, segmented, and optimized for cost and value.

Process excellence requires a full-scale Lean or Six Sigma organization. A small, fit-for-purpose reengineering team can drive significant, sustainable change without the permanent infrastructure of a Lean/Six Sigma program.

Top managers can dictate change. Just as front-line managers cannot drive the entire process, neither can the C-suite. Top leaders can articulate objectives, allocate funds, and demonstrate a commitment to fundamental change, but they can't make it happen on a day-to-day basis. Managers and staff from the middle of the organization down to the front line need the training, tools, and authority to carry out process improvements.

Avoid IT at all costs. Notwithstanding the risks and bottlenecks sometimes associated with technology implementations, no process improvement project can afford to be indifferent to technology enablement. Recent advances in robotics, digital machine-to-machine functionality, and other technology solutions produce step-change efficiency gains in many processes. Those who ignore these options forgo significant savings and risk falling behind competitors who can lead concurrent process and technology improvement programs.

You can't improve processes if you can't improve your systems. While IT improvements drive significant efficiency gains, don't overlook nontechnology solutions. Changing what you do, where you do it, and who does it may yield worthwhile improvements even without systems upgrades.

A Guide to Process Excellence

As you try to get your arms around a process excellence initiative, it helps to remember that virtually every company conducts business through four macro processes: *innovation* processes that create new products or services; *delivery* processes that make and deliver products or services; *sales and marketing* processes that drive revenue and margin growth; and *support* processes that enable a company to manage itself and deliver basic administrative support to its employees. Each macro process encompasses certain core business processes that support your differentiating capabilities, and each category requires a different set of techniques and tools to improve processes. Optimizing these core processes generates the greatest value in a process excellence initiative, so focus your efforts there.

Building best-in-class processes involves five key steps. Start by defining your core processes, then use a customer-back analysis to identify your challenges. Gather the data you need to fully understand the current performance and the root causes of performance gaps. Use this information to develop and pilot a solution. Last, evaluate results of the pilot against your expectations and then formalize your new processes (see Figure 10.3).

Step 1: Define Core Processes

Every process excellence initiative starts with identifying your macro processes and how they interact. You start by defining Level 1 and Level 2 processes that are essential to your business and your differentiating capabilities. During this task you need to identify your differentiated processes and key supporting processes, then create a blueprint to ensure a coherent approach across the value chain.

PROCESS EXCELLENCE APPROACH

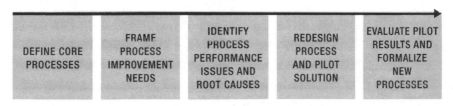

| DEFINE CORE PROCESSES | FRAME PROCESS IMPROVEMENT NEEDS | IDENTIFY PROCESS PERFORMANCE ISSUES AND ROOT CAUSES | REDESIGN PROCESS AND PILOT SOLUTION | EVALUATE PILOT RESULTS AND FORMALIZE NEW PROCESSES |

Source: PwC Strategy&

Figure 10.3

Levels of Processes

A foundational requirement for a successful process excellence program is to examine your existing processes at the right level of detail. If you look at your process at too high a level you will miss the opportunities to optimize, and if you get lost in the weeds of a process you will miss opportunities for more fundamental and cross-functional change. In our process excellence approach we rely on three levels of detail in a process.

Level 1: Value Chain. Take an end-to-end view of the major links in your value chain—processes such as R&D, manufacturing, sales, and marketing. The value chain view will be similar across companies within an industry. This high-level map helps define the primary processes and major steps within each.

Level 2: Process Overview. Break down processes identified in Level 1 into major capabilities. For example, a broader sales function might include capabilities such as sales planning and customer relationship management. The Level 2 process flow shows a comprehensive view of all capabilities within each step in the value chain, and how these capabilities are related in terms of inputs, outputs, and key interfaces to other processes.

Level 3: Activity Detail. Level 3 process maps break down each of the capabilities in Level 2 to the next level of detail. This often looks like a "swim lane" diagram, where each swim lane represents a participant role in the process, and captures sequential flow of step-by-step activities for each role, specifically calling out key decisions and systems involved in the process.

For example, a step in the Level 1 value chain of a manufacturer could be R&D. Level 2 for this process might consist of product strategy, design, prototyping, preproduction, and product lifecycle management. Level 3 would break down each one of these into specific steps, participants, and systems.

Step 2: Frame Process Improvement Needs

Your next task is to determine how well a process meets important expectations of internal or external customers. Use four primary investigative tools to pinpoint these improvement opportunities and frame the issues you need to tackle:

1. Cross-industry research that reveals best practices for each process;
2. An assessment of broader market trends and how they affect your processes;
3. A comparison of your current service levels with customer expectations and the service levels provided by competitors; and
4. Customer interviews, surveys, user groups, and statistical testing that will provide deeper insight into how customers perceive your products or services, what they value, and what they can do without.

Tools such as conjoint analysis, critical-to-quality driver trees, and design for Six Sigma can help pinpoint what customers truly value and identify improvement opportunities.

After identifying improvement needs, describe them explicitly and develop a theme for your improvement initiative. Specify what you aim to accomplish, how it will create value, and how you will measure results.

Step 3: Identify Process Performance Issues and Root Causes

To fix the flaws you've identified, you'll need a deeper understanding of the processes in question. Gather Level 3 process data, including process-step activity times, the number of workers per step, the volume and variability of demand for the process, and the labor and material cost for each step. Calculate process step capacity, overall process flow rate, labor and material content, and idle time. Identify over- or under-utilized resources by computing an implied utilization rate for each process step.

Identify all sources of waste in your processes. Waste takes many forms, such as overproduction, idle time, overprocessing, excess inventory, reworking of flawed products, and unnecessary movements on the production line. Work with the line management and staff to identify and eliminate root causes of waste. A number of analytical tools are available to baseline the current performance levels and identify root causes of waste (see "Analytical Tools for Process Excellence").

Analytical Tools for Process Excellence

Value-stream mapping. Captures the flow of material and information as a product or service makes its way through the value stream, along with labor consumed and performance measures at each activity in the value stream.

Workload demand profile. Documents the demand profile by time segments (e.g., time of the day or month of the year) to better match labor supply with demand patterns.

Time and motion study. Captures detailed observations of staff performing the processes, documenting the workload for and time required to perform a specific activity.

Value Add/Non–Value Add Analysis. Categorizes each activity in the value stream as value add, non–value add, or non–value add but necessary, to enable identifying and eliminating waste.

Seven-waste assessment. Used to identify inefficient or unnecessary parts of a process, testing for each of seven common wastes: defects, unnecessary motion, overproduction, ineffective transfers, waiting, inventory, and overprocessing.

Fishbone (root cause) analysis. Used to structure a brainstorming session and identify many possible root causes of a certain effect, asking probing questions to drill down to why waste occurs.

As your analysis progresses from the customer through the enterprise, opportunities to create additional value will become readily apparent. Based on this analysis, create a blueprint outlining the overall impact of process change across your organization. Developing the blueprint at the outset will enable you to quantify the benefits of process excellence and sequence the initiative to ensure that early stages generate enough value to self-fund later phases.

Step 4: Redesign Process and Pilot Solution

Launch initiatives to transform processes, relying on your analysis to determine which parts of each process to eliminate, consolidate, or automate. Use tools such as Lean to redesign processes, working with cross-functional teams of employees directly involved in each process under evaluation. Address the key factors that drive process efficiency, including the following:

- Determining the economic order quantity for each process—the optimal number of units that can be processed at one time to achieve the best trade-off between batching (which slows the process down) and inventory (which increases process costs).
- Establishing service-level requirements that will deliver the performance customers expect, and zero-basing all other activities that are not essential to delivering these outcomes.
- Smoothing production rates across each process by balancing work among various functions and process steps. Alternatively, explore pooling options to balance out the work.
- Realigning the organization structure of the process to match the throughput needed from each process step.
- Reducing variability of demand for process inputs, process steps, or the overall process. In cases where demand consistently exceeds supply, add capacity by replicating an efficient line, selectively adding workers, specializing tasks, or increasing automation.

As you plan your solution, consider all technology options for process improvement. For example, "smart factory" systems that track the location of labor and materials in real time enable manufacturers to smooth out production and maintain performance levels by anticipating production bottlenecks and reallocating resources accordingly. One manufacturer testing this technology already has seen significant benefits at the pilot plant: labor productivity up 20 percent; on-time deliveries up 15 percent; scrap and rework down 3 percent as a percentage of cost of goods sold (COGS); and total COGS spending down 10 percent.

As you standardize and simplify processes, make sure you balance the efficiency benefits of process standardization with the strategic value of customization. Building dedicated front-to-back business processes to accommodate every country, customer, and channel-specific requirement is most likely uneconomical. The trick is to "smart customize." This involves segmenting customer-facing processes from back-office processes. Back-office processes that cut across businesses, countries, and customer segments should be ruthlessly standardized with tailoring reserved for "must-have" regulatory and legal requirements. For customer-facing processes, the key is to identify the threshold value of business size or customer size, below which the cost of process customization far outweighs the revenue benefits achieved from providing a tailored process or service to the business or the customer. Once this threshold value has been determined, it is best to limit (or better still incentivize) the process-customization choices offered to businesses and customers that fall below this threshold value to preserve scale economies.

Step 5: Evaluate Pilot Results and Formalize the New Processes

Use the pilot to test your hypotheses and business case for process improvements. Ask yourself if the pilot yielded benefits in line with expectations across your overall blueprint for the core business processes. Make adjustments, and then accelerate implementation of process excellence initiatives in a series of waves to create value coherently throughout the enterprise.

Aligning Process Excellence with Other Cost Levers

Process excellence creates the greatest value when aligned coherently with other cost levers. For example, levers such as footprint optimization and digitization are closely tied to process excellence and should be sequenced appropriately.

Effective alignment raises important questions, including: Which processes can I combine into shared services? Should I transform a process first and then move it to a different location, or move it first? When should I digitize processes? How does process transformation change my talent needs? To answer these questions, you'll need a detailed understanding of the processes and challenges, as outlined in Step 3, and an overall view of how your processes align, as discussed in Step 1.

Start by establishing an improved target process and aligning it coherently with the other core processes. Then deploy other cost levers to drive significant additional value. Digitization should follow the initial waves of process excellence; large-scale implementation of foundational data and systems should wait until process excellence initiatives are well underway. Making process excellence tools and skills available across your organization will enable you to move and consolidate processes before they are fully optimized, and ensure that process optimization doesn't end when the initial transformation effort is over.

Process Excellence Best Practices

Win commitment to enterprise-level process change from senior executives. The core process excellence initiatives affect the entire enterprise; therefore, they require formal buy-in and commitment from most senior executives.

Put value capture first. Successful initiatives simplify challenges and isolate waste by segmenting processes across many dimensions. The most important segmentation is between activities that create value the customer is willing to pay for, activities that don't create value for customers but are necessary to operate a business, and activities that add no value at all.

Self-fund. Sequence process excellence initiatives to generate savings early in the transformations—even those requiring structural changes. These initial savings can be used to fund later stages of the program. Making a program self-funding will focus the team on high-value areas and generate the scale and confidence to pursue the overall program.

Eliminate steps. Elimination is often the best form of optimization. It creates dual synergies. First, it eliminates process steps that don't add value, driving savings and simplicity. Second, it raises customer and employee satisfaction.

Get and trust the data. Tools such as Lean often give executives their first look at detailed data that reveals process issues. Unlike anecdotal information that often obscures the real issues, these insights enable executives to make strategic decisions that will create value.

Keep the target blueprint in mind. Companies drive large-scale value only when they look beyond individual process initiatives to spur change across the organization.

Take advantage of technology. Automation has become an essential element of process optimization, reducing labor costs and eliminating human error that saps efficiency. Today's digital technologies can be implemented in concert with Lean process improvements, without a costly and time-consuming reconfiguration of underlying enterprise resource planning (ERP) systems. This combined "Lean *and* digitization" approach is a catalyst that scales up process excellence initiatives faster and accelerates improvement across a wide range of processes.

Create a "living will" for the project team. Plan for the eventual dissolution of the dedicated team formed to support a process excellence project, and make sure they transfer their skills to line workers and managers who must carry forward the process improvements.

Enlist employees to drive process improvements. Improve your employees' capabilities to identify process issues and improve them. Some tactics include:

- Create leading and lagging indicators to shed light on process performance.
- Meet with teams daily to assess performance, drive accountability, and foster teamwork.
- Coach teams on problem-solving techniques, including regular desk-side sessions to improve capabilities and increase motivation.
- Establish one "best way" of working to reduce variation in performance. Sustain the best way through regular process-checking procedures.
- Motivate staff by recognizing and reinforcing the behaviors that improve performance.

Pitfalls to Avoid

Allowing opt-outs. Unless there are significant timing issues, all four major processes must undergo the analysis phase of process excellence.

Ignoring the 80/20 rule. Not every process needs the full suite of Lean or Six Sigma tools. Blindly applying every available methodology consumes time and money without delivering more value than a smaller set of tools would produce in less time.

Overlooking variability and predictability. Failing to reduce or eliminate variability at every stage of a process—from inputs to outcomes—squanders opportunities to drive efficiency, reduce delays, and save money.

Leaving it to the line. Line managers have enough on their plates without taking responsibility for a companywide process excellence effort. Form a specialized team to spearhead the initiative.

Boiling the ocean. Improving all your processes a little bit will yield less value than improving your most important processes a lot. Focus on the core processes that drive your differentiating capabilities and look to eliminate the others.

11 | Spans and Layers

Flatten and Empower the Organization

Restructuring the spans and layers of management control within a company is one of the most effective tools for addressing organizational bloat. This lever reduces organizational layers and management overhead, which not only cuts costs, but also simplifies decision making, improves flexibility, enhances responsiveness, and unleashes innovation—positioning the company for better growth.

What Is a Spans and Layers Restructuring?

Restructuring spans and layers optimizes two critical aspects of organizational structure: the spans of control (the number of direct reports for each managerial position) and management layers (the number of hierarchical levels that distance the front line from the CEO). A spans and layers analysis enables a company to identify and eliminate narrow spans and excessive layers.

In our experience, even the best-run companies tend to lose focus on their organizational structure over time, at least in some businesses or functions, and end up with too many layers and too much management overhead. This may result from poorly integrated acquisitions, unregulated growth, or simple inattention. Unless periodically reviewed and adjusted, unwieldy organizational structures burden a company with high management costs and stultifying bureaucracy. Excess management layers with narrow spans of control slow down decision making, delay the flow of information from the top to the front lines (and vice versa), stifle creativity, and frustrate employees subjected to micromanagement by supervisors who don't have enough management work to do.

Before reading further, take a moment to review Figure 11.1, which illustrates management spans and layers, and defines key terms we'll be using throughout this chapter.

The "right" span of control for any managerial position depends on a range of factors. Particularly important is the complexity of the role—the scope and complexity of work overseen, the degree of judgment involved in day-to-day activities, the stability of work processes, and the amount of interaction with others within and outside the organization. Managers overseeing highly complex activities should have fewer direct reports, while those responsible for simpler functions can manage more employees without undue risk.

Generally, spans of control will range from 5:1 to 15:1 for most management positions. In transactional functions such as customer contact or accounts payable processing, each front-line supervisor can manage 8 to 15 line employees. The appropriate span for consultative roles, such as supply chain planning, finance decision support, and sales representatives, ranges from five to eight employees per manager. Expertise roles such as legal counsel, tax planning, or business development require a manager for every four to six employees (see Figure 11.2).

Wider spans of control force managers to focus on guiding, coaching, and managing, and empower individual contributors to make decisions and truly "own" their work. Wide spans also enable companies to reduce managerial ranks and eliminate layers of management. Reducing layers winnows bureaucracy, speeds up decision making, increases information flow up and down the organization, and brings senior management one or two steps closer to customers and front-line operations. With fewer midlevel managers clogging up the organization, accountability and transparency increase. Eliminating layers also pulls talented managers up from lower ranks, and improves career opportunities for others stuck in the middle.

ORGANIZATIONAL CHART AND DEFINITIONS

ILLUSTRATIVE ORGANIZATION CHART

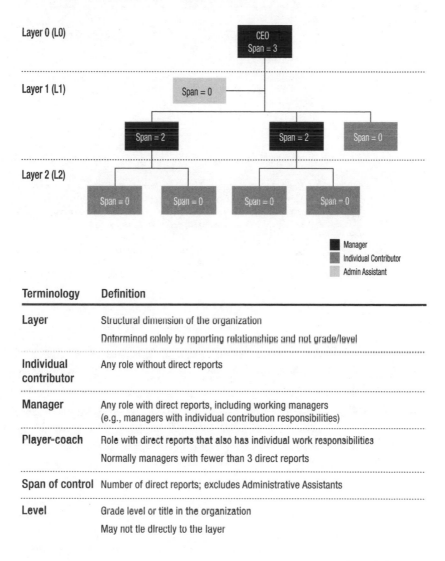

Terminology	Definition
Layer	Structural dimension of the organization
	Determined solely by reporting relationships and not grade/level
Individual contributor	Any role without direct reports
Manager	Any role with direct reports, including working managers (e.g., managers with individual contribution responsibilities)
Player-coach	Role with direct reports that also has individual work responsibilities
	Normally managers with fewer than 3 direct reports
Span of control	Number of direct reports; excludes Administrative Assistants
Level	Grade level or title in the organization
	May not tie directly to the layer

Source: PwC Strategy&

Figure 11.1

VARIATIONS IN SPANS OF CONTROL

Factor	Level 1	Level 2	Level 3
Functional diversity of work	Wide variety of functions performed (>10)	Significant diversity in functions performed (5–10)	A few different functions performed (<5)
Degree of process standardization	Processes are performed differently each time executed	50% processes standardized, others are customized	All processes are standard, with selective tailoring
Level of interfaces outside of organization	Extensive need to interface with people outside (>50% of time)	Significant need to interface with people outside (20%–50%)	Some need to interface with people outside (5%–20%)
Geographic dispersion	Resources and work dispersed equally across many locations	Resources and work dispersed equally across several locations	Work dispersed across locations, with one dominating
Span of control	4–6	5–8	8–15

Source: PwC Strategy&

Figure 11.2

In our experience, a range of benefits accumulate as management structures become more efficient:

- Employee engagement increases when decision-making authority devolves to front-line employees, micromanagement subsides, and opportunities for development and advancement increase.
- Decision making accelerates as information moves faster through a flatter organization, and cross-functional collaboration improves with fewer management layers in the way.
- Fewer managers means fewer meetings, resulting in less time spent on administrative meetings.
- Spending on salaried managerial staff declines by 10 percent to 15 percent as highly paid positions are eliminated and work shifts to lower-paid contributors.

For example, expanding spans and eliminating layers across an organization with 15,000 individual contributors will dramatically reduce management overhead costs. At an average span of control of 4:1, the company needs 5,000 managers to oversee 15,000 individual contributors. Doubling the average span to 8:1 means the company needs just under 2,000 managers for the same 15,000 employees—a 60 percent reduction in management overhead. At the same time, expanding spans of control reduces the number of management layers from seven to five, bringing top managers much closer to the front line.

Spans and Layers Myths Debunked

Some companies resist restructuring using the spans and layers approach, citing widely held but inaccurate objections:

Managers shouldn't just manage; they should "get their hands dirty." Although managers need to understand the work they oversee, that shouldn't become an excuse to meddle in front-line tasks, slowing down decision making and creating unnecessary work. Efficiency requires clear roles and responsibilities, and explicit decisions about who's a player and who's a coach.

My department is unique; it can't be benchmarked. Few business functions are unique to a single company. Almost all large organizations have similar functions (e.g., human resources, IT, and accounting), and, as we described, the span of control can be evaluated based on the complexity of the role across organizations. There are many external data points to guide decision makers seeking to determine the right levels of management for a company or functional organization.

My process is complex; it requires experienced people at every stage. That may be true, but they don't all have to be managers. Breaking down a complex process into discrete phases, such as data gathering, data entry, or decision making, enables you to determine the appropriate level of managerial oversight.

Top performers will leave if they don't get promotions. Standout individual contributors don't always make good managers. Promoting people into jobs they're not well-suited for is bad for the company and the individuals. Reward and motivate excellent front-line employees with other incentives, like bonuses, recognition, and important assignments.

My process is so risky it requires extra oversight. High-risk processes require enhanced controls and strict accountabilities, not excess management.

When to Restructure Spans and Layers

How can you tell if your organization's spans and layers are out of shape?
Look for these telltale signs of structural inefficiency:

- There are seven or more layers of management between the CEO and
  the front line.
- Managers oversee fewer than five employees on average.
- Decision making is slow and requires multiple levels of approval.
- Meetings typically include 10 or more people to assure that all stake-
  holders are represented.
- Bureaucracy is sapping morale across the company.

A dead giveaway is an organizational profile in the shape of an hourglass
or an inverted pyramid (see Figure 11.3). In an hourglass organization, wide

THE OUT-OF-SHAPE ORGANIZATION

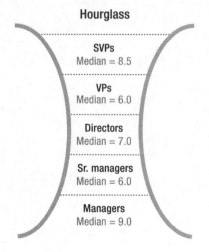

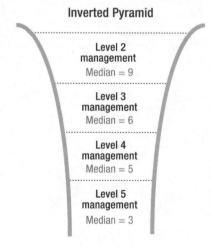

More common in companies with fixed
layer structure

Top layers set example with wide span

Middle managers try to reduce costs by
broadening lowest-level spans

Middle layers get squeezed

Example typically set at top levels

Result of overly senior work mix

Typically too many layers

Also common where there have
been layoffs

Source: PwC Strategy&

Figure 11.3

spans at the top and bottom are separated by multiple layers of middle managers with narrow spans of control. In an inverted pyramid organization, the picture is worse: front-line managers have the lowest spans of control.

Embedded in these structures is a tendency to manage by consensus and a fundamental aversion to accountability (or, in some cases, an unwillingness on the part of top management to hold their teams accountable). Overcrowded org charts insulate people from responsibility for delivering results and meeting commitments. Redundant layers of management encourage decision makers to protect themselves from the consequences of their choices. When spans of control are too narrow, even the most routine decisions require multiple managerial meetings. Mistrust flourishes and costs rise as highly paid managers do little more than attend meetings and "chaperone" employees through their daily tasks. Anxious to justify their own existence, managers burden subordinates with endless requests for information, reports, and other "make-work" assignments that leave lower-level staffers with less time for work of real value to the company.

If your organization fits these profiles, it's time to rethink your spans and layers.

How to Restructure Spans and Layers: Five Steps to a Leaner Organization

A spans and layers restructuring rationalizes management through a five-step process, starting with an "art of the possible" analysis that identifies all potential opportunities to expand spans and eliminate layers. From there, the process moves through baselining to redesigning upper management, functional hierarchies, and the rest of the organization, followed by transition planning (see Figure 11.4).

Step 1: Define the Art of the Possible

An exercise we call "the art of the possible" will reveal the full potential scope of a spans and layers restructuring of your organization. This top-down, analytical exercise highlights narrow spans of control and redundant management layers. It quantifies potential savings from expanding these spans of

SPANS AND LAYERS RESTRUCTURING APPROACH

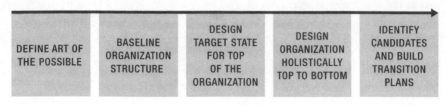

Source: PwC Strategy&

Figure 11.4

control and consolidating redundant layers. The art of the possible review comprises two main elements: an evaluation and breakdown of organizational hierarchies based on data from human resources information systems, and a comparison of spans and layers against appropriate functional benchmarks.

Rarely does an organization capture all the potential savings identified by the art of the possible exercise. A variety of risks and other practical factors limit the actual scope of most spans and layers restructurings to between 60 percent and 80 percent of the theoretical opportunity.

Step 2: Baseline the Organizational Structure

After completing the art of the possible analysis, develop a set of options for senior decision makers. Guide their deliberations with organizational charts highlighting low spans of control, a top-down analysis with cascading targets for spans of control at each level of the organization, point-of-view hypotheses for meeting span guidelines at the second level, and scenarios for eliminating management layers throughout the company.

Step 3: Design the Target State for the Top of the Organization

Work with the CEO to restructure upper management, designing logical, coherent operating models for functional organizations and business units. Consolidate major areas of activity by region, work type, or some other commonality that creates potential economies of scale across your operations. This top-down exercise moves beyond mere cost cutting to focus on organizational coherence. It yields insights that can guide later design choices, and helps senior leaders confront difficult decisions that may eliminate the positions of longtime colleagues.

Using the CEO's upper-management redesign as a blueprint, help executive leaders rationalize spans and layers in their organizations. Bring these executives together in joint design sessions to discuss possible consolidation of like activities across departmental lines, and challenge existing segmentation of work that isn't based on rational distinctions. The joint sessions also will reveal opportunities to accelerate decision making, highlight potential "quick wins," and identify top talent for leading roles in the restructured organization.

Step 4: Redesign the Rest of the Organization Holistically

Restructure the remaining levels of the organization comprehensively, rather than layer by layer. A holistic approach extends the coherence of your upper-level redesign throughout the company (see Figure 11.5). But rather than relying solely on upper management for guidance, it draws on insights from leaders at lower levels. They often have a better understanding of the rationale for existing management structures, and greater familiarity with the regulatory considerations, customer requirements, and other practical impediments to consolidating layers and expanding spans of control. Tapping a broader knowledge base also surfaces more opportunities to drive efficiency. Just as important, a comprehensive redesign prevents the talent drain that often results when a layer-by-layer restructuring discharges managers in successive waves, which can demoralize—and even paralyze—the whole organization. Instead, the company's entire talent pool is available to fill all management positions in the new organizational structure.

As you redesign your organization around new spans and layers targets for each function, your operations may have to change as well. For example, expanding spans of control may require consolidation of decentralized activities, standardization of common business processes, and upgrading of management talent to manage a diverse set of processes. Consolidation and

ORGANIZATIONAL REDESIGN TECHNIQUES

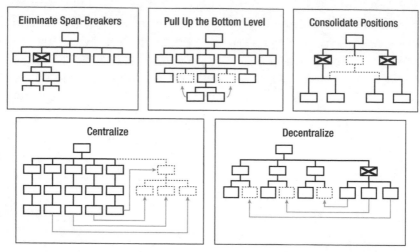

Source: PwC Strategy&

Figure 11.5

centralization, however, will eliminate layers of management, bringing P&L leaders closer than ever to the people who actually do the organization's front-line work. In parallel, strive to whittle down redundant levels of hierarchy above the natural business units. This may require eliminating management layers that were set up to manage risks, handle process exceptions, or create placeholder slots that provide regular promotion opportunities for lower- and middle-managers. Delayering also may elevate some roles and downgrade others: a senior management slot may move down a rung, while a midlevel role moves up.

Your organizational redesign should also include a reevaluation of seniority levels for each management position. This is an opportunity to combat the title inflation so common in the corporate world. You may find, for example, that a vice president's role could be assigned to a director-level manager with fewer years of experience but a strong grasp of the organization and its operations. In other cases, you will have to decide whether business objectives are best served by expanding a manager's span of control, or by creating a "player-coach" role for a manager who will perform work as an individual contributor while supervising and guiding others.

Redesigning your organization and streamlining management also requires defining new roles, responsibilities, and decision rights across the company. Often the most uncomfortable part of the adjustment process, this is also the most important thing you can do to ensure your new organization operates effectively. A well-designed and streamlined organization gives more decision-making authority and responsibility to managers accustomed to managing by committee. Clearly defining these responsibilities and decision rights—and linking them to performance criteria—is critical to success.

Step 5: Identify Candidates and Build Transition Plans

You'll need to redefine management roles for an organization with fewer management layers and broader spans of control. Rewrite job descriptions to suit these new requirements, and launch selection processes to find the right talent for managerial positions that may call for different sets of abilities. Also, prepare transition plans that identify the managers displaced by the reorganization, and outline redeployment strategies for those who will be transferred, temporarily retained, or terminated.

Intensely competitive global markets require flexibility and rapid responses to ever-changing conditions and customer preferences. Out-of-shape companies can't move fast enough to capture fleeting opportunities and neutralize onrushing threats. Restructuring spans and layers to eliminate unnecessary bureaucracy will not only reduce costs, but also give your company the flexibility and quickness to win in this ever-changing business environment.

Case Study: Getting Flat and Happy in CPG

A global consumer packaged goods company was groaning under corporate bureaucracy after an aggressive growth campaign gave rise to a complex organizational structure. SG&A expenses had swelled by 20 percent. The company passed these higher costs along to customers—a risky move in an industry where private label competitors offered

(continued)

(continued)

lower-cost alternatives in almost every product category. Rather than cede market share to low-price rivals, the company decided to rein in overhead spending.

Restructuring spans and layers played a key role in a broader transformation program. An organizational review revealed a classic hourglass profile, with costs concentrated in multiple layers of middle managers who supervised an average of four direct reports each. External comparisons showed the company had more layers of management and smaller spans of control than industry peers.

Company leaders believed a flatter, leaner organization would cost less, compete better, and execute more effectively. So they set goals of expanding average spans of control to between six and eight direct reports, and eliminating several of their 12 management layers in the process.

To achieve these ambitious goals, they streamlined and rationalized management activities in several ways. Strategic and operational management were separated, with senior managers focusing on strategy and coaching the managers responsible for daily operations. The performance management model was simplified, reducing the amount of information and the level of detail analyzed. Clearly defined decision rights eliminated the need for frequent, lengthy meetings to build consensus. Accountability and the corresponding decision-making authority was given to managers with P&L-level responsibility.

Ultimately, the company increased its median span of control to 6:1 and reduced the number of management layers from 12 to 8. Streamlining management generated over 25 percent of the savings from the cost transformation program.

The spans and layers targets also fostered cost discipline across the organization, instilling a spirit of "doing more with less," and catalyzing process reengineering efforts. Company performance improved dramatically, as earnings soared to record levels, profit margins reached their highest point in over a decade, and market share expanded in most key business lines. The CEO credited the spans and layers restructuring with sparking the turnaround.

Spans and Layers Best Practices

Avoid the allure of simplistic targets. Beware of targets such as "no more than five management layers" or "no fewer than five direct reports." Not all spans are created equal. Sustained improvements hinge on developing the right size and number of organizational building blocks for your organization, based on core business processes involved, the type of work, and the interactions required to drive smart decision making.

Create fit-for-purpose targets. Base targets for management spans of control on the nature of the work, the type of supervisory role, and decision-making responsibilities.

Start at the top. Work with the CEO to redesign the top three levels of the organization. This allows the CEO to shape the organization, create a model for others to follow, and short-circuit political interference. Redesign the rest of the organization holistically, to ensure a coherent structure, maximize efficiencies, and capitalize on insights from people at all levels of the company.

Implement measures and incentives. Aim to sharpen the organization's focus on accountability and the consequences of hitting or missing performance goals.

Design fulfilling career paths. Staffing strategies, including horizontal moves and increased compensation, should challenge and reward managers faced with fewer classic upward promotion opportunities.

Deprogram micromanagers. Train the next generation of middle managers to delegate more decisions to the front lines, where relevant information resides.

Modify job titles and compensation levels. They should reflect and encourage simplified and streamlined work processes.

Institutionalize communications vehicles. They should break through traditional roadblocks that impede the free flow of information.

Pitfalls to Avoid

Adhering to benchmarks that don't fit your company. Industry benchmarks are just a guide for sizing up potential opportunities. Actual program goals should be based on customized benchmarks reflecting the complexity and risks of your business.

Confusing operational experience with decision-making acumen and accountability. Establish clear decision rights and accountabilities for every management role.

Failing to distinguish management activities from activities performed by managers. People with managerial titles (and paychecks) frequently do the same work as those they nominally supervise.

Naming names. Spans and layers should be an objective exercise focused on roles, not individuals. Don't introduce subjectivity by putting names in boxes as you plan your new organizational structure.

Hearing too many voices. When too many people participate, every management post is defended. Remember, spans and layers isn't a democratic process. It's a top-down initiative that should be driven and controlled by senior management.

12 | Strategic Supply Management

Extract More Value from Your Purchases

Strategic supply management drives savings in nonlabor third-party expenditures, which can represent as much as 60 percent of costs at some companies. This fact alone makes strategic supply management an essential lever for any broad-based cost transformation. But it does more than simply reduce nonlabor costs; unlike traditional sourcing methods predominantly focused on price and supplier negotiations, strategic supply management aims to maximize value in procurement activities across the organization. This cross-organizational quest for value puts strategic supply management at the center of sustainable, strategic Fit for Growth transformations.

What Is Strategic Supply Management?

Vast nonlabor expenses are perennial targets for cost-reduction campaigns. Yet many procurement organizations have already consolidated suppliers, centralized purchasing, renegotiated prices, and pursued other supply-side measures to drive down this "spend" (as managers typically refer to a stream of expenditures). Successful as these efforts often are, most of them fall short of delivering all potentially achievable costs savings. The reason is that they are tactical, focused narrowly on competitive price and cost inputs, and overlook other levers and the impact of demand on procurement costs.

Strategic supply management, by contrast, is a comprehensive, holistic approach that addresses *all* price, cost, demand, and value levers for nonlabor spend, and reaches beyond merely "optimizing the buy" to maximize value in procurement. While price and cost savings usually are easier to achieve, significantly greater upside can be realized through the more complex demand and value levers, which require greater cross-functional collaboration.

Strategic supply management, for example, captures savings opportunities in categories that are often excluded from traditional procurement transformation programs, such as marketing and legal expenses. It's rooted in a deeper understanding of procurement maturity levels and opportunities for value creation in a company's direct and indirect spend.

Procurement maturity is defined by the depth and sophistication of the various levers applied in a spend category (see Figure 12.1). Potential savings opportunities can be significant in areas of lower maturity that have relied principally on price and cost levers. Conversely, more-mature categories may have less incremental savings potential.

Direct spend typically encompasses raw materials, packaging, transportation, and other expenditures directly related to producing goods. Most product-based companies have relatively mature procurement practices in these categories, which represent the majority of nonlabor spend. Direct spend is typically centralized under a sophisticated procurement organization that uses advanced techniques to reduce supplier costs and control internal demand.

Still, there's more value to be captured in direct spend categories. Strategic supply management expands on price-based measures by challenging product and portfolio decisions that drive up costs without creating distinct value in the marketplace. Product supply costs reflect an array of choices about materials, ingredients, features, the number of SKUs produced, and other factors that don't always matter very much to customers. Winnowing product lines, substituting less costly materials, or redesigning products through a "design-to-value" lens can reduce procurement costs without jeopardizing sales.

Potential savings (as a percentage of the spend base) are even greater in indirect spend—a surprisingly large percentage of procurement outlays that

STRATEGIC SUPPLY MANAGEMENT MATURITY FRAMEWORK

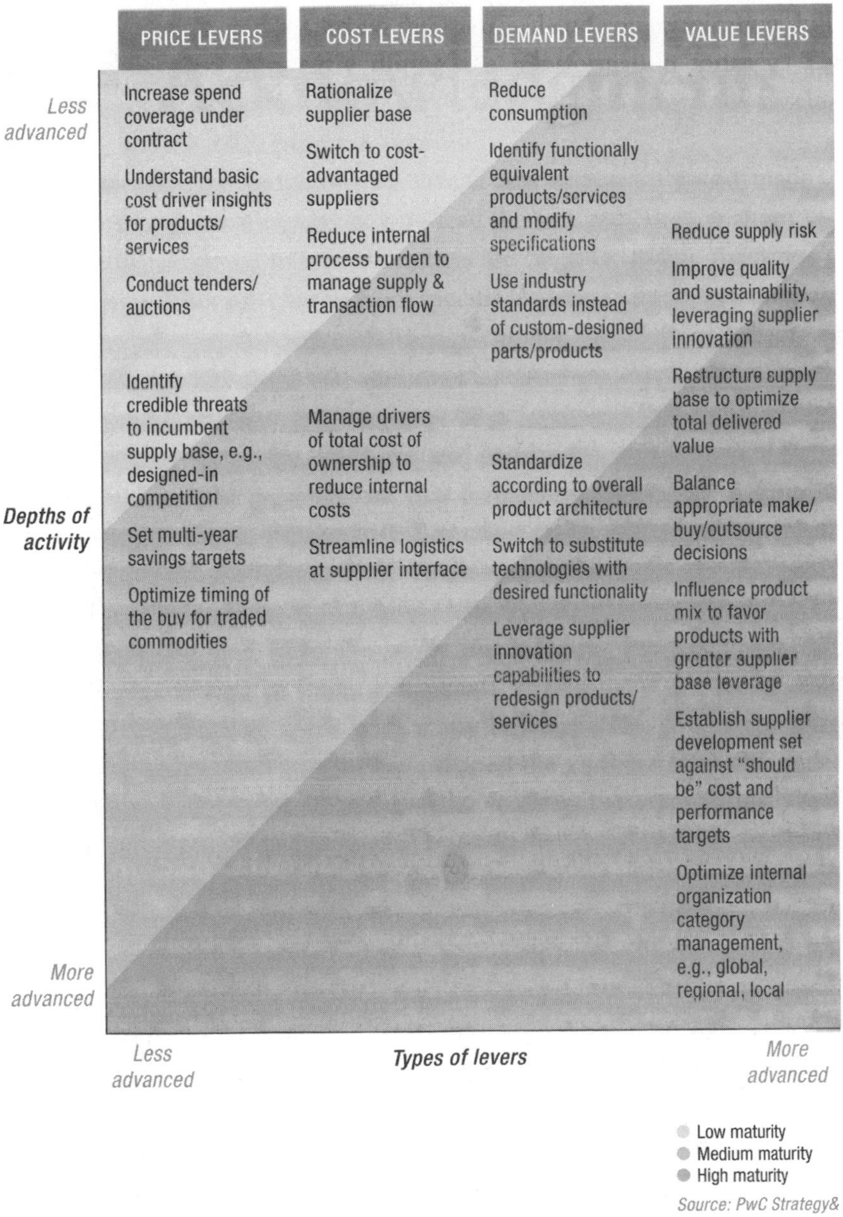

	PRICE LEVERS	COST LEVERS	DEMAND LEVERS	VALUE LEVERS
Less advanced	Increase spend coverage under contract Understand basic cost driver insights for products/ services Conduct tenders/ auctions	Rationalize supplier base Switch to cost-advantaged suppliers Reduce internal process burden to manage supply & transaction flow	Reduce consumption Identify functionally equivalent products/services and modify specifications Use industry standards instead of custom-designed parts/products	Reduce supply risk Improve quality and sustainability, leveraging supplier innovation
Depths of activity	Identify credible threats to incumbent supply base, e.g., designed-in competition Set multi-year savings targets Optimize timing of the buy for traded commodities	Manage drivers of total cost of ownership to reduce internal costs Streamline logistics at supplier interface	Standardize according to overall product architecture Switch to substitute technologies with desired functionality Leverage supplier innovation capabilities to redesign products/ services	Restructure supply base to optimize total delivered value Balance appropriate make/ buy/outsource decisions Influence product mix to favor products with greater supplier base leverage Establish supplier development set against "should be" cost and performance targets
More advanced				Optimize internal organization category management, e.g., global, regional, local

Less advanced	*Types of levers*	*More advanced*

- Low maturity
- Medium maturity
- High maturity

Source: PwC Strategy&

Figure 12.1

often elude cost-transformation efforts. Indirect spend represents the lion's share of nonlabor expenses at service companies, and up to half at some manufacturers. Most indirect spend appears in SG&A expenses for categories such as professional services, travel, IT, temporary office labor, overnight shipping, marketing, advertising, and office supplies. COGS also includes some indirect spend, in categories such as MRO, service and supplies, and temporary factory labor.

It's not hard to understand why most companies have made little progress optimizing indirect spend. Control of indirect categories—except for basics like office supplies and travel—often resides outside procurement's sphere of influence, scattered among various functional groups that may not have adopted effective policies or cost controls. This makes it difficult to clearly see the nature of spend in indirect categories, which is recorded piecemeal in departmental budgets across the company. Imposing spend discipline in these categories poses an even greater challenge. Indirect purchasing decisions can be fragmented among numerous individuals, undermining transparency and accountability for what is bought and from whom. Left to their own devices, these decision makers often ignore company procurement policies such as preferred supplier designations and spend thresholds for competitive bids.

A well-executed strategic supply management program encompassing direct and indirect categories can reduce total external spend by 10 percent to 15 percent, often within six to nine months. (See Figure 12.2.) And by expanding the focus of procurement from price to value, it establishes the foundation for a more strategic approach to cost management across the company.

Successful strategic supply management initiatives maximize savings by using the full suite of price, cost, demand, and value levers in every category. The savings generated by each lever varies among categories.

In addition to its own direct benefits, strategic supply management can enhance the impact of other cost levers. For example, the principles of strategic supply management also apply to outsourcing, which is, after all, a form of sourcing. However, the application of various levers in a broad cost transformation program should be coordinated to avoid unnecessary or redundant effort. There's little sense in optimizing sourcing for a function slated for elimination under a zero-basing initiative.

TYPICAL SAVINGS RANGES BY MAJOR CATEGORY

Plant	
Commodities	2%–5%
Engineered components	8%–20%
Equipment and construction	6%–14%
Finished goods/ contract manufacturing	5%–12%
Packaging	6%–12%
Plant materials and services	6%–18%
Transportation and distribution	8%–16%

Corporate	
Human resources	2%–12%
IT & telecom	5%–10%
Marketing and advertising	10%–22%
Office supplies	15%–30%
Professional services	10%–25%
Real estate/facilities	6%–12%
Travel	10%–25%

Source: PwC Strategy&

Figure 12.2

When Should a Company Use Strategic Supply Management?

Since strategic supply management can produce significant savings in a category of spending that encompasses a large portion of total costs, it is an essential lever for any comprehensive cost-transformation program based on Fit for Growth principles. In addition, it's a good place to start, since nonlabor cost savings are far less sensitive than headcount reductions and often can be implemented faster. Strategic supply management generates momentum for the broader transformation by locking up quick savings with little or no up-front investment. The cost transformation program, in turn, creates leverage with suppliers by sending a public message that the company intends to reduce costs in every spend category. Internally it breaks down barriers and opens up visibility into costs, revealing potential purchasing synergies and opportunities to create economies of scale throughout the supply chain. Most important, strategic supply management establishes sophisticated new procurement practices and a value-oriented mindset that will generate sustainable savings for years.

Companies need to use strategic supply management if their nonlabor costs have gotten out of line with their competitors'—either in the industry generally or in specific categories. But while industry and category spend benchmarks will help identify potential opportunities, they are merely guidelines, not definitive standards for every company and category. The right spend level for your company in any given category will depend on your product and customer mix, outsourcing choices, and scale effects. Nonlabor spend optimization is an ongoing capability for most companies, and we have found that a *procurement maturity assessment* is a better guide to savings opportunities. This maturity assessment, described in detail next, will help focus strategic supply management efforts, assess the size of potential savings, and determine which tailored approaches will capture the most benefits.

For each spend category, the maturity assessment will reveal key factors, such as:

- The rigor of systematic spend management efforts in the category;
- The level of supplier fragmentation;
- The level of centralization and coordination among procurement decision makers;
- The types of sourcing levers that have been applied in the past;
- The time elapsed since the last sourcing initiative (we recommend a formal sourcing review at least every three years); and
- Movement in the prices of raw materials, ingredients, and other inputs, as well as changes in market structure or technology in the category.

Strategic Supply Management Myths Debunked

Several widespread misconceptions often undermine efforts to maximize value in nonlabor spend.

Price is all that matters in sourcing. A focus on underlying cost drivers and value creation generates greater savings than narrow price-reduction efforts.

Supplier negotiations are adversarial, win–lose contests. An approach that balances cooperation and competition yields more value for both sides over the long term.

Anything purchased outside the procurement organization is poorly sourced. Marketing, legal, IT, and other functional areas can be sophisticated buyers of services integral to their activities.

You always need at least two suppliers. Sometimes it's better to have one "strategic partner" who understands your business well enough to help you achieve your savings and transformation goals. But don't get complacent; periodically test the market to make sure you're getting the best possible terms.

Always maximize price savings by consolidating spend with a few large vendors. The number of suppliers matters less than their capabilities. Create a customized supply base uniquely capable of meeting your specific needs.

Tough customers get the best deal from suppliers. Customers that reduce their suppliers' costs-to-serve can reap more value, provided they insist on a share of those benefits.

Making It Happen: A Guide to Strategic Supply Management

Like any cost-cutting method, strategic supply management starts with a baseline spend review and an overall savings target. Granular analysis of every spend category isn't initially necessary. You can move forward based on a high-level understanding of costs, relying on industry and maturity benchmarks to identify areas ripe for strategic supply management efforts. Perhaps you're spending more than peer companies on IT services, or your narrow gross margin may indicate an opportunity to reduce raw material spend.

Unlike traditional approaches, strategic supply management involves more than ballparking a savings goal, sending out an RFP, and hoping bids come in low enough to hit your target. It goes deeper by illuminating the underlying drivers of your costs, segmenting expenditures by category, and setting spend priorities that advance your transformation agenda and strategic goals. Our five-step programmatic approach analyzes baseline spend, engages with stakeholders to set savings targets, segments the efforts, and deploys a comprehensive array of tools to tap all sources of potential value (see Figure 12.3).

STRATEGIC SUPPLY MANAGEMENT APPROACH

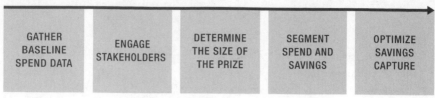

Source: PwC Strategy&

Figure 12.3

Step 1: Gather Baseline Spend Data

Establish a robust baseline and make visible recent spend by vendor, category, and business unit. This data is critical for evaluating opportunities, identifying spend owners, and setting targets. Sometimes this data is readily available, but in many cases you will have to gather it from a number of disparate sources to create a unified view of supplier spend across the enterprise.

Step 2: Engage Stakeholders

After establishing a spend baseline, engage procurement managers and budget owners to review each category. Spend data alone yields only surface-level insights into factors such as supplier fragmentation, cross-business unit commonality, and spend versus benchmarks. To uncover the fundamental drivers of nonlabor spend, you'll need input from a broad set of stakeholders. The inquiry focuses on the following:

- Validating spend and identifying decision makers and existing contracts
- Understanding underlying cost drivers and requirements
- Current sourcing strategies, levers addressed, and recent efforts
- Impact of zero-basing efforts on go-forward spend and requirements

Case Study: Strategic Supply Management in Banking

A major commercial and retail bank turned to strategic supply management as part of a broader cost restructuring aimed at freeing up resources for growth in core businesses. With just nine months to cut its $800 million external spend budget by a targeted $90 million, the bank unleashed a three-wave attack on discretionary expenditures across all categories, ranging from IT and human resources to travel and office supplies.

Rather than simply ordering a fixed amount of spend cuts in every department, the bank pursued greater value by challenging basic spend assumptions, entrenched vendor relationships, and longstanding procurement practices. Along the way, it enlarged and redefined the role of procurement.

Expanding procurement's mandate to marketing, legal, facilities management, and other areas brought new rigor to spend categories that had been loosely managed. Opaque "personal" relationships between managers and vendors became transparent business relationships based on competitive bidding and value creation, resulting in significant savings on many outside services.

The initiative found its mother lode in travel and entertainment, sponsorships, training, conferences, consulting, promotional items, memberships, and charitable contributions. These discretionary categories represented 20 percent of the total spend baseline, but had never been subjected to a thorough need and affordability analysis. The bank cut these expenditures by 35 percent, based on rigorous reviews with budget owners, benchmarking against industry spend levels, new ROI hurdles, and stricter procurement policies. It locked in the savings with additional controls and dashboards to monitor discretionary spend.

Traditional supply-side tactics were instrumental in achieving the overall savings goal. Competitive bidding, targeted negotiations, concession letters, and other methods drove down costs, mostly in areas where procurement had little previous involvement, or where personal relationships had undermined competition in the past.

(continued)

(*continued*)

But these familiar methods accounted for less than half the savings. Most came from demand-side measures that shed light on the true costs and benefits of various expenditures and reshaped procurement practices to optimize value for the dollar. For example, the bank reduced legal costs by reallocating outside assignments based on complexity and price. Expensive firms with specialized expertise got complex, high-risk projects, while routine matters went to lower-cost firms that could meet the bank's quality requirements for simpler legal work. Similarly, the bank found functional substitutes for costlier items in its office supply catalog. And it saved money on IT and telecom services by tailoring software and hardware packages to the actual needs of various user groups, rather than giving everyone multiple features and capabilities they would never use.

Within nine months, the program had reduced external spend by $110 million, or about 14 percent, exceeding the original 11 percent target, with additional longer-term upside.

As the procurement organization extended its reach, its role evolved in parallel. Once mere order takers, procurement managers took on greater responsibility as category managers accountable for spend and value creation. This enhanced stature attracted new talent to procurement and helped sustain savings over time.

This is a relatively straightforward exercise in most direct spend categories, which are consolidated under procurement managers with clear lines of responsibility. Validating spend estimates and savings targets for indirect categories is usually more challenging. These categories sprawl across multiple constituencies, many of whom have only a vague idea of how much they actually spend (vs. budgeted to spend), let alone the total expenditures for services ranging from legal advice to advertising and package delivery. You'll have to canvas the functional areas where these spend decisions are made. Discuss legal fees with in-house lawyers, media spend with marketing managers, software purchases with IT leaders, and so on. It is often practical to deploy a quick, efficient survey to systematically build the fact base, then follow it up with targeted interviews and workshops to fill gaps and clarify responses. Cumbersome as this process may be, it often reveals big opportunities.

This step should be closely coordinated with the zero-basing efforts described in Chapter 6. The visibility that procurement can bring into nonlabor spend and supplier choices helps separate the suppliers that support differentiating capabilities from other suppliers, and spotlights specifications or service levels that can be rationalized without undermining your key competitive strengths. Make these zero-basing decisions as you develop your strategic supply management strategy.

Step 3: Determine the Size of the Prize

The quantitative and qualitative information collected in Steps 1 and 2 can be synthesized into a top–down analysis of potential cost reductions for each procurement category, bearing in mind their relative maturity and address-ability. Your big wins generally will come from less-mature categories. Yet even mature categories can generate large incremental savings through more-sophisticated demand and value levers such as specification changes or outsourcing. Use maturity-adjusted savings benchmarks to set overall targets for each category. Build internal stakeholder support by highlighting specific examples of realized savings that prove your targets are realistic. It is critical that both procurement and budget owners endorse the savings goals and accept accountability for hitting the targets.

Step 4: Segment Spend and Savings

Nonlabor expenditures touch almost every aspect of the enterprise, com-prising multiple categories and thousands of suppliers. An undertaking of such vast scope requires segmentation and prioritization to concentrate effort against the biggest opportunities, and ensure the swift and complete capture of all potential savings. Start by segmenting strategic and nonstrategic suppliers; each group entails different risks and requires different tailored sourcing approaches. Further segment nonstrategic suppliers based on the size of go-forward spend to separate the 20 percent of vendors who generate 80 percent of the spend from the long tail of small vendors that have to be managed but provide limited services. Then apply relevant criteria to prioritize efforts, focusing on size of expected savings, ease of implementation, and budget owners' level of interest in addressing spend in the category. The outcome is a road map of strategic supply management initiatives and associated savings targets over time.

Step 5: Optimize Savings Capture

After defining your targets and timetable, choose the appropriate tools for driving value. A well-executed strategic supply management program takes

FIVE APPROACHES FOR CAPTURING SAVINGS

Savings capture approach	Description	Levers impacted	% spend affected	Expected savings	Time to achieve savings
Rapid sourcing	Capture immediate supply-side savings in centrally driven categories and from nonstrategic suppliers	– Price	<10%	4%–8%	1–2 Months
Strategic sourcing	Launch broader strategic sourcing efforts to capture the maximum opportunity across supply and demand levers	– Price – Cost – Demand – Value	30%–40%	10%–20%	2–3 Months
Policy changes	Reduce/redirect spend through enhanced policies and compliance (particularly for indirect or otherwise discretionary spend)	– Demand	10%	20%–30%	1–2 Months
Supply chain optimization	Analyze end-to-end supply chain cost drivers and work with suppliers to eliminate waste	– Cost	20%–30%	8%–12%	3–4 Months
Design to value	Optimize the design of products and services to better align cost with the value created	– Demand – Value	30%–40%	10%–25%	6–9 Months

Source: PwC Strategy&

Figure 12.4

full advantage of all available levers, maximizing savings with a holistic approach encompassing price, cost, demand, and value. Most transformation programs form a cross-functional team to capture savings, rather than leaving it all to procurement. While procurement may be able to manage price and cost levers alone, significant organizational engagement is needed to support or facilitate the trickier demand and value levers.

We generally find that there are five different ways to capture savings in a supply management transformation. The right approach for each category depends on size of spend, procurement maturity, strategic importance, type of goods or services purchased, supplier market dynamics, and fragmentation of internal stakeholders and requirements (see Figure 12.4). In some cases, multiple approaches may be applied to the same category.

Strategic Supply Management Best Practices

Cross-functional collaboration. Require committed participation across the company to attack costs at the source and move up the value chain—including procurement, research and development, marketing, and manufacturing.

Joint accountability. Share accountability for savings goals with budget owners in various spend categories to improve collaboration and ensure tough spend choices.

Supplier engagement. Take full advantage of vendors' insights into your cost drivers. They can point out excess spend or service requirements and help you close the cost gap with competitors.

Unrestrained change. Empower the procurement team to challenge embedded resource allocation policies, organizational roles, and decision rights that lock in unnecessary costs. Breaking through these constraints generates the greatest value.

Tracking and monitoring. Track savings generated by your program to prove its value and help prevent targeted cost reductions from "leaking" away. While cost avoidance and other "soft savings" are important, only bottom-line spend reductions move the needle.

Effective governance. Establish governance structures to oversee the program, ensuring that decisions are made at the right level, with an enterprise-wide perspective. It's especially important to create mechanisms for deciding whether procurement savings will be reinvested in functional activities or flow through to the bottom line.

Pitfalls to Avoid

Assuming that "one size fits all." Every category faces unique challenges. Tailor your sourcing approach to the specific economics and supply market dynamics of your spend categories.

Honoring sacred cows. Companies squander savings opportunities when they put any spend category off limits, regardless of the reason. Every category should be in play, and all expenditures can be addressed over the appropriate time horizon.

Seeking control. Procurement asks for trouble when it pursues outright control of spend categories. Instead, the organization should offer support and collaboration to functional departments, with a mutual goal of optimizing value.

Chasing every last dime. Full-scale campaigns in small-scale spend categories don't justify their own costs. Focus resources on larger categories where strategic sourcing will pay big dividends. In smaller categories, a lower-cost, standardized approach will do.

Overlooking change management. You can't change your spend unless you change your ways. Strategic supply management initiatives stall without a paradigm shift and the associated effective change management.

Focusing only on cost. Carefully evaluate the impact of cost reductions on quality and other performance metrics. Construct incentive schemes to guarantee minimum required performance and actively mitigate risks.

13 | Digitization

Make Technology a Game Changer

For decades, companies have used technology to do work faster, better, and cheaper than human labor. Fit for Growth transformations also take advantage of technology where possible, tapping the full power of digitization to increase productivity, improve quality, and build capabilities. This approach deploys technology in two stages. The first optimizes internal processes ranging from manufacturing to customer service and human resources, often in concert with other cost reduction levers. The second goes beyond the boundaries of the enterprise, using cutting-edge digital technologies to drive fundamental change by automating interactions with customers and suppliers, fully digitizing processes from end to end, and eliminating labor in all but the highest-value areas. Together, the two stages generate significant savings while positioning the company for more profitable growth.

What Is Digitization?

Digitization reduces costs throughout an organization, most obviously by automating manual processes from the factory floor to the back office.

Beyond that, digital technology creates additional value by improving quality, accelerating production, and replacing manual interactions. No company can afford to forgo the potentially significant contribution of digitization to a cost transformation program.

In the first stage, digitization applies technology to internal processes. This can be as simple as creating a spreadsheet macro to automate a single calculation performed thousands of times daily by employees across an organization. Or it may be as complex as installing an enterprise resource planning system to standardize end-to-end processes and automate numerous tasks. Indeed, with the advent of artificial intelligence (AI), robotic process automation, and the Internet of Things, we've reached a point where nearly any business activity can be automated to a degree unimaginable just a few years ago. Examples include the RFID systems many companies use to manage inventory, and shopping-cart scanners that enable grocery shoppers to avoid checkout lines.

The benefits go well beyond immediate labor cost savings. Digitization also eliminates costly human error and enables companies to handle an increasing workload without adding more employees. Another advantage of digitization is speed. Automated systems accelerate processes, which generates additional knock-on benefits. For example, speeding up bill collection through digitization enables companies to reinvest cash sooner.

In the second stage, digitization pushes a company's technological boundaries to encompass customers, suppliers, and other outside parties. Putting technology in their hands creates opportunities for low-cost growth through new channels and products such as online banking and a wide range of mobile apps. This is where the transformative power of digitization comes into play, enabling companies to build new capabilities and achieve step-change efficiency improvements.

E-commerce, for example, revolutionized retailing by allowing companies to expand their market presence at a fraction of the cost of building additional brick-and-mortar stores. Online marketing through platforms such as Google, Facebook, Twitter, and Instagram engages customers in a more personalized way than costlier mass-market advertising campaigns.

Business analytics turn a company's data into a strategic asset that provides never-before-available insights, which can be used to monitor product performance, improve efficiency, and develop new products and services. Examples of these data-driven service platforms include IBM's

Watson Analytics and auto insurer Progressive's Snapshot offering. Digital solutions also enable businesses to create, augment, and transform products and services at very low cost. Tesla, for example, has used the Internet to transmit software fixes to its electric cars, eliminating the need for expensive and disruptive product service visits or recalls.

At General Electric, digitization became the platform for an entirely new business model. The diversified manufacturing giant is shifting from a traditional, product-based industrial paradigm to a customer-focused approach. Seizing opportunities created by the Internet of Things, GE launched a new generation of connected products that generate streams of performance data from equipment in the field. GE developed the software and networking capabilities to interpret this information and turn it into new services that help its customers improve their own operations. For instance, a purchaser of GE diesel engines gained valuable insights that improved the average speed of its trains by 10 percent, and a hospital used GE data to reduce its "bed turnaround" time by 51 minutes. The digitization strategy paid off for GE, too, generating billions of dollars in cost savings and new revenue.

Along with its standalone benefits, digitization complements other levers in a Fit for Growth cost transformation. For example, it enhances process excellence initiatives by automating manual processes and eliminating delays in "handoffs" and information transfers. Similarly, automating basic lights-on activities supports zero-basing by minimizing spending on nondifferentiating capabilities. Real-time data flowing from connected equipment and devices helps a company optimize its footprint, while digital capabilities can become a key part of any company's business portfolio. Integrating digitization with these other levers maximizes efficiency in key operations, bolstering strategically differentiating capabilities. Indeed, we have seen end-to-end digitization spanning multiple processes serve as the "tent pole" that supports entire transformations.

When to Use Digitization

The fundamental rule of any transformation initiative applies equally to digitization: companies should pull the lever when it will yield an acceptable return on investment (ROI). Technology isn't free, or even cheap. In some cases, the cost of creating, implementing, and maintaining digitized processes equals or exceeds the benefits generated. That said, the sheer magnitude of labor expenses at most large organizations, and the enormous benefits of replacing manual processes with automated systems, lead many companies to launch technology initiatives when they need a step-change in efficiency.

But when does digitization produce the best results? Ideal conditions vary from company to company, but a few general guidelines help determine when a process is ripe for digitization:

- *When digitization will eliminate large amounts of labor*, because of the number of people or working hours dedicated to overly manual and error-prone processes.
- *When processes are well understood, mature, and standardized.* The costs and benefits of automating murky, ill-defined processes can't be estimated with any certainty. Attempting to automate an evolving process becomes too costly as continual process changes beget multiple technology updates. Similarly, the cost of automating every permutation of a highly variable process will quickly outstrip any benefits. (Warning: Tempting as it may be to use digitization as a forcing tool for standardization, such tactics often spark internal resistance.)
- *When there are opportunities to shift work to others.* With digitization, customers and suppliers can take over tasks such as status updates and data entry.
- *When manual activities are slowing down processes that are integrated across your organization and external parties.* Digitization can automate handoffs and data exchanges among existing systems.
- *When you know exactly how technology will reduce human involvement in a process.* You need a clear vision of the specific aspects of a process that can be taken over by technology.
- *When others have shown the way.* Proceed only in areas where others have marked out a path to digitization. The first company to automate a particular process endures an expensive learning experience, replete with wrong turns, unforeseen obstacles, and other setbacks that dilute benefits.
- *When new technology is disrupting your business.* You have no choice but to keep pace with technological advances that alter the competitive landscape.

Digitization Myths Debunked

A few common misconceptions often deter or undermine digitization initiatives.

This process can't be automated. Often heard from defenders of the status quo, this argument overlooks the fact that 80 percent of virtually every process is standardized and can easily be automated. A small number of variations doesn't undercut the business case for digitization. Even processes that involve complex decision making can be automated, especially with improvements in AI and analytics. Natural language processing enables digital systems such as Apple's Siri to interpret voice or text instructions and take appropriate action. Machine learning technology "teaches" a system to perform tasks, while deep learning systems actually figure out better ways of doing things. More and more often, combinations of these enabling AI technologies are eliminating the need for human workers to answer difficult questions and fulfill complex requests.

Digitization always pays off. Digitization can be costly. In some cases, the costs of automating highly variable processes exceed the labor savings. In others, ongoing support costs offset the savings.

Don't bother digitizing a process unless you can automate every step. Partial digitization often yields meaningful savings and quality improvements, while avoiding the more complex parts of a process that could make the digitization effort too risky or expensive.

Digitization is only for front-end, customer-facing activities. "Customer-centric design" and self-service principles used in front-end digitization also simplify and improve internal processes. Digitized data, harvested from sensors through the Internet of Things, for example, enables automation of processes like replenishment or diagnostics.

Digitization will be easy and painless. In digitization, there's rarely any gain without some pain. Large-scale digitization requires companywide efforts and can affect thousands of people across an organization. A strong change management program is essential, particularly when digitizing deeply ingrained processes.

How to Digitize

There are many approaches to managing digitization initiatives. The one that is right for you will depend on your choices of scope, technology, development approach, and users of the new technologies. Despite the myriad choices, there are five common steps (see Figure 13.1).

Step 1: Analyze and Prioritize Requirements

You can digitize anything, but not everything. Determine where digitization will generate the highest returns, then prioritize processes, rules, and analytics that are integral to your strategic capabilities and that can best produce labor cost savings, quality improvements, and better decision making. Look for highly structured, repetitive processes and rules that can be automated with proven technologies whether they sit within or outside your firm. Customers, trading partners, and suppliers should be key contributors to your digitization requirements. Information exchanges and approvals among groups can be tackled through workflow and collaboration solutions. Where possible, however, digitize the core processes prior to addressing information exchanges. Last, you should capture a number of additional requirements in this initial phase, including data, security, infrastructure, underlying software components, performance, and availability expectations.

Conduct a high-level analysis of likely costs and probable benefits of digitization, considering not only upfront implementation expenses, but also the cost of supporting and maintaining technology over time. Assess these factors independently—don't rely on the rosy forecasts of systems vendors

DIGITIZATION APPROACH

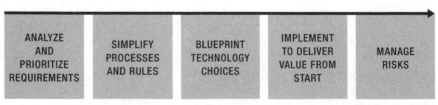

Source: PwC Strategy&

Figure 13.1

vying for your business. Consider the downside risks of automating a process, and heed your gut-level instincts. Move forward only in areas where the odds favor success, and the expected returns justify the expense, effort, and organizational change required to automate core business operations.

Step 2: Simplify Processes and Rules

Align your digitization effort with any business process optimization efforts you are pursuing. Before automating a process, ask yourself if it's really necessary. If not, stop doing it. If a process is necessary, get rid of any superfluous steps. After distilling the process and rules for computation and decision making down to their essentials, eliminate variations where possible to create a standardized format that can be automated. In some cases, you may conclude that a process is necessary, but your customers or strategy partners are better off doing it themselves.

Step 3: Blueprint Technology Choices

The technology blueprint is a critical step that determines success of a digitization program, as measured by time to market, adoption, and sustainability of the resulting process. As in the case of constructing a skyscraper, where the blueprint must account for everything from building materials to emergency exit routes, the technology blueprint addresses a number of foundational questions that must be answered prior to implementation. These include choices about technology solutions, sourcing, development methodologies, and how people at your company will engage with the new technologies.

- *Technology solutions.* You'll have to decide what type of technology solution suits your needs and objectives. Some companies opt for an overarching ERP system, while others select individual, best-in-breed software for each process they're planning to automate. An ERP implementation may be the right choice if you need to digitize multiple processes across a large organization with relatively few automated systems in place. Best-in-breed solutions work better for more targeted improvements in smaller or technologically advanced organizations. As you consider your options, be mindful of emerging technologies that can fundamentally change your solution design. You don't have to embrace every new concept, but you can't afford to miss major technological leaps that your competitors are sure to capitalize on. Many systems can be designed with flexibility to incorporate future technological advances. An architecture that describes the business processes, users, technology solutions, and supporting organization is a key deliverable for the blueprint phase.

- *Sourcing*. Technology sourcing decisions often come down to a choice between commercially available off-the-shelf (COTS) software and customized systems designed and built for your individual needs. Each option has its pros and cons. Bespoke technology fits better but costs more, potentially eroding your ROI. COTS software costs less up front, but the low up front price on an entry-level package may be only a down payment on the additional fees you'll incur to add all the capabilities you need.

- *Development methodologies*. Options include "Agile" approaches and their variants—industrial agile and extreme programming—and traditional "waterfall" approaches, among many others. Agile methodologies are well suited to projects that require significant input from users, such as the development of digital user interfaces. Waterfall methods, which march steadily from the requirements phase through design, build, and testing, work better for complex programming challenges involving extensive logic that is hard for users to "touch and feel."

- *User engagement*. Putting technology in users' hands from the start reduces costs and enhances buy-in, but adoption may lag if they lack the skills to make the jump on their own. Evaluate the technological sophistication of users to determine who can teach themselves to use new technology, and who will need help from peers or a dedicated team of trainers.

Step 4: Implement to Deliver Value from the Start

With all the planning that goes into a digitization initiative, the rubber does not hit the road until implementation starts—and there is not a construction project that has not run into its share of challenges. As you begin implementation, you often find your team size and the number of stakeholders involved increase three-fold, and so does the complexity of your project. As far-reaching as your goals may be, and as tempting it is to get everything done at once and ramp down the project, it is important to show results as soon as possible. Break up larger projects into smaller stages, focusing first on improvements that will produce quick returns. Savings from these "quick wins" will help fund the project, help manage complexity of implementation, and demonstrate the value of automation and digitization.

Resist the temptation to hold back delivery until every process has been automated. The "big bang" approach carries big risks and often leaves users feeling underwhelmed. Build support by rolling out multiple iterations, starting with early versions that offer basic functionality, then gradually add bells and whistles. From day one you should plan to have resources that will continuously fine-tune the technology and add new features after initial implementation. Institute a system of "check-ins" to make sure the project stays abreast of changing business needs, meets users' expectations, and pays for itself over the long term.

Step 5: Manage Risks

Like any technology, digital solutions come with risks that can undermine their benefits. Among them is adoption risk—the very real possibility that users within or outside your organization won't embrace the technology, robbing it of any chance to deliver the cost savings you hoped for. Another is the risk that outside vendors or your own internal technology organization won't support, maintain, or upgrade infrastructure and software. Such neglect allows value to erode over time. Sometimes a project is simply too ambitious for the team assigned to carry it out, resulting in an outright failure to deliver. In other cases, the technology itself will fail to live up to expectations. Technology owners should monitor and measure these risks, along with the benefits expected from digitization. And they should have authority to intervene if they see value eroding. Monitor financial risks as well, revisiting your business case periodically to make sure your technology implementation costs don't exceed the expected savings. Last, build in strong data security protections—recent digital intrusions at major companies show that a single breach can cost far more than your digitization program will save.

Case Study: Digitizing a Financial Services Company

Digitization is powering a $1 billion Fit for Growth transformation at a global financial services company.

When the company publicized its ambitious cost reduction goal, it employed about 10,000 people in various roles across a vast back-office operation. These employees recorded trades, performed account reconciliations, authorized cash transfers, and recalculated asset valuations, to name just a few of the hundreds of different transaction types flowing into the company every day. As the large headcount suggests, many of these processes were heavily manual, with employees entering data by hand and shuffling through paper trading records.

High labor costs sat atop an outmoded technology base rooted in a customized IT infrastructure that wasn't easily scalable. The company hadn't adopted many common digital capabilities (e.g., smart order-routing and real-time client interaction) that could streamline operations, drive down cost, and reduce risk.

To address these shortcomings and achieve its cost reduction goal, the company shifted to a fully digitized, data-centric business model. A new, nonproprietary technology infrastructure based in the cloud gave new resiliency, stability, and scalability to core operations. Digitizing key processes, such as pricing lightly traded securities, drove down transaction costs. New digital customer interfaces enhanced client service by providing access, transparency, and control to clients across the transaction life cycle.

The company automated hundreds of processes representing about 70 percent of the total workload. As a result, operating costs and risks declined while operating leverage and quality improved. IT systems also became more reliable, with an availability rate of nearly 100 percent. What's more, the new technology made the company nimbler and quicker to respond when markets moved and client needs changed.

Today, the company is on track to exceed its $1 billion savings target.

Digitization Best Practices

Focus on outcomes. Your goal is to drive efficiency and cost savings or build new capabilities, not merely to automate manual processes. To ensure that digitization serves business objectives, include business teams in the planning and execution of the project.

Bring a digitization mindset to the transformation. Identify opportunities to use technology early in the cost transformation, and optimize processes with digitization in mind.

Create a digitization cadre. Form a dedicated "SWAT team" of people who understand both technology and your particular business requirements to drive change. This team becomes accountable for the overall solution architecture, and has decision authority on strategic solutions for the implementation teams. The team develops the overall digitization blueprint, working with the day-to-day operations teams, and ensures that the hard decisions get made, so that digitization initiatives deliver the expected value.

Manage your data. Technology systems are only as good as the data they run on. As part of your technology initiative, take time to clean up and govern your data and the processes that touch it, and make sure it is properly secured.

Clarify your vision and take your time. A strategic, long-term view of evolving technologies and their role in your business should inform digitization decisions. Deploy technology gradually, so you don't outpace your business and the sophistication of your users. For example, don't jump to AI analytics if your organization is not yet comfortable with building its own reports. Approach digitization as a journey, not a race.

Own the thinking and the result. Set your own course and make sure you have the talent on staff to manage a technology vision and implementation. If you outsource strategic thinking to a systems integrator, prepare to exceed cost estimates and fall short of savings targets.

Prioritize your digitization initiatives and commit to them. Few companies have the breadth of resources and talent to take on all potential digitization initiatives. Clearly prioritize those that are essential to your Fit for Growth program and commit the right talent and resources for execution.

Act decisively. Analysis of costs, benefits, and risks is essential, but shouldn't become a chokepoint. Determine if there's a business case for automation or not—and act accordingly.

Pitfalls to Avoid

Overreaching. Overly ambitious programs often spiral out of control, driving up costs and undermining the benefits of digitization.

Losing focus on capabilities. A program that overemphasizes technical functionality may short-change the few critical capabilities needed to achieve
business objectives.

Paving the cow paths. Companies squander value when they automate
inefficient processes without optimizing them first.

Not committing to the full complement of required talent. Digitization requires the
best business, technology, innovation, and engineering talent. Successful
digitization requires a commitment to all of these skills.

Forgetting to plan for the future. Every digitization program should plan for
ongoing challenges such as system maintenance and future upgrades, as
well as major organizational changes like mergers and acquisitions.

Expecting results too soon. The full benefits of large-scale digitization programs
accrue over a period of years. ROI calculations and internal support for
the program will suffer when transformation leaders promise too much
value too soon.

Coping with Cost Restructuring

How to Manage and Sustain the Change

14 | Running a Cost Transformation

Mobilizing, Scaling, and Sustaining

Now that you have learned the strategy behind a Fit for Growth transformation (Part I of our book) and are familiar with the various cost levers a company has at its disposal (Part II), we will next discuss the *process* needed to transition your organization to be Fit for Growth.

Companies are forever making themselves over in response to performance goals and strategic priorities. The usual way these changes are implemented—by embedding them in business plans, then having managers throughout the company execute them—works well when the goals revolve around a specific function or business unit and involve relatively incremental changes. In these situations, the changes can often be included in an annual planning and budgeting process and executed as part of business as usual.

But when a true transformation is needed—when the company is setting out to dramatically reshape its cost structure and organization—the typical business-as-usual approaches are insufficient. Transformations of this sort include five to 10 simultaneous, large-scale initiatives. They cut across the lines of businesses and functions, and affect the entire organization. They require meticulous planning and execution to achieve their objectives, and take 12 to 24 months to complete. Given their level of complexity, such transformations cannot be executed as part of business as usual—they require something different. They require a *programmatic approach* (see Figure 14.1).

A programmatic change for a Fit for Growth transformation comprises four elements:

1. The transformation is undertaken over three distinct phases, each with a specific purpose.

COMPARISON OF A PROGRAMMATIC AND TRADITIONAL APPROACH TO DRIVING CHANGE

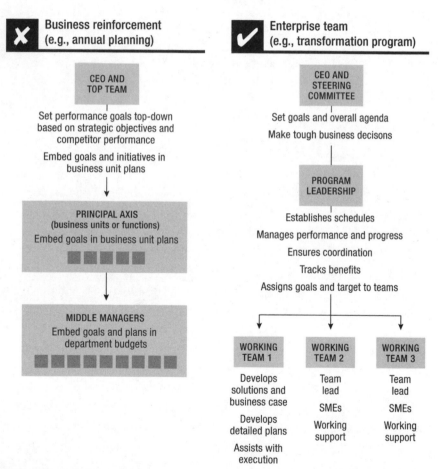

Figure 14.1

2. The transformation is owned and led by the CEO and a subset of the CEO's direct reports.
3. A dedicated transformation team, separate from the day-to-day organization, manages the detailed design, and the line owns the execution.
4. A disciplined working process is put in place and managed by an empowered program management office (PMO).

Transformations following the Fit for Growth approach typically begin by conducting a diagnostic exercise and building the case for change (Phase 1). Next, they build a detailed design of the transformation (Phase 2); last, they are executed (Phase 3; see Figure 14.2). Each phase is unique in purpose and outcomes targeted: each is different in the work undertaken, the governance of the transformation, the makeup of the transformation team, and the working process followed (see Figure 14.3). We discuss each of these three phases in turn.

Phase 1: Diagnostic and Case for Change

The purpose of Phase 1 is to set the direction for the program, prioritize opportunities to pursue, and create the case for change. While cost reduction is top of mind in Phase 1, investments in differentiating capabilities are equally important—a Fit for Growth transformation always seeks to strengthen the company's capabilities system as a simultaneous objective. Thus, the CEO and the executives spend significant time aligning on the company's differentiating capabilities and determining how much to invest in them. Last, Phase 1 is the time to build the transformation's case for change, detailing why a change is needed, the vision for the future, the benefits of the transformation, and the outlines of the transformation road map.

How It Is Governed

Phase 1, like other phases of the transformation, is led by an *executive steering committee,* which owns and leads the transformation program. The steering committee is almost always chaired by the CEO. Sometimes the CEO delegates the responsibility to another senior executive, such as the CFO or COO, and is not a visible champion of the transformation. The CEO may

THE THREE PHASES OF A TRANSFORMATION

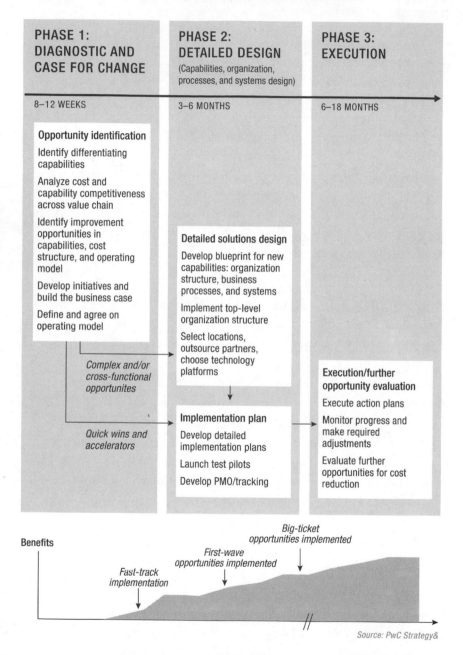

Figure 14.2

SUMMARY OF TRANSFORMATION PROGRAM ELEMENTS

Program elements	Phase 1: Diagnostic and case for change	Phase 2: Detailed design	Phase 3: Execution
Purpose of the phase	Define the future state vision and the case for change Prioritize initiatives to pursue	Develop detailed plans to design the future organization, cut costs, and strengthen differentiating capabilities	Execute the plans and achieve the targeted objectives
Program team makeup	Small, senior team—select part-time CxOs and a 3–4 person team for analyses	Expanded program team, with dedicated, high-potential team members for each workstream	Small PMO team to coordinate and track execution, and line executing as part of day-to-day work
Governed by	CEO and 2–5 CxOs	CEO and direct reports	Line and Staff Leaders
Executive steering committee role	Set a stretch target Define the future state vision Define the case for change	Ensure designs are consistent with the vision Resolve dependencies and issues Begin to role-model the future state behaviors	Maintain momentum Ensure plans are executed and objectives realized Resolve major issues
Steering committee meeting cadence	Every 2–3 weeks, for 3–6 hours	Every 3–4 weeks, for 4–8 hours	Every 4–6 weeks, for 2–4 hours
Size of the working team	1 Full-Time Lead 3–4 Team Members	1 Full-Time Program Lead and 3–8 Team Members per initiative (30–80 people)	1 Full-Time Lead 3–4 Team Members
Role of the program management office	Lock down the baseline and scope Establish program processes	Drive the workstreams to achieve their targets Surface and manage dependencies, issues, risks Integrate the opportunities into a solution Ensure the program is on track	Track all key measures (change initiatives, benefits, costs, risks, employee satisfaction, customer satisfaction) Ensure teams keep true to the vision and Phase II designs Transfer ownership to the line organization

Source: PwC Strategy&

Figure 14.3

have reasons for such a hands-off posture—providing a development opportunity for another executive, letting the executive team find (rather than be told) the solution, or simply having too many other time commitments. But in our experience, such an approach does not work well and almost guarantees poor results. Either purposefully or inadvertently, the CEO signals to the organization that the program is not important enough to merit his or her attention. Only the CEO can make calls that reshape the company's future; delegating to the next layer down constrains the questions that can be addressed, or limits the quality of the solutions because peers around the table may not agree.

The steering committee at this stage includes several senior executives, including the senior-most business and staff function leaders, such as the CFO, the chief human resources officer, and heads of business units. While steering committees with eight or more members may be inclusive and help with organizational buy-in, they may also be too large to effectively debate the issues and make decisions.

The Transformation Team

In addition to the steering committee, leaders select a small but vital transformation team to define opportunities, size the benefits and transition costs, and develop the road map to follow. The team is led by a senior, full-time *program lead*, who is two to three layers below the CEO. The program lead manages the effort day to day, brings facts and recommendations to the steering committee, and champions the change effort.

The choice of the program lead is the first critical decision the CEO and the steering committee make about the program. Who the program lead is speaks volumes about how the C-suite sees the program and the weight they place on it. Assigning a senior leader with a history of results in important line positions, or a high-potential rising star, will signal to the organization that the CEO means business. On the other hand, appointing a "has been" who needs a bridge role prior to retirement, or a mediocre manager who's been stuck in midlevel roles with few accomplishments, will signal that the program lacks serious support and can be ignored.

The ideal program lead is a naturally respected leader within the organization with a strong track record of accomplishments. He or she gets things done, is credible with other executives, has an open mind, and takes an enterprise view, unencumbered by current organizational lines. The ideal candidate also has a strategic perspective, yet can immerse himself or herself in the details, and has strong interpersonal and communication skills, which will be used frequently during the transformation journey. The program leader sets up the PMO in Phase 1 to lock down the baseline and scope, and establish program processes.

In addition to this program lead, a small *working team* is formed, made up of a few full-time team members who lead the fact gathering, analyses, and recommendation development. Members are often front-line managers or senior analysts. They are chosen from specific business units or functions and need not be fully representative of the organization—the skills and characteristics they bring to the team are more important than where in the organization they sit. They need to be strategic, open minded, and analytical; have a reputation for getting things done; and be able to take an enterprise view.

Last, the transformation team will need access to subject-matter experts in finance and HR, to help with data collection and specific questions, such as what assumptions to use for business case calculations or severance policies.

The Working Process

During Phase 1, the program lead and the working team work closely with the executive steering committee. The team first baselines the company's performance—gathering facts on the company's performance, assessing capabilities through interviews with process owners, and conducting benchmarking exercises to understand any gaps with leading performance. The baselining work typically includes interviews with 20 to 30 of the seniormost executives in the company, and seeks to understand their perspectives on the company's performance and where they see improvement opportunities. The team then conducts additional targeted analyses to test the opportunities that benchmarking suggests, and begins to form a view of the changes required and a vision of the future state.

The steering committee meets several times during the course of Phase 1's eight- to 12-week duration. Each meeting should be lengthy enough (three to six hours) to allow sufficient time to review the fact base and discuss the recommendations. Armed with the facts and analyses the working team provides, the executive steering committee debates options and then decides, through these meetings and working sessions, the future-state vision, the improvement target, and a set of prioritized opportunities. While the analyses are often straightforward, the steering committee members often need "soak time" so that the changes they are being asked to make sink in. They often need time to have discussions with their peers in small groups to absorb facts and recommendations, evaluate scenarios and their larger implications, contemplate the magnitude of the decisions they are making, and get comfortable with it all.

Phase 2: Detailed Design

Phase 2 takes the directional findings of Phase 1, translates them into a detailed design of the future processes, organization, and systems, and develops a detailed plan for moving from the current to the future state. The savings opportunities and investments that were broadly sketched in Phase 1 (in many cases based on top-down analysis and benchmarks) now need to be validated bottom up by creating a blueprint for what the future will be.

Phase 2 also jump-starts the change management process by identifying what will change, describing who change will impact and how, and developing a detailed plan to enable the organization to change.

In parallel with the future-state design, some "quick wins"—changes that can be realized with little planning and few systemic or process changes—should be executed, such as a reduction in discretionary spending, or seeking concessions from vendors.

How It Is Governed

The governance of the program evolves from Phase 1 into Phase 2 in three possible ways. First, the composition of the steering committee may broaden, especially if the Phase 1 steering committee included only a few members. In Phase 2, the steering committee may expand to half a dozen or more to include all major line and staff functional leaders. As in Phase 1, there is a trade-off between being inclusive and facilitating buy-in, and allowing for candid and effective discussions among senior leaders. In this phase, the steering committee's role is guidance and oversight: ensuring the program is moving toward the vision and goals set at the end of Phase 1, and resolving issues raised.

Second, as the scope and the complexity of the program increases from Phase 1 to Phase 2, a C-suite-level *executive sponsor* is appointed to guide the program on behalf of the CEO and the steering committee, to ensure the program is on track, address issues, and remove roadblocks. The executive sponsor spends about one day a week on the program and is one step closer to it than the rest of the steering committee.

Third, each of the CxOs plays a *workstream sponsor* role for one or more of the workstreams launched as part of Phase 2. Each sponsor owns a workstream and is ultimately accountable for its success. Sometimes we see clients assign two sponsors per workstream to ensure constructive tension and collaboration among key stakeholders. Sponsors set the vision and the overall direction for the workstream, select a team leader to run it, staff it, and engage the workstream team periodically to ensure high-quality analysis and recommendations. They also address thorny issues, such as having delicate conversations with uncooperative or resistant senior managers, or resolving complex dependencies with other sponsors. Sponsors must become champions for their workstream's recommendations when presented to the steering committee (see Figure 14.4).

The Transformation Team

In Phase 2, the transformation team evolves in two ways. First, the working team expands to a larger number of workstreams, each with dedicated staff; second, more team members are added to the PMO to guide, align, and track the program.

The workstreams are launched to develop a detailed design of the opportunities prioritized in Phase 1. Each of these workstreams is staffed by a team leader and several members, whose skills and characteristics resemble their predecessors in Phase 1. Team members should be high performing, analytical, inquisitive, and open minded; they should include a mix of subject matter experts in specific processes, functions, or businesses and strong

PHASE 2 TRANSFORMATION TEAM AND GOVERNANCE

SAMPLE PROGRAM STRUCTURE

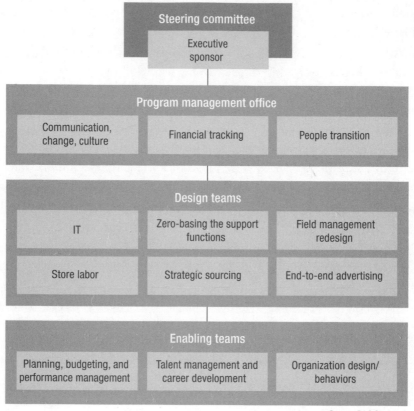

Source: PwC Strategy&

Figure 14.4

generalists. Team leaders should be seasoned, respected, accomplished leaders with strong interpersonal and management skills. They should be subject matter experts, credible among their peers, and be direct reports to function or business leaders.

The PMO manages the complex program as its moving parts, dependencies, and risks multiply. It is the central hub for the program and has three roles: guide the program, align it, and track it.

In its first role, the PMO guides all the workstreams toward the program objectives defined in Phase 1. The PMO, which at this stage functions in the same way as the program lead did in Phase 1, proactively communicates with workstream leaders and their sponsors on the expectations from each workstream. The PMO also provides the workstreams with a set of templates to fill out during Phase 2 to guide the work and ensure basic quality output. These templates typically include baselining (financial, headcount, org chart), savings (drivers of savings, cost reduction, headcount reduction), issue tracking, dependency identification, risk identification, and an implementation plan. If a workstream is straying or falling behind, the PMO intervenes directly and through the sponsors and the steering committee.

In its second role, the PMO aligns the program by proactively solidifying senior stakeholder support (working with the executive sponsor, workstream sponsors, and the steering committee) and integrating the solutions developed independently by each workstream. The PMO identifies dependencies across the workstreams and ensures the resolution is effective through the workstreams.

Third, the PMO tracks the program: the financial and headcount baseline, progress against the milestones, and resolution of issues and risks surfaced.

To cover its scope and responsibilities, the PMO assembles a few team members to focus on classic project management and tracking, financial baseline-setting and savings tracking, and workstream coordination. In addition to this small dedicated team, the PMO also oversees planning around people transitions (discussed further in Chapter 15), and change management and culture evolution planning (discussed further in Chapter 16). To manage the activity, the PMO puts in place processes to engage the workstreams and track the progress in a fact-based way.

The Working Process

During Phase 2, there are three critical interactions, each with working processes around them: the steering committee with the workstreams; the PMO with the workstreams; and workstreams among themselves.

In the first critical interaction, the steering committee engages the workstreams through regular meetings. The content of these meetings evolves throughout Phase 2. Early on, the meetings enable the steering committee to stay informed of the workstreams' progress and also guide them. In the later stages, these meetings evolve into decision-making forums, where future processes and organizations are defined, cost savings are confirmed, and agreements on reinvestments into differentiating capabilities are concluded.

The steering committee meetings take place about once per month, and should take a half to a full day. In our experience, adapting a "T-shaped" agenda in these meetings is the most effective approach (see Figure 14.5). The horizontal bar of the T refers to broadly reviewing the status of the

SAMPLE T-SHAPED MEETING AGENDA

"T-SHAPED" STEERING TEAM MEETING STRUCTURE

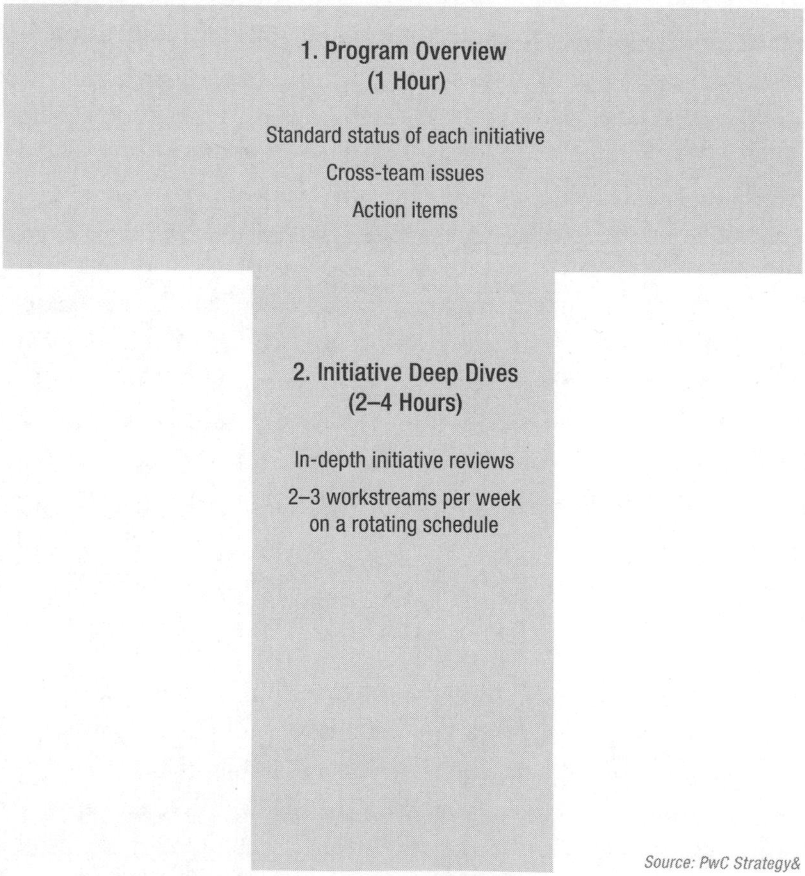

**1. Program Overview
(1 Hour)**

Standard status of each initiative

Cross-team issues

Action items

**2. Initiative Deep Dives
(2–4 Hours)**

In-depth initiative reviews

2–3 workstreams per week
on a rotating schedule

Source: PwC Strategy&

Figure 14.5

program and each initiative, and making calls on program-wide priorities. The vertical bar of the T refers to going more deeply into two to three workstreams at each meeting, where facts and analyses are presented, options debated, and decisions made. These workstream-specific meetings should be long enough to allow in-depth reviews and discussions.

In the second critical interaction, the PMO engages with workstreams through weekly "deep dive" or "double-click" meetings lasting about an hour. These meetings generally include the PMO leader, the workstream team lead, the sponsor of the workstream, and one or two workstream and PMO team members. These meetings enable the PMO to guide and to track the work: the PMO reviews the workstream's progress, understands the content of the work, surfaces any issues that need to be resolved with other workstreams, provides input as needed, and ensures the workstream is on the right track.

In the third interaction, the PMO facilitates workstream-to-workstream interactions through weekly cross-workstream lead meetings. The PMO typically brings workstream leads together to jointly discuss the program's progress, share program-wide information, and review priorities for the next few weeks. The PMO also facilitates information sharing across workstreams, by going around the table and allowing each team lead to raise and discuss issues that are important for their team.

Phase 3: Execution

In Phase 3 of the transformation, the focus turns to execution. The transformation is no longer an esoteric exercise; it is the new normal for everyone in the company. No more is the success of the transformation in the hands of the sponsors or working teams. Workstream leaders turn their meticulously developed plans over to line managers to execute.

How It Is Governed

There is a temptation in many organizations to disband the program structure and processes once Phase 2 is over. There is an understandable fatigue among the executive team after heavy involvement during Phase 1 *and* Phase 2. Yet little has actually been executed by the beginning of Phase 3, and the

TRANSFORMATION TEAM EVOLUTION
THROUGH THE PHASES

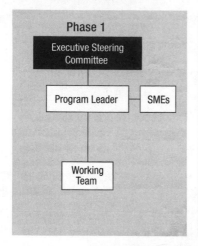
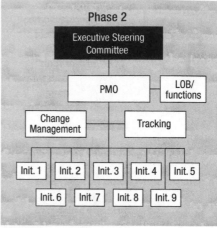
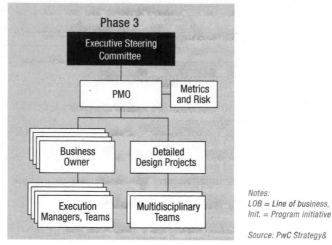

Notes:
LOB = Line of business,
Init. = Program initiative

Source: PwC Strategy&

Figure 14.6

discipline of Phase 2 must be maintained into Phase 3, where a lot could be lost in translation and fall through the cracks during hand-offs between the transformation team and the line managers who will execute the plans.

During the first 12 months of the execution, the governance structure should continue from Phase 2 with some modifications. The steering committee members remain in their roles and continue to oversee the execution, ensuring the program stays on track, and resolving issues submitted to it. The frequency and duration of the meetings could be scaled back, as there are fewer decisions to be made at the steering committee level.

In the latter stages of Phase 3, however, the steering committee can be disbanded and program tracking can devolve into regular business-performance management processes.

The Transformation Team

In Phase 3, the dedicated transformation team shrinks as initiatives are approved and turned over to the business owners, and execution gets under way. After a period of hand-offs, the team leads and working teams go back to their day-to-day jobs (or assume new roles in the organization after the program). They are still available as questions come up, but now middle managers, empowered to make decisions, play the biggest role—along with employees—in pushing the transformation forward.

As the Phase 2 team winds down, new teams are built under each business owner (a line or functional leader) with an initiative to execute (see Figure 14.6). If an initiative cannot be clearly assigned to a line manager, business owners appoint *execution managers* to run and enact initiatives in their areas, leveraging dedicated or part-time team members as needed. In addition, these execution managers play project management roles to help business owners coordinate and track initiatives in their areas.

In some cases, however, a smaller transformation team should remain in place (or be created anew). When new initiatives are identified or initiatives with lower priorities are put back on the table for detailed design, they will require the same level of attention and resourcing (i.e., staffing at the same numbers and with the same skill sets) as the earlier Phase 2 initiatives.

The PMO retains a critical role in Phase 3, especially for the first 12 months. The PMO tracks progress against the planned savings and execution schedule—using key performance indicators, team scorecards, and other tools—and pushes for results to be realized. It coordinates the milestones and sequence of multiple initiatives that are mutually dependent. It takes steps to ensure that improvements (both on the capabilities and cost sides) will be sustained. And when it needs to, it enlists the steering committee to help put derailed initiatives back on track.

The Working Process

A key activity during Phase 3 is tracking the execution of and progress toward the chosen objectives. To this end, the PMO establishes a tracking process, works with the business owners, and reports periodically to the steering committee.

Tracking in Phase 3 has two broad elements:

1. Are the initiatives being executed as planned?
2. Are the results being achieved as expected?

The PMO sets up a process to engage with the business owners periodically to understand the execution progress, similar to workstream deep dives in Phase 2. Business owners report their progress against the plan and discuss any issues they are encountering during execution. In addition, the PMO continues to orchestrate steering committee meetings during Phase 3, where the business owners describe their execution progress. These meetings allow the steering committee to remain informed of progress and resolve issues raised to their level.

In Phase 3, the PMO and the steering committee need to ensure the plans are executed as envisioned, and not allow managers to substitute across-the-board cost reductions not envisioned in the transformation plan without changing how and what work gets done. If not closely tracked, the anticipated savings still may be achieved, but they may come from the wrong places, the work may not go away, and ultimately the fitness of the organization and the sustainability of the changes may be at risk.

Fit for Growth Cost Transformations Best Practices

Do use a dedicated team to execute the transformation and carry out the vision. Most transformations happen at a time when things are not going well—and are in danger of deteriorating. This is not a time to be unrealistic about what people can accomplish, or expect them to perform magic. The people who are part of the transformation must be allowed to temporarily step away from their day jobs.

Do pick your best people to head the transformation. In a change this big, the future of your organization is at stake. Assign your highest-potential people to the task—people you expect will make even bigger contributions to the organization in the future—even though you may have to back-fill their roles to keep the business running.

Do push every workstream to meet or exceed objectives. Not every workstream will produce the planned savings. Pushing for even more savings than you think you actually need is the best way to ensure against slippage in one or more workstreams and meet the overall objective.

Do err on the side of over-communicating. Especially in the early part of a transformation, people often don't understand everything that's happening, and it's a mistake to assume they do. Communicating clearly and frequently is an important part of keeping the workforce focused and energized.

Do stay ahead of the program. To ensure momentum across phases and to ease changes in ownership as work is handed off from the transformation team to the business owners, plan a few steps in advance. The PMO plays a crucial role here by anticipating issues and next steps.

Pitfalls to Avoid

Executives should not be too hands-off. Senior leaders may feel tempted, after they have provided direction, to get out of the way. After all, delegating is their normal mode of operation. In a transformation, however, it's important for executives to remain not just visible but also engaged. It is management's role to ask tough questions and challenge the team to overdeliver.

Don't let siloed thinking get in the way of sharing great ideas. Transformation is not a time for turf-protecting or siloed thinking. In fact, it's important that change ideas be shared and that others be allowed to improve on them.

Don't disband the PMO too early. Many executives believe that the most substantial part of the transformation is wrapped up once the Phase 2 (detail design) is done. However, while accountable line managers should be in the driver's seat for implementation, the PMO should continue to play a critical role as the conscience of the transformation.

Don't allow teams to short-change detailed design. Ensure working teams take the time to document and explain line and staff responsibilities, cross-functional process interactions, and the impact of the operating model on day-to-day process. Otherwise, the intended changes may not be fully understood by the line managers who will execute them.

Don't allow executives to claim "I will get my number." Sometimes executives get frustrated by the process imposed on them, want to shortcut, and say. "Tell me what you need, and I'll get my number." While these executives are likely to get their number, the number tells only half the story. Fit for Growth transformations call for changing the organization and the spend profile to invest in differentiating capabilities. *How* the cost reductions are achieved and sustained are as important as the cost reductions themselves.

15

Morale, Emotions, and Expectations

Leading during a Restructuring

Until now we have focused on the actions and roles of those who initiate and run a Fit for Growth transformation and are most directly responsible for its success. We have described the responsibility they have to strengthen their company's differentiating capabilities, how they can use various levers to cut costs, and how they can manage a programmatic transformation journey.

But the people on the transformation team who are *changing* the business are not the only ones dealing with challenges during a transformation; the senior, middle, and front-line managers who are *running* the business bear a heavy burden, too. These managers must guide, coach, and support their employees through months of uncertainty. And when the transformation design is complete, it will fall to these managers to stand up the new organization, convince a reduced workforce to implement and adopt improved processes, and transition to working in a different way, while also managing the business. Their role will include helping employees adapt to the changes and often will also include the agonizing business of managing headcount reductions. In this chapter, we discuss how these managers can surmount the challenges of a transition—and how they can rally their employees to do the same.

To augment our experiences in helping clients accomplish Fit for Growth transformations with additional first-hand perspectives, we interviewed several mid- and upper-level managers who lived through transformations in recent years. All of these managers have either remained in their positions at their companies or moved into positions of greater responsibility, so they bring the perspective of the before, during, and after. Their stories and the lessons they have learned inform the discussion in this chapter.

Uncertainty and Anxiety

For managers and their employees, a transformation is a time of tremendous personal uncertainty. After that first all-staff memo from the C-suite, noting that a reassessment of the business is underway and that it may be accompanied by a major restructuring, there are invariably months in which there is little to no further communication, and everyone—from vice presidents on down to hourly workers—is left in the dark. "Everything went quiet" is what one manager remembers of the period after his own company announced plans for a large-scale restructuring. Although the manager was considered a top performer and has since been promoted, he adds, "I was very worried about what was going to happen to me and whether I was going to have a job. No one was giving me any reassurance. And no one could."

This is the crux of the issue for those on the receiving end of a transformation: they naturally view everything from their own perspective. This is true in the literal sense that the first thought of receiving managers (everyone outside the transformation is in a sense a "receiver" of it) is for their own job security, the protection of their domain, and what they personally may need to do differently. But it's also true in the figurative sense of taking something personally: as the period of time without any clear communication lengthens, frustration, resentment, anger, and depression set in, at various times and to varying degrees.

Among front-line managers and employees, there is often a perception that corporate management is removed from the rest of the organization. This perception becomes more pronounced during a transformation. The small group of executives who have responsibility for the overall transformation can't say much about it themselves, initially because they are still figuring things out and later because of the implications of misspeaking. What little they do say only reinforces the perception that they are out of touch, especially if they stick to limited talking points about the importance of the transformation to the business. The other managers who are brought in to design pieces of the transformation are likewise asked to treat the plans as confidential and speak in only the most general terms. In the information vacuum that develops, the receiving managers themselves end up having to articulate a message to keep their teams going and prevent morale problems from getting out of hand.

There is only so much a manager can do during a transformation to address employees' anxiety. As information leaks out—or doesn't—employees ride a roller coaster of emotions, veering between hope, anger, fear, frustration, depression, and relief. In the rest of this chapter, we focus on what receiving managers encounter during a transformation: from the rumors early on when senior leaders are still debating the cost-savings number and scope of the restructuring; to the intensifying water-cooler speculation as more managers get drawn into private planning sessions; and last to the tectonic shifts of the last phase, when the plans become public and execution begins. Through it all, receiving managers, far from being passive, have a chance to influence pieces of the transformation and use it to shape their own careers. (See "The Upside of a Transformation for Midlevel Managers.") Their chances are improved if, throughout the transformation, they remain committed to open communication; express optimism about the changes that are brewing; and resolve to handle the inevitable setbacks to come (including staff departures) in the most thoughtful, productive way possible (see Figure 15.1).

The Upside of a Transformation for Midlevel Managers

For the vast majority of managers, transformations are a trial by fire. Yet there is a flip side to all the challenges: transformations teach managers new skills, allow them to demonstrate leadership under adverse conditions, rid their departments of low-performing workers; and gain the trust of the executive team. In short, transformations offer a stage on which managers who haven't led the change effort can nonetheless become a part of it and shine.

"You have to take the perspective of, I'm going to learn a lot. I'm going to try to provide value, and hopefully by doing that, be looked at as an asset," said an IT director at a company that recently went through a Fit for Growth transformation. "Worst-case scenario, I'll learn what to do, and what not to do" during change programs "and be able to apply that at my next company."

An even more tangible upside relates to the creation of new leadership roles. This is especially true at organizations known for being top-heavy and for not presenting opportunities for advancement. At these organizations, a transformation can present high-potential managers with rare opportunities to move into positions of greater responsibility.

Phase 1: Opportunity, but for Whom?

The diagnostic and case for change phase is when the senior management determines the broad outlines of the restructuring. This includes setting an overall vision and target, prioritizing changes, and putting in place a road map to achieve them. While employees may know that a major analysis of the organization and costs is underway—based on the memo from the C-suite—the specifics are unknown.

What Employees Go Through

For everyone outside the executive team, Phase 1 is a time of uncertainty. Questions surround the vaguely described "project." Unless employees know with absolute certainty that they are "indispensable," many feel vulnerable about their own future. And even employees handling those seemingly indispensable activities—and who are considered top performers—rarely see their positions as secure. With the company sharing so little, rumor and speculation take the place of information in this phase. Hoping for the best, some employees predict it will end up just like the last time the company announced a reorganization, when it petered out a quarter of the way through and nothing changed. Other employees will express a more

MORALE AND EXPECTATIONS
IN EACH TRANSITION PHASE

	Phase 1: Diagnostic and case for change	Phase 2: Detailed design	Phase 3: Execution
What happens	Top-down performance analysis Opportunity sizing Prioritization and planning	Detailed design for new organization, processes Pilots and quick wins Detailed execution plans	Execution of plans Headcount reductions Transition to a new way of working
How people feel	Lots of uncertainty Range of emotions from anxiety, to skepticism, to some optimism	Anxious about own job Concerned about the company's future Low morale due to uncertainty	Optimism for the future and new model Survivor guilt and sadness for separated colleagues Fatigued from absorbing changes in their departments Confused by new ways of working
What leaders should do	Support team Build credibility by being candid, transparent Focus on cultural values Create an energizing case for change	Manage day-to-day work Set a positive example to keep up morale Engage staff to minimize attrition Support the transformation	Manage employee transitions Support the team; adapt to new ways of working Role-model new behaviors

Source: PwC Strategy&

Figure 15.1

pessimistic view: that there will be radical changes, including large layoffs, that will directly affect them and hurt the company. In a matter of weeks, what is or isn't going to happen with jobs and organizational changes becomes the dominant topic of discussion in the office. Few people see the possible upside—that the transformation will fix broken processes and reduce bureaucracy, leaving the company (and many of its employees) better off.

What Managers Are Up Against

Middle and front-line managers who aren't involved in designing the transformation usually bear the brunt of employees' questions in this phase. These managers rarely have an idea of what is being discussed at the executive level and what might come out of the initiative. Often, they don't know what their own futures look like. Yet they have to manage the morale and expectations of their people, who often don't realize or believe that a manager could be as much in the dark as they are. This puts managers in an awkward position: not knowing much about what is going on, but still having to say *something* to address the rumors, support their people, and maintain productivity.

What Managers Can Do

The best that managers can do in this phase—where they have no real information and nothing has been decided—is to be as truthful and transparent as possible. They need to reinforce the case for change as communicated by the CEO in everyday language that will resonate with their teams. In addition, they need to find a way to keep their teams focused on day-to-day business. One effective way to do this is to take actions that reinforce the company's existing culture and values. For instance, a manager might find a way to get staff to focus on an individual performance metric in which people naturally take pride. In an operation focused on customer service, for example, a manager might launch a customer satisfaction survey and share results with employees. A retail operations manager might remind employees to keep focusing on their customers and delivering the best service they can.

"I encouraged people to control what they could control, to try to stay positive, and to focus on their key objectives," said an IT director at a company that went through a Fit for Growth transformation in 2015. "My feeling was we could all take one of two roads. We could either sulk, not do the work, or not act in the right way—in which case we would be making the decision to let us all go much easier and our fears would become a self-fulfilling prophecy. Or, we could continue to work on what we were supposed to work on, try to help the company, hope for the best, and go from there.

"At the end of the day I knew I might not have a job, but I didn't feel that it would do me any good to take a pessimistic position."

Phase 2: Anxiety Surfaces

The detailed design kicks off with the public articulation of a savings target, often quite aggressive. With the target identified, shared with outside stakeholders, and broken down by function and business unit (at least internally), the transformation moves into a more intense phase. If there was skepticism, however faint, in the previous phase that things would just blow over, it diminishes in Phase 2. A select few colleagues and managers get pulled out of their day-to-day jobs to help design the detailed expense-reduction plans. Some early cost-savings initiatives—hiring freezes or restrictions on travel, for instance—get implemented. In whatever department one happens to be in, there is an unmistakable sense that things are speeding up.

What Employees Go Through

With something very sizable in the works but no details on how it will be achieved, people's anxieties come to the surface. In some cases, good people—exactly the people companies want to keep—become frustrated with the uncertainty about their futures, seek other opportunities elsewhere, and leave. The majority of employees don't go anywhere, but as the rumors continue to fly, morale dips and anger and resentment mount toward the company and the executive team, who are often invisible to employees at this point.

"You almost have to see it" to understand how disruptive the experience is, said a manager at a large company who believes that the transformation at his organization was particularly difficult because of how much like a family it had been previously. "There would be days when everybody was in tears, and nothing had even been announced yet."

What Managers Are Up against

In Phase 2, managers' own worries deepen. On top of being concerned for their own jobs, they also worry about whether long-time colleagues, some of them personal friends, will survive the restructuring; about the fate of their executive sponsors and others who have mentored them; about what it will take to grow and advance in the restructured organization, should they be fortunate enough to be offered a position in it; and about whether the new company will be a good place to build a career.

Part of the problem for managers in Phase 2 is that they don't have a lot of support. By necessity, the change management and communications work is focused on the transformation initiatives, all critical undertakings. In the face of these larger priorities, there is often little time to help middle and front-line managers figure out what they should be saying to people further down the organizational ranks, which increases the unease in that part of the organization.

"There was no talking point we were given that made any real sense; there was only a talking point to the business piece," said the manager at the family-like large company. "And most employees could care less about the business piece when something like this is going on. 'Talk to me as a human, as part of your family.' That's what people wanted."

What Managers Can Do

For managers, three things are particularly important in Phase 2. First, they must continue to communicate with their employees. Much of a manager's success during this phase comes down to people skills: the quality of relationships the manager has, and his or her ability to convey empathy and communicate a realistic optimism. As in other situations in life where one has a leadership role, it's sometimes useful to project the opposite of what others are feeling: optimistic when others are gloomy, confident when others are insecure. These positive attitudes send an important signal to other members of a team.

Second, managers should communicate employee concerns and suggestions *up* to the executives and the transformation team. Midlevel managers should use their access to senior leaders to inform them of what's happening in the trenches and the overall morale of the front-line work-force. Senior leaders are often so consumed with shaping the future that they lose track of the feelings within the organization at large. Friendly prompts about what's happening in the trenches help remind them to address the communication vacuum and support the day-to-day business.

Last, managers should support the transformation. This means providing information accurately and promptly when someone on the transformation team requests it. It may also mean volunteering for the workshops and solution-development sessions that the company is likely using to shape the future.

Phase 3: Turmoil, but also Glimmers of Something Better

In the execution phase, the uncertainty that has pervaded the organization starts to recede. Decisions about new operating models and the required headcount changes are finalized and announced. Implementation teams are formed to act on the decisions that have been made. Employees at every level see what the new organization will look like and how individual roles will change. Communication that was once minimal moves into overdrive in the form of memos, town hall meetings, staff meetings, training, and team-building sessions.

What Employees Go Through

The transformation is now in high gear. Employees are told how reporting lines and organizations will change. They may learn of plans to consolidate functions across business lines or geographies, to implement new processes or IT systems, to outsource work, to move some work to a new city, or to shut down entire offices. In some instances, early retirement and enhanced severance programs will be announced, giving employees even more to think about.

Not everybody will like what they hear. As in previous phases, there will be a lot of bias in how employees interpret information—*what's in it for me?* Some employees will think the changes take the company down the wrong path. Others will believe that the essentials that made the company great are being abandoned. A few will be disappointed that the changes don't go far enough.

At the beginning of Phase 3, the question that looms largest for every employee still has not definitively been answered: *do I still have a job?* This is because the decisions about organization changes, process redesigns, and upcoming cost cuts (all of which are now being discussed openly, at least in broad terms) must still be translated into names of who stays and who goes. So the bulk of the emotional bumps still await the employees, and the uncertainty about the personal situation remains.

In addition to the psychological and emotional toll of daily worry, there are practical adjustments to make. Every department is starting to hear about new systems or processes they will be implementing. There is talk about changes in the metrics that employees will be held to, and about the new measures that will be used to judge their job performance. Everyone will need to work in a new way and demonstrate new behaviors. This will lead some people to ask, "Can we really pull this off? Can we work this way in the future?"

What Managers Are Up Against

For all the turmoil, the beginning of Phase 3 can also be a time of relief and renewed optimism, certainly for managers. The stage has been set for a recovery of the department's morale, and there is a vision of the stronger company that will emerge as a result of the transformation. But there is a lot of work to be done before reaching the promised land, and there is one especially difficult obligation to fulfill: managing headcount reductions, if the plan calls for them.

In a large-scale change, many managers will face the difficult obligation of having to let some of their employees go. In some transitions, existing performance data may be used; the data is applicable to the future and is of high enough quality. In other transitions, where the data is not applicable or not trusted, managers need to conduct special assessments to evaluate their employees. Once the assessment is done, the manager, with help from HR and Legal, will select who in the team stays and who goes. During this time, until the selection is complete and the official communications and severance packages are ready, the manager cannot tell the employees anything.

"You get the pressures of people calling you who are your friends, saying, 'Come on now, what's going on? You've got to tell me something. Am I safe?'" recalled a manager of the period when he was huddled in meetings related to employee selection. "To have to turn them down"—that is, not be able to answer them—"is a tough thing," this manager added.

On the flip side, managers should expect that some of their high performers will leave in Phase 3, generally for jobs at other companies. Some employees will put out feelers that turn into offers, and some others, especially in the middle to senior management positions, will be approached by recruiters. Unwanted attrition is part of the fallout of a transformation. Despite the risk of losing their top performers, managers should resist the temptation to make promises to employees about their jobs during a restructuring, but instead discuss the benefits of the transformation to the company and to the employee.

Last, a manager must be prepared for the emotional fallout that the retained team will experience once their friends and colleagues are let go. For the remaining employees, the relief of knowing they have a job is often quickly followed with something akin to survivors' guilt. "I felt like I had been hit by a truck when [my closest colleague and peer] told me that his role had been eliminated and that there were no additional roles available for qualified talent like himself in the company going forward," said a regional vice president of a retail bank. People decisions will be scrutinized and conspiracy theories about favoritism may arise. This dampens team morale and adds to the concerns over what new expectations will mean for the remaining employees personally, how they can perform the work with fewer staff, and whether those new expectations are realistic.

What Managers Can Do

The manager has two roles during Phase 3: to ensure that his or her employees transition into the new world as quickly as possible; and to manage the selection and departure of the employees being laid off.

In the first role, the manager is the field leader who will take his or her employees from the old to the new, helping them learn new processes and systems, adapt to a new organization structure and hierarchy, and change behaviors to move to a new way of working. Most if not all managers will face some challenges with their teams; some employees will need help and coaching to learn the new ways; others will miss the old and resent having to learn the new.

To minimize the time and pain associated with the transition, the manager must demonstrate absolute leadership to the team, starting with internalizing very quickly the "why" and the "what" of the transformation and accepting that he or she will be part of the future. Employees will recognize immediately if the manager is not 100 percent committed, and use it as an excuse (perhaps subconsciously) not to make the transition. The manager's role, then, is to show the employees, in words and actions, that he understands the changes, is convinced that they make sense, and will adapt as quickly as possible. To do all this, the manager must be immersed in all the organization, process, and systems changes in order to explain them to his team without hesitating or wavering.

The manager must also be an empathetic coach to his team; even when employees want to make the transition, the change is not necessarily easy. The manager must patiently coach the "willing" so they become "able" as quickly as possible. This may also require requesting additional help from the transformation team and HR for more training or better communications and training packages.

And while the manager is patiently supporting the "willing," he must also identify the "unwilling" in his team and either bring them along or move them along. Despite best attempts, there are often a few employees who will not be able to break with the past and who will continue to be "derailers" of the transformation. The manager must spot these naysayers early and engage to bring them along. Tactics could range from extended conversations to explain the changes, to blunt direction to shape up or else. And if the behavior does not change, the derailers may need to be let go so they don't poison the well and set a bad example for the rest of the employees.

In the manager's second Phase 3 role, he or she must navigate the set of tasks involved in headcount reductions. Everything connected with reductions—the selection of the people who will end up without jobs, the communication of the unwanted news to those people, and the process of "managing them out"—is a difficult experience. This is a part of a transformation where *process* is especially important. With any luck, the company has taken a rigorous approach to performance reviews before the transformation, and the existing data can be used to select who is let go. If not, the company likely needs to deploy a special assessment to objectively evaluate employees, and separate top, average, and poor performers. However it is accomplished, the selection process as layoffs begin must be as objective as possible, and the company must avoid any hint of favoritism or bias. The human resources and legal departments will help line managers get through this tricky time.

It's impossible to completely avoid pain during headcount reductions, but many companies seek to minimize the pain to the extent they can. Voluntary severance or early retirement programs might be options in certain cases to reduce involuntary reductions. (See "Managing Voluntary and Involuntary Separations.") For those let go, outplacement services can likewise be useful, both in lifting morale and in encouraging cooperation.

Managing Voluntary and Involuntary Separations

As companies proceed with the transformation journey, it is inevitable that some employees will be separated from the company. How these actions are handled can affect how the company is perceived by employees and the public. Most companies first and foremost want to ensure that people are treated fairly, but even within that guideline, a range of options are available.

You must first address how the separations will occur: over time through attrition, through voluntary separation programs, or through involuntary separation. Many companies institute a hiring freeze early on—even while still fact finding—to enable attrition to have the largest impact possible before taking other actions. In turnover-intensive areas, attrition may even allow companies to change much of the organization and the work rapidly enough to minimize further effects.

In many cases, however, the need for change is more urgent and it is not possible to reorganize based on voluntary attrition alone. If it is clear that further incentives will be required, some companies implement voluntary separation programs that feature cash payments, early or enhanced access to retirement or pension benefits, and continued medical benefits. Companies select voluntary options for one of two reasons. First, enabling employees to "opt in" will put the program and corresponding separations in a more positive light for employees and the community, as the decision to leave remains with the employee. Second, some companies with defined benefit plans are able to offer a voluntary early retirement package that minimizes up-front cash impact (but which may increase the company's pension benefit obligation).

On the downside, however, voluntary separation programs may lead to unexpected outcomes for the company. Acceptance rates of voluntary programs can range from 3 to 10 percent for voluntary severance and upward from 60 percent for early retirement, depending on the generosity of the package, employee engagement, and the perception of impending layoffs. Often the roles of some critical, high-performing employees who opt for voluntary separation will need to be backfilled. To mitigate such risks, it is possible to exclude certain employee groups from the voluntary package—such as those without whom the business cannot run or roles that are in high demand. Such exclusions are more probable in voluntary severance programs; defined benefit plans may have more regulatory restrictions on what can and cannot be done.

Involuntary programs are the fastest and most precise way to reduce headcount. They also come with choices, such as the type of package to offer and when and how to communicate management's intentions. Many companies have historical severance guidelines used in other involuntary exits, such as a fixed amount plus two weeks of salary per year of service.

When it comes to communication, regardless of the type of separation, it is critical to ensure employees are notified about impending downsizing at the right time and at the right level of detail. Communicating too much too soon will cause undesired attrition; too little too late will result in a major loss of employee goodwill. And in a voluntary scenario, people may feel threatened or forced into accepting a package. A good rule of thumb is to not announce any people actions until the organizational design is complete and you know exactly how many positions the new organization

(continued)

(continued)

will need by department. In cases of voluntary separation, it is customary to give employees 45 to 90 days to evaluate and accept the packages. In cases of involuntary separation, individuals should be notified as soon as decisions have been made. Retention bonuses may be offered to select critical employees to mitigate the risk of top performers proactively leaving or employees who will be laid off leaving before a natural transition point.

The costs to implement voluntary and involuntary separation options are not radically different, but they each offer trade-offs in the level of flexibility provided to employees, the level of complexity and administration required on the company's behalf, and the level of precision in addressing specific changes in the organization. Moreover, companies can use both options at the same time. Begin evaluating these options early, as programs can take months to design and eventually execute.

Around the same time that they are handling the departures of laid-off employees, managers should also begin the more intrinsically rewarding task of managing and motivating the remaining organization. The staff and managers who are still at the company need to know that their former colleagues were treated with dignity and respect, but more importantly—now that the focus is turning to the future—they need to understand their role in making the new organization a success. This is a big turning point in the transformation, both practically and emotionally. "As soon as people knew their options, they were able to say: 'Okay, it affects me,' 'It doesn't affect me,' or 'I've got to think about this,'" said one manager. "At that point, we were good. I mean really, we were good."

The forward-looking communication that is necessary once a transformation has reached this stage is not something that can be accomplished in one or two executive-run town hall meetings, important as those are. There also need to be targeted team discussions led by the immediate managers that the employees trust the most. This is the time to start implementing the new organizational structure, and to codify the decision-making process and how information will be shared and how incentives and motivators will be used to influence behavior. In other words, this is when everybody starts to execute the changes that were being talked about and worked on a few months earlier behind closed doors.

With most transformations, the changes that begin at this point, with new processes, new ways of doing business, and often a refined strategy, need to be jump-started in order to take hold. Corporate culture is an essential tool in making the changes of a transformation stick, with mechanisms like peer interactions and informal leaders reinforcing the most important new behaviors. How to do all of this is the subject of the next chapter, in which we discuss culture-led transformation, an approach that can add immensely to the success of a Fit for Growth transformation.

16 | The Human Element

Getting People Ready, Willing, and Able to Change

A Fit for Growth transformation asks a lot from all the employees in the company—from the CEO down to the most junior front-line employee. Once it's all said and done, many employees will have learned new processes and IT systems, and will be working with a new set of colleagues. Some will have stepped into altogether new roles, while others may have relocated to new offices. For almost all, there will be new expectations for performance, new measures, and new ways of working in a more cost-conscious organization.

But all the elegant plans to transform the organization will come to naught if the employees do not get on board with the transformation. Its ultimate success will hinge on how successfully employees adapt new ways of working. For that to happen, employees need to understand why such a big change is necessary in the first place, agree that *this* change is best for the company and for them personally, and be inspired by what the future promises.

"Change management" is an all too familiar concept for executives and managers. Indeed, large-scale initiatives such as Fit for Growth transformations do require thoughtful change management to help bring the employees along the transformation journey—to educate them on the what and the why of the change, train them on new processes and systems, and motivate them to sign up for the future. The basic change-management building blocks include leadership alignment, change impact assessment, stakeholder engagement, employee communications, training, and measurement and tracking.

These basic building blocks of change management are absolutely necessary during a Fit for Growth transformation, but they are not sufficient to ensure that change is adopted. For large-scale change to succeed, the leadership team needs to work with and within their company's culture to motivate and mobilize the employees. Yet some executives assume that a rational explanation of the need for change, backed up by facts, catchy slogans, and well-crafted memos will be enough to convince employees—that if leaders simply make the case clearly and strongly enough, people will be motivated to act in the organization's best interest. These same leaders also tend to focus only on the rational and formal aspects of the organization—like governance, process, and structure—that are familiar and easy to see. But they forget about the emotional and informal aspects of the organization, which play an essential role in how people behave. These emotional and informal aspects are embedded in the company's culture—the self-sustaining patterns of behaviors, thoughts, feelings, and beliefs that determine "how we do things around here."

Those on the front lines have to embrace the change, and to get them on board and keep them on board, you have to enlist your organization's culture and leverage what works within your culture. The Fit for Growth journey will require employees to change not only what they *do* but how they *behave* on a day-to-day basis. That is a considerable ask, and it will go unanswered unless you are able to put your culture to work.

Leveraging the culture throughout the transformation—in making the case for change, building alignment among leaders, communicating the plan to the broader organization, and driving acceptance and enthusiasm—can accelerate the transformation, deepen its impact, and increase the likelihood that the changes will succeed and be sustained. A recent PwC Strategy& survey of more than 2,200 executives and managers about change management programs[1] showed that the number of informal elements brought to bear throughout the transformation significantly increases the transformation's success and sustainability. Respondents who leveraged the existing culture throughout the transformation were more than twice as likely to deliver sustainable change as those who didn't.

Thus, the Fit for Growth transformation approach emphasizes culture-led and behavior-based change. A company's culture holds within it a tremendous source of emotional energy, which can either hinder or catalyze large-scale change. The transformation needs to build on the company's existing organizational and cultural strengths. Mind you, it's not about *changing* the culture—a company's culture is its basic personality, and changing it takes several years, even decades, far beyond the time horizon of the transformation. Instead, it's about *harnessing* the positive aspects (which every culture does have) and emotional forces in the existing culture to motivate and mobilize people around the task at hand—the business of transforming the company for the good of all.

Elements of a Culture-Led Change Management Program

The work of change management is ultimately about helping employees adapt to new ways of working. Employees make the transition from the current state to the future state in four stages, in which they move from becoming *ready* for change to becoming *willing*, *able*, and *committed* to the transformation. In the first stage, to become ready, employees first need to be *aware* of the change coming their way and understand it. In the second phase, to become willing to change, they need to be motivated. The case for change and the future state of the company must be broadly compelling to them, and individual employees must be inspired by the future-state vision and be able to see themselves as part of it. While sticks—like threats of job loss or career derailment—can "motivate" people, carrots—the promise of a better future for themselves, their colleagues, the company, and their communities—are more likely to truly energize them to adapt the change.

In the third stage, to adapt to the change, employees need the requisite knowledge, skills, and competencies. They will need to be educated on the new processes and IT systems, and be equipped to demonstrate the new expected behaviors. In the fourth and final stage, to become committed to the transformation, employees must fully embrace the change and demonstrate the new ways of working. They are incentivized and recognized for demonstrating the new behaviors.

To help employees traverse the path of becoming ready, willing, able, and—ultimately—committed to change, the transformation team must employ the following change management elements.

Align Leaders

Leaders must own the transformation and thoughtfully steer the organization through it, providing the right levels of inspiration, action, and pacing. Change will be very difficult if people in formal positions of power talk or act in ways that do not visibly and actively support the transformation; being neutral won't cut it. In times of change, employees naturally look to their mentors and direct supervisors for honest information about "what this means" to the team and to them personally—as well as for motivation to "get on board." So an effective transformation effort will anticipate this need and prepare leaders at all levels to manage through their own personal change journey so they can authentically demonstrate their commitment and "walk the talk" as the transformation plan is developed and executed.

Communicate Changes

Change communications are typically aimed at creating *awareness* and *understanding* through a wide variety of methods, such as formal executive communications (memos, e-mails, and videos), conference calls, town-hall presentations, staff meeting discussions, one-on-one meetings, employee newsletters, FAQs, conference calls, and many others. During a major transformation, however, the changes are so sweeping, and such large shifts in behavior are required, that communications need to drive *acceptance* and *adoption* as well. Leaders can make communications more effective by leveraging the culture. Transformation leaders should therefore plan from the start to make communication programs people focused and encourage participation and a two-way dialogue. They should use formal methods such as official memos from the CEO, a transformation intranet site, or town halls with open question and answer sessions, and informal methods such as informal conversations with mentors and peer coaching. Last, it is important to measure on an ongoing basis how well the messages being communicated are actually being interpreted, and, if necessary, to clarify and adjust the messages to make them more relatable to the organization.

Engage Stakeholders

There is no silver bullet for getting all your employees thinking and feeling the "right" way. Because the employee population is not uniform, each person will interpret and react to what is happening differently, depending on their role, function, location, age, previous experience, and myriad other factors. Change affects each employee segment differently, so a stakeholder engagement plan is needed to educate and motivate each employee segment. In addition, personalized impact assessments and engagement plans need to be developed for executives, so their issues are addressed directly, they can be true champions of the transformation, and they can bring along employees who look up to them.

Train Employees

Getting your employees to believe in the objective of the change is only part of the journey. Helping them learn how to change, what to do, and not be paralyzed by uncertainty requires targeted training and patience. In order to change, employees will need extensive training in new skills and capabilities, processes, and systems. Such extensive training often requires not a one-time day-long session, but rather a hands-on immersion experience in which managers lead by example on the job. A skillful combination of the training delivered in formal sessions, combined with informal peer guidance and direct manager coaching, is invaluable for helping employees learn from mentors and peers.

Drive New Behaviors

Change becomes sustainable when culture enables the transformation, rather than hindering it. As discussed, however, culture cannot change swiftly and on demand to perfectly align with the aims of your transformation program. The key is to focus instead on a *critical few* behaviors—behaviors that some people demonstrate regularly now; that would make the transformation smoother, speedier, and more successful; and that would lead to tangible business results if everyone adopted them. The focus is on *behaviors* because the culture—what people feel, think, and believe—is reflected in and shaped by daily behaviors. The focus is on a *few* critical behaviors because changing behaviors is difficult, and trying to change more than a handful at the same time is an impossible task. When everyone in the organization focuses on these critical few behaviors, they are able to act their way into a new way of thinking, while seeing rapid, tangible results.

As we have discussed in earlier chapters, Fit for Growth transformations unfold over three phases, each with its own purpose and focus. In each phase there are distinct change management activities to plan and execute, from developing the case for change, understanding its impact on employees, crafting detailed engagement plans, to execution and making the change the new normal (see Figure 16.1). We will discuss the change management work during each phase in turn.

SUMMARY OF TRANSFORMATION PROGRAM ELEMENTS

Program elements	Phase 1: Diagnostic and case for change	Phase 2: Detailed design	Phase 3: Execution
Focus on change management	Align the leadership on the case for change	Prepare for the change	Facilitate the change
Change management actions	Develop case for change	Prepare leaders to champion change	Roll out communications
	Align leadership	Assess stakeholder impact and develop engagement plan	Deliver training
	Assess cultural strengths and derailers	Identify critical few behaviors	Engage employee segments
		Develop communications plan	Translate behaviors into actions
		Identify training needs	Measure adoption

Source: PwC Strategy&

Figure 16.1

Phase 1: Diagnostic and Case for Change

To recap, Phase 1 of the transformation focuses on identifying the opportunity and defining the direction and focus areas for the Fit for Growth transformation. This is a time when a small, focused team is working closely with executive leaders to assess the organization and cost structure, set a target for the overall transformation, identify opportunities and quick wins, and develop the road map to achieve the goal. In parallel, the team lays the foundation for the culture-led change management effort by developing a case for change that the management team will stand behind and that will resonate with the average employee. The team also needs to assess the company culture in order to understand which aspects are strengths to be leveraged, and which are obstacles that could derail the transformation.

Develop the Case for Change

To capture the hearts and minds of your employees, you need to build a case for change that is both rationally and emotionally compelling. A good case for change outlines the rational explanation for the transformation, explaining the driver for the change (why are we doing this?) and its purpose (what are our goals?). It also sketches a picture of the future state (what will change and what will not change?), and makes the benefits tangible (what will this mean for employees, customers, and the company as a whole?). A better case for change, however, goes beyond the rational explanation to encompass emotional factors—it is aspirational and motivating as well as logical. In addition to discussing financial objectives (such as revenue growth and margin improvement), it appeals to shared sources of pride (such as service to customers, industry leadership, and company mission, values, or history), recognizes the company's strengths and accomplishments, and paints a vivid picture of a future that people want to be a part of.

At one U.S. health system, for example, profits were falling as new competitors entered its markets, and margins were pressured following the enactment of federal healthcare reform. To shore up the bottom line, the CEO initially cut costs across the board. This stemmed the profit declines to some extent, but also negatively affected investments in patient experience—which in turn caused an uproar within the organization. Recognizing that systemwide cost cutting was not a sustainable long-term solution, the CEO launched a Fit for Growth transformation. He defined the case for change around the two primary sources of employee pride: helping patients live better lives, and being an industry leader. He made the case for putting the health system on a solid footing, which would enable the system to continue serving its communities, reinvesting into the patient experience, and reclaiming its historical leadership position. These aspirations all connected emotionally with the employees, who were vested in the well-being of their patients and proud to be part of "the best health system" in their region.

Assess the Culture

In Phase 1, you baseline and diagnose the key qualities of the existing culture using a combination of interviews, focus groups, and surveys to identify the cultural traits that make the company tick. Understanding the emotional forces that drive the company will be helpful in evaluating the potential difficulty of realizing specific transformation opportunities. A company typically has four to six dominant cultural traits. These traits have both positive and negative implications. For example, a company with a strong entrepreneurial trait may be great at identifying and capturing market opportunities but may be challenged when driving cross-organizational enterprise initiatives from the top down, as entrepreneurial managers may bristle at their "freedom" being taken away. The team can develop aspirational cultural traits based on the current cultural traits, emphasizing strengths while mitigating challenges. For example, a company that is very purpose focused could tap into employees' emotional commitment to the mission (e.g., saving patients' lives for a health system) to connect the transformation goals to that overarching organizational purpose.

One multinational energy infrastructure company included a full-on cultural diagnostic for its transformation program during Phase 1. Leadership knew that marketplace dynamics meant the transformation would need to accomplish radical changes, but they also knew that the company had changed very little over its history, and worried employees would resist. One "aha!" moment came when the analysis revealed executives knew only half the picture about the company's culture. For example, before the diagnostic, leaders felt "we don't have a culture"—or that it was very fragmented and distinct across divisions, with no unifying traits or commonalities across. To the contrary, the diagnostic revealed that there *were* some common threads, sources of pride and root causes of the operating model dysfunction. The intensity or expression varied from group to group but the essence of culture traits were strongly similar, with useful insights on what people were proud of that could be leveraged to drive change.

In addition, the diagnostic revealed attitudes toward particular cultural themes by level. There was a big difference between leaders and front-line employees. Some things that leaders were proud of were seen as problems by the front line. Senior managers, for example, were proud of being entrepreneurial and willing to do "whatever it takes, at any cost" to meet their objective. But the front line viewed this kind of behavior as perpetuating silos and discouraging collaboration. This provided useful guidance on ways leaders would need to role model new behaviors.

Align Leadership

The transformation team and company leadership need to align on the transformation vision, objectives, and opportunities early in the process, so that they will be ready to drive the transformation throughout its duration, and will be motivating spokespersons and sponsors who will bring the broader organization with them. They must be unified, aligned, and committed to transforming the company. But that's rarely, if ever, easy. Some well-intentioned executives will find the change unnatural, no matter how hard they try. Some others will lack the capabilities, mindset, and willpower to execute the program. A few will resist if the change challenges their power and status.

Aligning the leadership will likely take the duration of the entire Phase 1, and then some. The CEO and the few other early zealots will have to bring along the rest of the executive team, while recognizing some may never make it through and need to part ways. Alignment is never achieved in one meeting or conversation; it needs to be built over time. The three of four formal steering committee meetings during Phase 1 are the first vehicle to establish alignment; reviewing the facts and debating options with peers will convince some of the executives. Yet those three or four meetings will not be sufficient for all; some others will need one-on-one, candid conversations with their trusted peers and the CEO. They need to air their concerns and be heard: "Will we break the company? Will this really be good for the employees? Do we really have the stomach to pull this off?" While the facts may be clear, these leaders need to come to terms with the implications on their own terms. This is where the CEO and the executive sponsors make a difference: understanding where each executive stands rationally and emotionally on the transformation, and "lobbying" them to convert them to zealots.

By the end of Phase 1, there is usually a public commitment to the change. For example, one CEO asked each of her reports directly in the final Phase 1 steering committee meeting two simple questions: "Do you believe in this change and will you move forward with me?" All but one said yes; the one outlier declared he did not agree with the direction and he could not do it. Shortly after the meeting, he voluntarily resigned and cleared the way for the change.

Phase 2: Detailed Design

The change management focus in Phase 2 turns to supporting the transformation's design teams as they design sustainable solutions and develop an integrated transformation plan. The change work in Phase 2 goes through a natural shift. Early on there is little information, so it's much more about continuing executive stakeholder engagement and leadership alignment, and guiding the design teams to consider and capture change implications. About halfway through, as the future state emerges and the changes are more defined, the focus shifts to understanding employee impact and developing the change plans: stakeholder engagement plan, communications strategy and plan, training plan, identification of critical few behaviors, and approach to measuring and tracking change adoption.

Prepare for the Change

The hard work of leadership alignment that began in Phase 1 continues into Phase 2. At this stage, the leadership should be largely aligned on the transformation themes. The focus at this point turns to bringing on any stragglers, and aligning on and testing the signaling behaviors the leaders are adopting to demonstrate their commitment to the transformation goals. The number of individuals involved with the transformation is still a small percentage of the workforce at this stage, but they are often the very people who are respected and can informally influence their peers as they demonstrate the critical few behaviors in their day-to-day work on the transformation team.

In addition to the executive leaders with formal authority, this is when authentic informal leaders (AILs) should be identified and brought into the transformation. These are people who may be at lower levels in the organization, possibly without formal management roles or authority, but are looked upon as role models and trusted sources by others. They already demonstrate the future state's cultural traits and critical few behaviors—they personify the positive elements of the company's culture. Since they are visible to others, they can play a quite powerful role in motivating those around them to understand and accept change and adopt new behaviors.

Stakeholder Engagement

Early in Phase 2, you need to understand the key stakeholders and how they view the upcoming transformation. Many of these stakeholders will either directly execute the planned changes or be influential in how they are accepted broadly in the organization. Hence you need to understand who is affected and how, and determine what you need to do with them: who are the zealots, and who can be your allies? How can you get them to be ambassadors for change? On the other hand, who are the opposition leaders? What do they oppose and why? And how can their opposition be overcome?

Stakeholders are segmented by degree of influence (in the outcome) and level of change required (by the change program). The segmentation helps prioritize stakeholders to address the concerns of critical stakeholders first while highlighting allies to enlist in spreading the change (see Figure 16.2).

Once the initial segmentation is done, the team needs to develop a stakeholder engagement plan, in particular for those who face significant change but are not yet supportive. The plan typically documents the concerns of the stakeholder, how to address those concerns, and who should engage the stakeholder and how. Each engagement is documented with clear next steps until the stakeholder moves to the "supportive" category.

EXAMPLE STAKEHOLDER SEGMENTATION

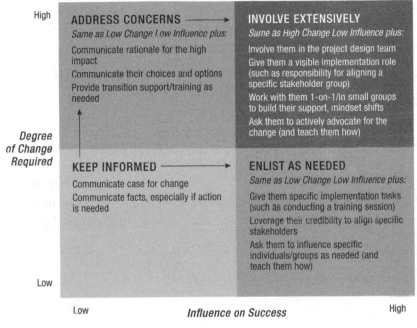

Figure 16.2

Employee Impact Assessment

As Phase 2 moves further along and the future state begins to solidify, how employees will be affected also emerges. You need to identify how various employee segments will be affected by the change, so they can tailor engagement, communications, training, and behavior change plans to help employees transition to the future state.

The impact assessment begins by segmenting employees into natural categories. Segmentation should be informed by the transformation changes, and is typically driven by roles, functions, business lines, and geographies—call center agents in U.S. offices, for example, or field sales reps, or finance managers and analysts focused on planning and analysis. Impact is defined as changes to roles and responsibilities, locations, processes, tools, skills and knowledge, behaviors, and performance. The impact assessment should be conducted by the transformation workstream teams that are designing the

EXAMPLE OF STAKEHOLDER IMPACT ASSESSMENT

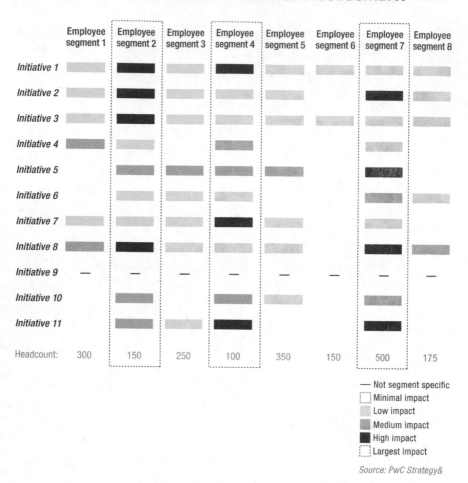

— Not segment specific
☐ Minimal impact
▨ Low impact
▨ Medium impact
■ High impact
⌶ Largest impact

Source: PwC Strategy&

Figure 16.3

future state organization and processes, as they will be in the best position to articulate the impact (see Figure 16.3).

Once the nature and magnitude of the impact by employee segment is understood, the transformation team can move to develop targeted plans.

Communications and Engagement Plan

You develop the communications and engagement plan during Phase 2. The work initially focuses on developing a "core message platform," which builds general awareness of the program, introduces the key concepts and reinforces key messages, articulates why change is needed, and instills a sense of urgency. It also includes external messaging to prepare responses for media inquiries and to communicate the cost savings targets to investor and internal communities. The message platform forms the single source from which the many more detailed communications that follow will be developed.

As Phase 2 progresses and employee impact is understood, detailed communications and employee engagement plans are developed. The engagement plan defines the actions and messages that will engage and mobilize each employee segment through the execution. It is informed by the employee impact analysis, and must be tailored to each employee segment, working with and leveraging the company's culture for maximum effect. It defines in detail the first few engagements with an employee segment: who engages, what are the key messages, what is communicated, what are the follow-ups.

There is a critical set of engagements during Phase 2 with the middle-management population. Middle managers are often the management team tasked with driving changes in the execution phase, and the quality of their leadership and their adoption of the change can make or break the transformation. This is a segment, however, that can be quite resistant to change: some of our clients refer to middle managers as the "calcified middle"—highlighting how stuck in their ways many of them can be. They are used to running their organizations and processes a certain way; they were promoted to their roles because they demonstrated the behaviors relevant in the current organization, and they expected that continuing to do what they have done would advance their careers in the future. Then along comes a change initiative, and they are told to forget much of what got them where they are, and instead to learn new ways of working.

In our experience, successful initiatives engage these middle managers *during* Phase 2—not after the fact. Early in the phase, detailed design workstreams engage these middle managers to understand how things work today and where the issues are, through one-on-one interviews or focus groups. As the work advances, the workstream leads engage the middle managers on jointly developing solutions or refining the workstream team's proposals. In this way, potential issues are addressed up front to ensure the design is robust. In addition, the middle managers see that their voices are being heard and that their contributions are valued.

Another aspect of engagement is selecting the transformation team, which becomes very important to the success of the program in Phase 2. Ideally, the workstream leaders are chosen because of their credibility in the organization, content expertise, and interpersonal skills. At this point, they leverage their credibility, knowledge, and skills to effectively engage the middle managers.

The communications plan is a subset of the overall employee engagement plan. It includes a granular list of communications to be delivered throughout the transformation. The plan should include, by employee segment: communication objectives, employee segment concerns, core messages, communication methods, and timing (see Figure 16.4).

For example, a retailer built a comprehensive engagement and communications plan to help employees transition to deliver a stronger customer experience. The retailer developed tailored plans for major employee segments in the stores: managers, assistant managers, and hourly employees. The engagement began with cascading conference calls with the leadership: from divisional presidents to regional VPs to district managers to store managers. First, the store managers verbally informed their employees of the high-level changes. Then, within several days, district managers delivered detailed communications to groups of store managers in "awareness presentations." After the presentations, the district managers had one-on-one meetings with their store managers to discuss how the performance expectations and bonus plans would change to reinforce the desired customer experience. The store managers then disseminated the information to their employees in store meetings, leveraging talking points, hand-outs, and job aids. Several weeks later, store managers received more targeted communications and training on the changes to specific processes.

This plan was informed by—and leveraged—the retailer's culture. The overall messaging explained why the change was necessary to improve the customer experience—something many of the store employees felt strongly about. The cascading messaging respected the hierarchical nature of the company and allowed managers to connect with their direct reports in more informal settings. The more challenging conversations were handled one on one between a manager and the employee, again in complete alignment with the company's culture.

EXAMPLE OF A COMMUNICATIONS PLAN

Channel	Content Overview	Target Audience
Town Hall	Inform all employees of the new operating model, new ways of working, and go-forward plan	Entire Organization by location
Road Show	Visit geographical hubs to inform about and discuss new operating model, new ways of working, and go-forward plan	Employees by location
E-mails	Inform all employees of the new operating model, new ways of working, and go-forward plan Address questions (e.g., FAQs), recap the changes, acknowledge the challenges, and explain the path forward	Entire Organization
Functional All Hands	Inform employees how the function is specifically changing, how it impacts individuals, and the new expected behaviors Provide employees the opportunity to ask questions	All Function Employees
Coffee Chats	Informal discussion with employees by function to discuss new org structure and future of the function	All Function Employees
Teleconferences	Inform employees how the function is specifically changing, how it impacts individuals, and the new expected behaviors	All Function Employees
Leadership Meeting	Update on the progress made by functions to date and any challenges	Leadership Team
Blog	Provide organization-wide update on the project and address most pressing questions regarding the change	Entire Organization
Video	Inform all employees of the new operating model, new ways of working, and go-forward plan	Entire Organization
Company Newsletter	Inform employees of how the organization is specifically changing and the new expected behaviors	Entire Organization

Source: PwC Strategy&

Figure 16.4

Training Plan

An important part of Phase 2 is to identify future training needs and develop the road map for an integrated training plan to support the new workforce skills, behaviors, and performance the transformation will require. Training will be needed to provide the employees with the knowledge and skills they need to perform their new jobs (e.g., around the new processes or how to use new systems), improve leadership or interpersonal skills, and adapt new behaviors.

The training plan should be developed top-down, reflecting the overall program needs, and bottom-up, reflecting the individual work-stream needs. The top-down training needs are identified by the PMO and the change management team, and cover training that enables the overall program, such as critical behavior changes. The bottom-up training needs are identified by individual workstreams, as part of the stakeholder impact assessment. These needs tend to be more granular, both in the specific training need as well at the audience affected, such as training retail bank-branch associates to use a new customer relationship management application.

The learning and development organization should gather all these requests and develop a comprehensive training road map at the end of Phase 2 and early in Phase 3. The training plan needs to be coordinated with the overall execution road map and communications and employee engagement plan.

The retailer we mentioned earlier developed and executed a three-year learning and development agenda to enable store employees to deliver a better customer experience. In the first year, the training agenda was designed to educate employees on a core set of customer experience behaviors and process changes in the stores, such as how to help a customer who seems to be searching for a product. In addition, the managers received leadership and performance management training so they were better equipped to coach and guide their employees. In the second year, the training targeted store managers and focused on sustainability of the trans-formation. The managers enhanced their skills in developing their teams and learned about driving customer behaviors. The third and final year delivered additional training on customer experience behaviors that were not being adapted in the stores and needed reinforcement.

Culture Impacts and Critical Behaviors

During Phase 2, the transformation goals developed in Phase 1 need to be filtered against the insights gained from the cultural assessment.

Transformation opportunities that sound great on paper, for example, may be tremendously difficult to implement due to emotional sources of resistance—they may be viewed as counter to the culture and values of the people in the organization. While this does not mean that an opportunity should not be pursued, you should use culture as a lens through which to evaluate opportunities. For example, in an entrepreneurial company where individual managers have significant power, creating shared services and consolidating resources away from local managers will likely run counter to the culture and will be an uphill battle. If the improvement opportunity is significant enough, the executive team can still choose to pursue it, but with eyes wide open for the potential cultural challenges to be addressed. Understanding the culture allows smart decision making in the near term and can avoid setbacks as the transformation moves into the implementation phase.

Phase 2 is also when the transformation team identifies the critical few behaviors that will have the most impact on the change effort, by drawing from the aspirational cultural traits developed during Phase 1. For example, if the transformation requires the company to focus more on execution speed than getting to a "perfect" solution each time, critical behaviors should focus on making the right trade-offs between perfection and speed. How many critical behaviors should a company aim to adopt? Usually three is a good number; focusing on a few allows energy to be spent where it matters most.

These high-level behavioral themes, however, must be translated for specific functions or teams within the company, and by role and level. Critical behaviors can manifest in simple ways, such as requiring that memos be kept to one page or less, or stipulating that leaders from two separate functions be present whenever a key decision is made.

For example, at a consumer packaged goods company focused on better managing trade spending, the transformation team identified a critical behavior to be "collaborating to work through unfamiliar situations and iterate on solutions." This was important for the company because the current practices of continually rehashing and escalating reasons for why an idea or approach would not work were resulting in significant rework time for whole teams. Eliminating this wasted time was a critical enabler to the success of the transformation. Leaders chose to signal this in two ways: first, by explicitly using part of every team meeting to collaborate on solutions to new trade-spending problems, and second, by actively and publicly making key decisions on those solutions within two weeks (rather than months).

Phase 3: Execution

In Phase 3, as the execution gets underway, plans developed meticulously in Phase 2 are rolled out to the broader organization and put into action. This is where change management gets into high gear: communicating detailed changes to the organization at large, delivering training, driving behavior changes, tracking change adoption, and intervening where needed.

Leadership Engagement

Senior leaders need to be engaged and visible throughout the execution. But in many transformations, once the design is finished and the direction set, leaders re-focus on other priorities, making them invisible or absent to the average employee. Instead, their roles should expand to include responsibilities for communications, engagement, and role-modeling the critical few behaviors. Senior leaders should use the core messaging to deliver consistent messages in their own voice—to "talk the talk"—and make sure their next-level leaders can do the same at the appropriate time to engage the broader organization. Leaders should connect on a regular basis, at least monthly, to discuss employee feedback and the challenges they are facing.

Even more important than talking the talk is walking the talk by using role modeling. As part of the process of getting to acceptance and adoption, people usually look beyond the words they're hearing to the actions they're seeing from their leaders. This makes it critical that leaders at all levels behave consistently with the transformation goals and messaging.

Critical Few Behaviors

In Phase 3, the critical few behaviors identified in the earlier phases are translated into specific actions at different levels of the organization and for key groups of employees. Leadership demonstrates signaling behaviors that show commitment to the goals. Middle managers role-model the critical few behaviors that in turn encourage the front line to adopt them. For example, a critical behavior may involve having explicit conversations about trade-offs among quality, speed, and budget. Leadership can signal this behavior by defining principles behind acceptable trade-offs and emphasizing when to prioritize each consideration. Managers can role-model the behavior by sharing stories during team meetings of appropriate trade-offs and impact on results. The job of front-line managers and employees then is to proactively identify trade-offs and risks and initiate discussions around them.

You can facilitate the adoption of critical behaviors by incorporating the culture insights distilled in Phases 1 and 2 and using a combination of formal and informal communications to instill the new behaviors throughout the organization. For example, a North American energy company launched a transformation that defined a new way of doing business. Underlying these changes was an important culture shift: to push for a performance culture in which employees would hold one another accountable for performance. Leaders prioritized four enterprise-wide performance behaviors: to apply a "can-do" mindset to execution, to take an enterprise-wide perspective, to demonstrate active accountability, and to develop the company's people. Within each business unit, top leaders and small groups of authentic informal leaders came together to translate these four behaviors into local behaviors— for example, translating what "active accountability" would look like in the company's utilities business versus its generation business, or at different levels. The CEO introduced the behaviors in a firm-wide webcast, and each business-unit leader followed up with their teams, including a series of "critical conversations" with their direct reports. These behaviors were later embedded into the performance review system company-wide.

Informal Leaders

Your network of AILs is expanded and rolled out in Phase 3, to spread the critical few behaviors and catalyze a viral movement to accelerate adoption and acceptance. The transformation team members themselves are the quintessential "early adopter" type of AIL. They usually go through their own journey from basic awareness to commitment to the transformation effort, and along the way become enthusiastic supporters and adopters of the transformation principles and behaviors. When the execution phase begins, their personal journeys can be compelling stories and points of influence for their peers as the wider network of AILs throughout the firm are engaged. You can use many methods to identify AILs, including scouting potential candidates via regular project interactions and forums, crowdsourcing nominations (and then conducting interviews to validate), or leveraging organizational network-analysis data.

We have worked with AILs in a variety of ways: to provide insight about the culture and what behaviors are likely to lead to success, to spread messages virally, to help overcome cynicism about the change, and to enlist others to join the movement. They can serve as role models at all levels of the company, and the fact that they already display the desired behaviors serves to reduce resistance around change.

Delivering Communications

As execution begins, communications focus on helping people adopt new behaviors, showcasing wins and exemplars, creating a storyline that artic-ulates and reinforces the key topics and messages, making strategic linkages to tangible transformation activities, and reinforcing the critical few behaviors. The dedicated engagement and communications mechanisms developed in Phase 2 are rolled out, and communications required by program work-streams are added to inform employees of specific changes and impacts. New mechanisms such as advisory councils—made up of people who represent stakeholders who are not part of the transformation team—can provide feedback on what people want to know and what they're are worried about, and how the messaging will be received. It is important to ensure that the communication is not a one-way lecture, but a two-way dialogue with both sides listening and asking questions.

Delivering Training

Communications are a great tool to educate people on what is happening, what is expected of them, and when it will happen. However, communi-cations alone do not arm an employee with the skills they need to be successful in a new model. Training must be delivered in a timely manner as the organization, processes, and systems change to ensure a smooth transition to new ways of working. At this point, diligent impact assessment, engage-ment and planning, and training-plan development combine to pay divi-dends by addressing the most critical new skill needs that arise out of the transformation. The timing of training should be aligned with the timing of the changes themselves, often preceding the change. For example, employ-ees need training to be able to transition to a new process with new workflows, or to new IT systems.

Many organizations have operations training and HR learning and development departments, which are leveraged in transformations to develop and deliver the training needed. Depending on the nature and magnitude of training, these departments may need to be supplemented by short-term external training services. Often, a "train the trainer" approach is followed, where the central training team trains the managers of departments, who then train their employees in a cascading approach. Beyond helping with scalability, this approach also reinforces the overall change message, by having managers own the change and lead their teams.

Measuring Change Adoption

You need to monitor behavior adoption and gauge the impact of behaviors and culture evolution so that the transformation team can assess and adapt—to find out what's working or not, adjust next steps to ensure the change sticks, and continue to lead the change until new behaviors are embedded. When organizations think about assessing traditional change management efforts, they often don't progress much beyond assessing awareness and understanding. Because transformations require fundamental shifts in behaviors—and therefore more emphasis on acceptance, adoption, and commitment—the approach to measurement needs to shift as well to include a broader suite of monitoring and tracking activities and tools, including monitoring and measurement of leadership activities, communications and engagement plans, effectiveness, and the overall success of the transformation. Thoughtful measurement of adoption will help the organization identify when certain communications need to be reinforced, when a critical assumption did not pan out as expected, or when additional training may be required.

Success of a Fit for Growth transformation hinges on how well employees adapt to new ways of working and change their behaviors. The changes called for are almost always large and will not be accepted by employees naturally; they will need a proactive, well-planned, and coherent change management approach to help them transition from the old to the new. Beyond simple communications and training, the change effort needs to embrace the organization's culture to be as effective as possible.

Large-scale change does not happen overnight, or even over months. The key is to stay focused on outcomes and on helping your organization—and to keep nudging in the right direction.

17 | Staying Fit for Growth

It used to be that a business transformation was a once-in-a-lifetime event, the sort of fundamental reset prompted by a rare, short-lived disruption—such as a new technology, a devastating scandal, or a dramatic shift in costs. But if recent events in our global economy have revealed anything, it's that change truly is constant. Companies of all sizes, in all industries, are operating in a more volatile, less predictable environment. To navigate successfully, companies must repeatedly transform themselves—indeed, institutionalize the capacity to change themselves—again and again, as market conditions require.

Very few companies are competent at doing this, and not for lack of trying. Our research suggests that less than half of all performance transformation initiatives actually achieve their goals. Even when companies see the need, mobilize their forces accordingly, and act with good intentions, the overall capacity to seize an opportunity or dramatically cut costs—and then *sustain* that performance benefit—is simply not there.

For all the attention these efforts get within their companies, the positive impact tends to be short-lived, as individuals revert to past behaviors and spending habits. No organization can operate indefinitely in transformation mode; as normalcy returns, so too do costs and headcount. The program management office is disbanded; the "best and brightest" who staffed the various workstreams return to their normal duties—and the urgency and strict oversight that characterized the company at the height of a Fit for Growth program naturally subside.

So, how do you keep the spirit alive? How do you create a cost-conscious culture like the one we described at IKEA in Chapter 1, where everyone is proud to declare, "Our employees spend the company's money as if it were their own"? In such a true "ownership culture," cost consciousness becomes an organizational capability and a shared mindset, rather than a bunch of rules that are resented and resisted. Even when no one is watching, employees treat every spending decision as if the money came from their own pocket.

We believe there are four primary sets of levers available to senior leaders when it comes to stimulating such a cost-conscious mindset and culture, and they map to the Fit for Growth principles we introduced in Chapter 2. (See Figure 17.1.) The first are *strategic* levers and involve tying the planning and budgeting process more closely to your strategy so that resources are reallocated to your differentiating capabilities. The second are *operational* levers you can apply to align your cost structure to your strategy on a continuous basis. The third are *organizational* levers you can pull to motivate and empower employees to act in the company's best financial interest on a day-to-day basis. Last, there are *cultural* levers that help reinforce a value system that encourages cost-conscious behaviors over the long haul. The first two can be described as rewiring the institutional "hardware" of your company; the latter two, recoding its "software."

Strategic Levers: Translating Strategy into Performance

As we've noted, most companies cannot sustain the energy—and hence results—of a programmatic cost transformation effort. It's treated as a contained event, and when the objective or deadline is reached, things "return to normal."

FIT FOR GROWTH LEVERS TO DRIVE SUSTAINABILITY

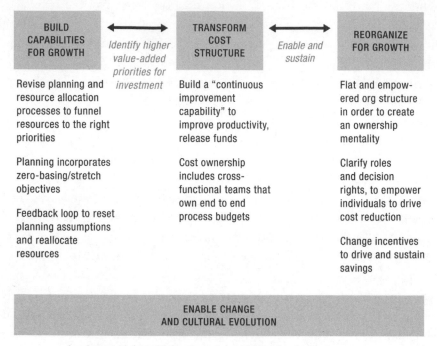

Figure 17.1

We find many companies do not effectively align performance with their strategy through a robust business planning and performance management system, and as a result strategy development and resource allocation become decoupled. Managers cannot confidently commit capital to unfulfilled or unfulfillable objectives and capabilities. Moreover, the company cannot make good portfolio management decisions, as it can't accurately assess if a business is worth more to shareholders or to outside buyers.

Revise Resource Allocation to Funnel Investment to Strategic Priorities

The need to reallocate resources to your strategic capabilities and highest-growth businesses is constant. Otherwise, investment will drift back to your established, mature businesses—your "cash cows" or, worse, your "dogs"—those with the most entrenched lobbying power and resources in the existing system.

The way to keep your resource allocation focused on priority, high-growth opportunities (i.e., aligned with your strategy) is to marry your financial planning and budgeting process and systems to your strategic planning process, so that they are fully synchronized on an ongoing basis. What happens during a cost transformation program—that is, cutting costs in lights-on and table-stakes capabilities and redirecting them toward differentiating capabilities—must happen on an ongoing basis through the annual budgeting and in-year resource allocation processes.

Zero-basing budgets, as we detailed in Chapter 6, is one way to level the playing field, so that investment dollars are redirected from mature and declining businesses to strategic growth priorities. In general, financial systems should create more transparency around "good" costs—those associated with differentiating capabilities—and dispensable "bad" costs. Strengthen your budgeting process to have explicit discussions around the spending levels for differentiating, table-stakes, and lights-on capabilities, and whether each set of capabilities receives the "right" amount of resources. Refine your resource allocation capability—for example, with new "business case" templates that bring transparency and new decision-making roles that ensure the right people are at the table to ensure investment decisions are in sync with your capability choices and strategy.

Adopt a Dynamic "Sense and Adjust" Planning Process

Leading-edge companies are increasingly investing in building "sense and adjust" capabilities to anticipate rather than merely respond to business transformation triggers. As the name implies, this dynamic approach allows companies to deftly modify business planning as economic and market conditions warrant. The aim is to completely avoid the wrenching effects of a transformation.

The *sensing* part of the planning process continuously gathers and analyzes data to understand current and future business conditions, and, importantly, translate these inputs into likely outcomes. It leverages existing baseline planning information—what's currently captured in strategic and operating plans—and synthesizes it with key performance data to form a single "dashboard" of actionable information for subject matter experts and business leads throughout the company.

Adjusting is the tandem part of process that alters the business based on sensed outcomes. Functional and business leads assess resource and capability trade-offs and their impact on people, processes, and technology, and develop a consensus on what strategy to pursue in order to build or maintain competitive position. As the adjustments are made, the sensing capability picks up again and continues the cycle, by scanning the horizon for market shifts and monitoring the execution of these flexible responses. Sensing does little good in the absence of adjusting, and vice versa. The two parts of the cycle complete each other and must be deployed in concert to be effective.

Unlike the traditional annual planning and budgeting process, in which business units are summoned every year to present their take on the market and their performance expectations, the sense-and-adjust process is continuous. It is always incorporating new information and translating that into adjusted outcomes and expectations.

Some of the world's leading companies have successfully developed full-fledged sense-and-adjust capability systems that constantly translate market signals into business and associated organizational adjustments. They have mature, advanced planning processes and deep leadership bench strength, as management has grown up in a sense-and-adjust environment. This is not to say that these companies are never caught flat-footed, but they generally see megatrends before they hit.

To support sustainable business transformation, a sense-and-adjust capability cannot reside purely in the planning functions; it must be inculcated throughout the organization. While strategic planning may lead the sensing part of the cycle, it must link directly to execution capabilities and organization design to drive the necessary adjustments.

Operational Levers: Executing Against the Plan

It's in the execution that so many good strategic intentions are derailed. Having gone to the trouble of developing a strategic cost management plan, too few companies actually track and enforce performance against it. Therefore, they fail to address and contain the inevitable cost creep until it becomes endemic to the system once again.

Ask a typical middle manager what causes him or her the greatest angst on a daily basis, and their immediate, unguarded answer may well be the planning, budgeting, and performance review cycle. It's not competitive threats or supply chain issues that keep these up-and-coming executives awake at night, it's the ever-changing expectations and unarticulated accountabilities inside their own organization. They don't have a clear sense of their marching orders.

So, how do you help employees make the right spending decisions—decisions consistent with your strategic objectives—on an ongoing basis? We have three suggestions.

Educate Employees on "Good" Costs versus "Bad" Costs

First, shed light on what it means to be cost conscious. Specifically, help employees to differentiate between "good" and "bad" costs—it's not as cut and dried as you might think. Costs that might seem wasteful or unnecessary in one context can be mission critical in another (such as car allowances for salespeople who use their cars to generate business, versus car allowances for executives).

Give people the information they need to make a direct connection between their individual decisions and the organization's performance. With more transparency around cost drivers and a stronger understanding of how the economics of decisions flow through the business, people are better equipped to make intelligent choices on how best to spend the company's money.

The failure to furnish such information in a timely manner can contribute substantially to organizational inefficiency and hence to higher costs. This is common with spending on internal shared services. If business units do not have clear and accurate information on what a service costs, they behave as if they have a blank check. Why not? For example, at a consumer services company, IT spend was not charged back–or even disclosed–to the business units, so naturally the business units asked for whatever they wanted and then waited in a brutally long queue for the requests to be fulfilled. They had no idea what it cost to provide the service, and the IT department had no idea how critical their demand was. Not surprisingly, IT costs went through the roof.

Few people willfully spend company money irresponsibly. If they waste money, it's usually through ignorance, not malevolence. So, rather than dealing with the problem by imposing restrictive and elaborate spending policies, management should provide people with the knowledge needed to make smart choices and the incentives to do so.

Build a Continuous Improvement Capability

To compete in today's fast-moving environment and drive sustainable improvement, companies need to embed continuous improvement (CI) principles across the enterprise. This is a leadership philosophy based on driving CI in the organization and its processes, using various improvement methodologies, such as Lean, Six Sigma, or others. The aim is to maximize customer value by creating a long-term vision of excellence and a culture of continuous learning that extends from the executive suite to front-line staff.

To guide and coordinate CI initiatives, many companies establish a center of excellence (CoE). The CoE can be small (a handful of people), where its role is limited to providing tools, methodologies, and a consistent vocabulary, delivering training to the organization, and tracking CI initiatives. In some companies, the CoE can be larger (dozens of people), where its role expands to staff "internal consultants" who are deployed on CI projects across the organization.

While CI programs can take various forms, the basic aim is to establish an internal capability that enables constant self-improvement through the training and empowerment of rank-and-file employees, the engagement of senior leaders, and the establishment of appropriate tools and metrics. In time, the CI capability becomes central to your company's identity and culture and makes challenging the status quo a behavioral norm.

We find that such CI capabilities are more successful when leaders create an (artificial) burning platform to generate "pull" for CI initiatives. Frequently, the CEO will assign an annual productivity improvement target at the enterprise level and at each department. The senior executives' performance goals and annual incentives are then tied to achieving these goals.

Assign Cross-Functional Process Owners

Another tactic to align your cost structure on a continuing basis is to assign specific end-to-end business processes to cross-functional process owners. The process owner's mission is to make sure the company's key processes are delivering competitive advantage—or if not, that the right fixes are on the way to address practices and procedures that complicate work or slow it down and add unnecessary expense. Then their challenge is to find better ways to get the work done.

Coupled with CI approaches, process ownership can be an effective way to improve end-to-end process performance. And it has the added benefit of motivating employees to make their work more effective and fulfilling. Rote tasks, unnecessary activity, fragmented responsibilities, and superfluous approval requirements not only render processes inefficient, they dispirit employees. When they have free rein to re-architect the process start to finish, employees come up with astonishing savings both in terms of work and cost. Process owners aim not just to address a performance crisis, but also to improve performance on broad customer-defined measures that cut across functions and need sustained attention.

Organizational Levers: Assign Accountability and Reward Cost Consciousness

Organizations win when the right people, armed with the right information and motivated by the right incentives, are in the right position to make critical decisions. If organizations want to sustain cost savings and performance gains, they should focus on two levers: decision rights and motivators.

Clarify Roles and Decision Rights to Reinforce Cost Accountability

Decision rights describe the underlying mechanics of how decisions are truly made and by whom. Sadly, decision rights often do not coincide with formal lines of authority or official accountability. Too often at too many companies, it is not apparent who has the final say and who gets the ultimate credit or blame. Decision rights are either ambiguous or misaligned. To apply a baseball metaphor, you either have all your outfielders yelling "Mine!" or declaring "Yours!"

This is especially true when it comes to cost. Misallocated or ill-defined decision rights are central to the cost management challenge at a great many companies. Managers often dodge responsibility by claiming that cost is a "specialist" area—the province of the finance department. To fight this tendency, you need to make it clear that every manager, including front-line and middle managers, are accountable for managing their costs. Managing to and meeting their budgets must be sacrosanct. The finance department can support their analyses, but the decision rights lie with the person running the business. Similarly, process owners need decision rights to manage end-to-end process performance and costs. If costs are hitting or exceeding budgets because, for example, costs are being allocated from another department, managers need decision rights to directly influence those allocated costs.

Some managers may need training on financial acumen to manage their costs. For example, a consumer services company trains their new operations managers on basic financial statements so they understand how their actions (or inaction) affects their budget performance, and eventually their individual performance and bonus.

Motivate Performance, Not Politics

An exhortation to follow the vision and pursue the strategy—to run faster, row harder, whatever the chosen sports analogy—is only so much air if the organization's objectives and incentives send contradictory signals. To be effective, motivators need to be aligned with the overall direction of the enterprise as articulated in its strategy.

What gets rewarded gets done, and when blatant maneuvering is rewarded, it breeds a culture of resignation, cynicism, and—ultimately—

mistrust. Corporate headquarters and field operations don't trust each other. The business units and support services compete rather than collaborate, and managers and their subordinates wage a passive war of attrition. At best, unmotivated employees and managers demonstrate apathy and mediocrity; at worst, they engage in short-sighted, counterproductive behaviors that undermine performance.

To overcome this "short-termism," change your incentives to encourage employees to take ownership for cost savings. We have found that incorporating specific targets for reaching Fit for Growth performance goals into short-term incentive compensation plans for the executive team drives accountability to ensure financial outcomes. Including both joint and individual goals in the plans tend to provide positive "peer pressure" among the group to collectively solve issues that may arise. Goals should be focused on a small number of metrics, for example: meeting or exceeding the approved plan for one's own function that includes the transformation financial goals, or meeting or exceeding the approved plan in total to drive cross-functional ownership.

Cultural Levers: Unleashing the Individual

As we discussed in Chapter 16, a company's performance—including its cost consciousness—ultimately resides in the behavior of the individuals who comprise it. So, how do you create a tight and enduring linkage between employees' individual behavior and the success of the organization as a whole? The answer lies in culture.

Model Frugal Behavior at the Top

To foster a culture that rewards and reinforces sustained organizational performance rather than short-term individual gain, start at the top. It's hard to motivate the rank and file to conserve resources when they see the executive team living large. Leaders must personally model cost-conscious behavior in visible ways. They need to demonstrate through real and symbolic steps that they are "proud to be frugal," thereby dispelling the skepticism—prevalent at so many companies today—that cost reduction is something the top tells the middle to do to the bottom.

Earlier, we referenced a media company that eliminated all executive frills, starting with its spectacular headquarters building, which had been a crown jewel but was physically removed from the rest of the company's operations. IKEA executives fly economy and proudly entertain VIPs in the company's in-store cafeterias, arguing that the customers should not have to underwrite their expensive business lunches.

A consumer goods company we worked with simply opened the lines of communication with staff by visibly embracing a set of cost-conscious values and hosting events like "Weekly Talks"—a forum where people from across the organization could ask senior executives hard-hitting questions about the company's future. These sessions were quickly redubbed "Straight Talk" and inspired leaders and staff to work together to overcome obstacles and improve performance.

Recognize Employees for Cost-Conscious Behavior

We talked about changing the financial incentive system to reward cost-conscious behavior, but nonfinancial rewards can be just as powerful. Many companies are explicitly anointing "cost champions" and giving them purview over the drivers of cost in an entire category (such as IT, facilities, and procurement). Simpler methods of acknowledging and appreciating outstanding achievement are powerful as well, such as prizes and awards—even if the monetary value isn't that high. In fact, our research shows that pride matters more than money in motivating people to change their behavior.

A few important guidelines in rewarding cost-conscious behavior. First, take care to specifically identify the actions that positively impact Fit for Growth goals. Get clear and granular about the ways employees at different levels and in different departments can contribute. Recognize consistent and steady achievement as well as outstanding achievement. When you observe someone "in the act" of being cost conscious, provide positive and immediate feedback. Also, provide the employee with a permanent record of achievement—a certificate, medal, trophy, or paperweight. Have senior leaders acknowledge the work both publicly (in an event such as a town hall), and privately (through a personal phone call). And celebrate successes through simple gestures such as a happy-hour celebration in honor of an individual or team who has gone above and beyond. Last, it is important to remember that a thank-you note will never go out of style.

Engage the Front Line through "Pride Builders"

Front-line employees are in the best position to assess what expenses can be cut and what processes can be streamlined without compromising quality or client satisfaction. So it's important to enlist their support in maintaining a cost-conscious culture. That's seldom easy. People have to feel good about tasks that are not financially rewarding or intrinsically motivating.

You accomplish this feat by identifying "pride builders": fellow employees who—through the force of their personality or the power of their example—are able to inspire their peers to work together for the common good. Working through these pride builders, companies focus on those critical few behaviors that will have the biggest and deepest impact on enhancing performance.

Our work with clients confirms that these front-line opinion leaders can generate broad-based support for cost-management efforts far beyond what any corporate-sponsored effort can achieve. These influential employees have high credibility, and if they can be convinced of the virtues and benefits of cost management, then they will help model winning behaviors. Companies entrust and empower these pride builders to build teams to suggest and drive cost management improvements throughout the organization.

Admittedly, motivating employees to reduce costs can be challenging, especially if the initiative involves headcount reduction, but if you can paint a picture of a higher-growth, less bureaucratic organization that is focused on work that matters, you can secure their rational and emotional commitment to company decisions and behavior change.

A few companies are able to do this systematically because they have built a culture that, from the beginning, has focused their people on cost and value. Southwest Airlines, for example, is built around the value proposition of making safe, comfortable air travel available to the average American. At Southwest, employees have been known to pay for energizing events, such as holiday celebrations, out of their own pockets to save the company money.

Sense and Sustainability: Getting from Here to There

As we noted at the outset of this book, companies have long recognized that the pace and magnitude of change is far faster and greater in today's global, technology-enabled market—and that becoming Fit for Growth is no longer something they can avoid, defer, or outrun. They need to institutionalize the capacity and the capabilities to change quickly and comprehensively and, often, continuously.

In our experience assisting clients with major change campaigns, we've seen companies adopt one of two approaches based on the nature and timeframe of the transformation required. Most often, companies default to the first—a reactive initiative, as they have little to no advance warning and must respond to the crisis swiftly and aggressively. We spent Part II of this book detailing the various levers management can pull in such situations to swiftly yet strategically cut costs.

The second approach is a programmatic transformation—the full, coordinated Fit for Growth campaign that we have described. Companies launch a comprehensive initiative, typically led by the CEO, across the organization. A program management office is set up, specific initiatives are identified, milestones are established, a communications program is launched, and progress is tracked, as we discussed. These programs can be highly effective in dealing with a contained event or threat, and are clearly more sustainable than the reactive approach, but as the name implies, the transformation is a program, and eventually things "return to normal" and costs can creep back.

To remain Fit for Growth, you will need to exercise the sustainability levers discussed in this chapter—strategic, operational, organizational, and cultural. Yes, you will need to design and implement the requisite systems and processes to manage change and adjust performance accordingly—whether that's through a full-fledged "sense and adjust" capability or a facility for using the select cost levers described in Part II. But ultimately, your fortunes rise and fall based on the decisions and trade-offs that individual employees make every day. Will those decisions benefit the firm as a whole or maximize the self-interest of the person making them? It's only when you reinforce a capabilities-driven strategy with both organizational design and cultural prompts that you succeed in becoming and remaining Fit for Growth.

Notes

Chapter 1

1. Jessica Sackett Romero, "The Rise and Fall of Circuit City," Federal Reserve Bank of Richmond, *Econ Focus*, 3Q (2013): 31–33, www.richmondfed.org/~/media/richmondfedorg/publications/research/econ_focus/2013/q3/pdf/economic_history.pdf.
2. Ibid.
3. Don Eames, *Circuit City Six: Six Fatal Mistakes of a Once "Good to Great" Company* (Minneapolis, MN: Eames Management Group, 2009), www.eamesmgmt.com/circuit-city-six-ebook.
4. John R. Wells, *Circuit City Stores Inc.: Strategic Dilemmas* (Cambridge, MA: Harvard Business School, 2005).
5. Anita Hamilton, "Why Circuit City Busted, While Best Buy Boomed," *Time*, November 11, 2008, http://content.time.com/time/business/article/0,8599,1858079,00.html.
6. Erica Ogg, "Circuit City Gets Delisting Notice from NYSE," *CNET.com*, October 31, 2008, www.cnet.com/news/circuit-city-gets-delisting-notice-from-nyse.
7. Romero, "Rise and Fall."
8. Ibid.
9. Paul Leinwand and Cesare Mainardi, *Strategy That Works: How Companies Close the Strategy-to-Execution Gap* (Boston: Harvard Business Review Press, 2016).
10. Deniz Caglar, Marco Kesterloo, and Art Kleiner, "How Ikea Reassembled Its Growth Strategy," *strategy+business*, May 2002, http://www.strategy-business.com/article/00111?gko=66b6e.
11. Ibid.
12. Ibid.

13. Ibid.
14. Fit for Growth is a registered service mark of PwC Strategy& LLC in the United States.
15. Vinay Couto and Ashok Divakaran, "How Ready Are You for Growth?" *strategy+business*, August 2013, http://www.strategy-business.com/article/00199?gko=edc83.
16. TSR scores range from 0 and 100, with 100 representing the company with the highest returns in its industry segment, and 0 representing the one with the lowest. This form of normalization insulates TSR results from external factors that might affect some sectors more than others.

Chapter 4

1. Paul Leinwand and Cesare Mainardi, *The Essential Advantage* (Boston: Harvard Business Review Press, 2010).

Chapter 16

1. DeAnne Aguirre and Micah Alpern, "10 Principles of Leading Change Management," *strategy+business*, Summer 2014, www.strategy-business.com/article/00255?gko=9d35b.

Acknowledgments

This book represents the collective thought leadership, dedication to client service, and over 100 years of experience in what is now PwC Strategy&, formerly known as Booz & Company. This book would not be possible were it not for the expertise, foresight, and mentorship of partners that came before us and laid the groundwork that formed much of our thinking.

This project also could not have become a reality without the wisdom, vision, and experience of our PwC Strategy& colleagues today. A special thank you to Miles Everson, Mohamed Kande, Ash Unwin, Les Moeller, Joachim Rotering, and Mike Connolly, for believing in our concept and providing what it took to make it happen.

We are fortunate to work with many brilliant colleagues, present and past, whose wisdom and insights have shaped the performance of countless companies and industries. Among these colleagues, several have been working on some of the ideas in this book for years, and have contributed to developing or enhancing them. Gary Neilson has ushered in new thinking on organization design; DeAnne Aguirre and Jon Katzenbach have shown how to evolve an organization's culture in a practical way and enable change; Paul Leinwand and Cesare Mainardi have crystallized the role of capabilities in the success of companies; and Jaya Pandrangi, Matt Mani, and Ashok Divakaran are among the initial leaders on the Fit for Growth idea. They have helped pave the way.

We want to recognize the experts in our firm who contributed their time so generously to supporting the development of this book. Their knowledge and expertise enabled us to provide deep and practical insights into the many different topics that we discuss, and ensured that we provided a global, cross-industry perspective. Special thanks to Eduardo Alvarez, Reid Carpenter, K. B. Clausen, Carl Drisko, Mike DuVall, Andreas Eggert, Kristy Hull, Hasan Iqbal, Seema Malveaux, Tim Pagels, Jason Palmenberg, Josh Peters, Laurens Petten, Caitlyn Truong, and Martha Turner for their contributions to specific chapters.

There is a strong community of hundreds of PwC partners, principals, and directors who help their clients get and stay fit, and who advance the ideas we have shared in this book. These leaders include Peter Bertone, Briggs Briner, Sarah Butler, Ivan De Souza, Eric Dustman, Ben Gilbertson, Jayant Gotpagar, Peter Heckmann, Rodger Howell, Gil Irwin, Ashish Jain, Namit Kapoor, Rich Kauffeld, Anil Kaul, Chris Manning, Kelley Mavros, Carlos Navarro, J. Neely, Yogesh Pandit, Earl Simpkins, Patty Riedl, Thomas Ripsam, Andrew Tipping, Tom Torlone, and Luiz Vieira. While there are many others we cannot explicitly name here, we still would like to recognize their contributions.

We would also like to acknowledge the debt we owe to our clients, who gave us the opportunity to develop our insights by working alongside them and benefitting from their wisdom and experience. A special thank you to the clients who we interviewed and consulted in the course of writing this book.

We want to thank PwC Strategy& editor-in-chief, Art Kleiner, who helped assemble the team to make this project a reality—and who set a standard for quality a firm can be proud of. Thanks to our editing and project management team of Boris Abezgauz, Rob Norton, and Jennifer Zelinsky for their endless commitment to keep us on schedule, and for creating a book that is easy to read for nonconsultants, yet deep enough to deliver value. Writers Tara Owen, Joe Cahill, and Rob Hertzberg, and graphic artist Kris Tobiassen, provided essential assistance in developing the book's content.

We also want to acknowledge our firm's supporting staff for making sure the book meets PwC Strategy&'s standards for quality and independence, including Kiran Chauhan, Ann-Denise Grech, Nadia Kubis, Jeannette Leong, Manish Mahajan, Debra Page, Christina Rockwell, Katrina Sellers, Ilona Steffen, and Linda Watts.

This book would not be possible without the vision and support of our publisher, John Wiley & Sons, and their representatives, Richard Narramore and Tiffany Colon, who provided us with the right balance of direction and guidance, while being flexible enough to let us develop a book we can be proud of, even when it did not confirm to norms.

To others who deserve credit, but whose names were inadvertently left out of this list—thank you.

Finally, we would be remiss if we did not mention how grateful we are to our families, for their never-ending understanding, patience, and inspiration. They were tremendously supportive during the development of this book, making it possible for us to spend late nights and weekends drafting it. Beyond this project, they have been tireless supporters of our careers and our work, taking care of everything else so we can focus on our clients and the firm. We accomplish what we can because of their limitless understanding and unwavering support. From the bottom of our hearts, thank you to Lynn and Suhail; Lisa, Ellery, and Nick; and Christina, Jacqueline, and Gerry.

Thank you.

About the Authors

Vinay Couto is a principal of PwC's Strategy& in the people and organization strategy practice based in the Chicago office. He leads this practice and leads the global Fit for Growth platform. He has worked with clients in the automotive, aerospace, pharmaceuticals, life sciences, media and broadcasting, consumer packaged goods, retail, banking, technology, and insurance industries. Mr. Couto is a recognized thought leader; has contributed to numerous *strategy+business* articles, including "Headquarters: Irrelevant or Irreplaceable?," "How to Be an Outsourcing Virtuoso," "Making Overhead Outperform," "The Globalization of White-Collar Work," and "The New CFO Agenda: Global G&A Survey Insights and Implications"; and is the coauthor of *CFO Thought Leaders: Advancing the Frontiers of Finance*. Mr. Couto is a three-time recipient of Strategy&'s prestigious Professional Excellence Award, which was given in recognition for innovative work with clients. Mr. Couto holds an MBA from the Columbia Graduate School of Business and a First Class Honors Degree in Chemical Engineering from the Imperial College of Science and Technology, London University.

John Plansky is the U.S. leader of PwC's Strategy& and is a principal in the financial services practice based in the Boston office. He is an expert in restructuring the global information technology function and back-office operations to enhance value for financial institutions. He has deep expertise in applying information technology to launch new products and enable global operating models for securities firms. Mr. Plansky has written or cowritten numerous articles, including "Is Your Company Fit for Growth?," "A Strategist's Guide to Blockchain," and "The Digitization of Financial

265

Services." Prior to joining Strategy& as a senior executive advisor, Mr. Plansky was CEO of NerveWire and chief executive, securities industry, at Wipro. Mr. Plansky has a BS degree in biophysics from Brown University.

Dr. Deniz Caglar is a principal of Strategy& in the people and organization strategy practice, based in the Chicago office. He has deep expertise in organization design, corporate function efficiency and effectiveness, shared services, and outsourcing/offshoring. He primarily serves clients in the consumer packaged goods and retail industries, and has also served clients in the automotive, consumer services, financial services, health care, industrials, life sciences, transportation, technology, and utilities industries. Deniz has coauthored multiple articles, including "Is Your Company Fit for Growth?," "Seven Value Creation Lessons from Private Equity," "The Redefined No of the CFO," "The New Functional Agenda," and "Be Your Own Activist Investor." Dr. Caglar earned his PhD in operations research at Northwestern University, and holds BS and MS degrees in industrial engineering from Northwestern University.

Index

Note: Page references in *italics* refer to figures.